I'D KILL
FOR YOU

M. WILLIAM
PHELPS

PINNACLE BOOKS
Kensington Publishing Corp.
http://www.kensingtonbooks.com

KENSINGTON BOOKS are published by

Kensington Publishing Corp.
119 West 40th Street
New York, NY 10018

All Kensington Titles, Imprints, and Distributed Lines are available at special quantity discounts for bulk purchases for sales promotions, premiums, fund-raising, and educational or institutional use. Special book excerpts or customized printings can also be created to fit specific needs. For details, write or phone the office of the Kensington special sales manager: Kensington Publishing Corp., 119 West 40th Street, New York, NY 10018, attn: Special Sales Department, Phone: 1-800-221-2647.

Kensington and the K logo Reg. U.S. Pat. & TM Off.

ISBN-13: 978-0-7860-3497-0
ISBN-10: 0-7860-3497-1
First Kensington Hardcover: March 2015

eISBN-13: 978-0-7860-3498-7
eISBN-10: 0-7860-3498-X
First Kensington Electronic Edition: March 2015

10 9 8 7 6 5 4 3 2 1

Printed in the United States of America

*This book is dedicated to my longtime editor
at Kensington Publishing Corp., Michaela Hamilton,
who has been by my side for every true crime title I've written.
This is our twentieth book together!
What an incredible milestone.
Michaela has done more for the world of true crime
than anyone else I know. She is an expert editor and
true friend and colleague.
I am grateful to have met her
and humbled by the opportunity to work with her.*

"*Behold, in example I grieve my heart out for that so sweet young girl; I give my blood for her. . . . I give my time, my skill, my sleep; I let my other sufferers want that so she may have all.*"

—Bram Stoker, *Dracula*

CHAPTER 1

TO FEEL THAT sun on his back for the first time a free man:
Oh, how warm and liberating.

He took a breath. A deep one.

In through the nose, out through the mouth.

Life on the outside.

It had a ring to it.

On September 4, 2001, a glorious Tuesday afternoon,
exactly one week before terrorists would attack New York and
the world would change forever, eighteen-year-old Kyle
Hulbert found himself standing in court. Not the criminal
kind, but probate. On this day, Kyle was set to be released.

"He's turned eighteen," Kyle's social worker explained to
the judge. Kyle sat quietly, listening; his eyes, like his mind,
darted back and forth, a million miles a second. "He's not
showing any signs of psychosis. We want to have him released.
Declare him an adult."

Emancipation.

Kyle said the word to himself.

"Emancipation."

It sounded so historical and unassociated with his life. Yet
here he was.

The state spoke, claiming its position was that they didn't
think Kyle was well enough to leave the facility just yet.

The judge heard the evidence and sat back to think about it.

Kyle stood and thought, *Come on . . . let me go.*

"Release him," the judge uttered.

Kyle had been a ward of the state.

Not anymore.

Funny, he didn't feel that much different when the doors of the courthouse closed behind him and Kyle found himself exiting the courthouse, now his own "man," breathing that fresh Virginia air into his lungs as a free young adult for the first time. It was a day he had looked forward to over the past year, especially. With all of the problems Kyle had gotten himself into at the foster homes where he'd lived, in school, and within his community, Kyle viewed this day as a new beginning. Now here he was, walking out the door an independent man, dependent upon nobody but himself.

"They gave me a bus ticket," Kyle said of the court, "and cut me loose."

Emancipation. Stepping onto the concrete outside the courthouse, looking back one last time, Kyle considered what was in front of him. This was it. He *was* on his own. He'd have to fend for himself from this point forward. Think for himself. Feed and clothe himself.

Survive.

More important (or maybe *most* important), he'd have to medicate himself. It was up to Kyle now. No one would be asking if he had taken his meds. Or hand him a little paper cup with the day's rations inside, making sure he swallowed every last bit. It would be Kyle's decision. His alone. The state had given him a three-month supply of the psychiatric prescriptions he needed to feel right; yet it was going to be up to Kyle to go to the pharmacy, actually pick up the drugs, and then ingest each pill.

Every. Single. Day.

"I didn't stay on them very long," Kyle explained. "It's a bad cycle. A minor manic phase will set in and I'll forget to take the medication."

And then the Catch-22 effect: Because he was not on his meds, he didn't feel he needed them.

Kyle was a boy in a man's body. Truly. The state of Virginia, however, by law, claimed he was old enough (sane enough) now to make adult decisions on his own. Average height, quite skinny—"lanky" or "scrawny" is what they'd call him—with dark, silken black hair, slick like oil, Kyle had a gaunt look to him. He had chiseled and bulimic-like weight-loss facial features: pointed cheekbones, sunken eyes, and the somewhat obvious, cerebral wiriness of a hyped-up meth addict—although Kyle claimed he never dabbled in the drug. He didn't need it. Kyle was amped-up enough already by what were voices and characters stirring in his head like a thousand whispers. This, mind you, even with a dozen years of psychiatric treatment and medications behind him.

Kyle had what some may view as a strange look on life. His birthday, for example, was not a day like most: cake and ice cream and feeling special. Kyle never did feel special—not in the traditional sense of a kid wearing a pointed cardboard birthday hat, which was tethered by a too-tight rubber band pinching his neckline, ready to blow out candles, with his family and friends surrounding him, did. Kyle called it—the day he was born, that is—his "hatching day," as if he had emerged from a cocoon, slimy and gooey and ready to take on the world, born out of some sort of metamorphosis. And yet, as he thought about it while walking toward the bus stop on that emancipation day—on his own for this first time, no counselor over his shoulder, no psychiatrist telling him what he should do or how he should think anymore—this was Kyle's *true* hatching day. His rebirth. A time for Kyle to take on life by himself and make decisions based on the tools he had been given.

"I am constantly struggling with a question," Kyle observed. "Psychology teaches us that a person's personality and psychological makeup is a composite of past experiences . . . and I am suffering from a complex network of fantastical memories of things that never actually happened."

Despite his often volatile and strange behavior while in mental hospitals and in group and foster homes, along with Kyle's biological father's request that his son be continually detained and treated, the state had to cut Kyle loose. In fact, Kyle's father, who had given up custody of Kyle when Kyle was twelve ("I was too much to handle. . . ."), had always kept in contact and, as Kyle had said, "He kept tabs on me and my entire life, and he knew about my behavioral problems. And he knew, which is why he fought against me being emancipated, that letting me off the leash was not a good idea at the time, because it was *not* going to end well. In fact, he told them: 'You let Kyle out and he is going to kill somebody.'"

The judge decided, however, it was time. Kyle Hulbert was eighteen. And Kyle, as it were, was not going to argue with being given a free pass for starting a life.

"Kyle Hulbert," one law enforcement source later analyzed, "has been, since he was six years old, in and out of mental institutions. Kyle's world includes a number of darker characters . . . demons or presences . . . that live in his head."

And now this "man" was free to roam the world and do what he wished. Thus, on September 4, 2001, Kyle found himself on the street, walking, with literally nowhere to go.

No home.

No friends.

No family.

There was a certain "high," Kyle recalled, about being freed from the structured, routine life inside an institution. It felt good. It felt right. It felt redemptive.

"I was happy that I was free! No more leashes. No more having to worry about institutions. I was . . . free. Those are the only three words that I can say describe how I was feeling."

Kyle had been told to have a plan. And he did. Kyle said his "plan" on this day, as he walked down the street in front of the courthouse toward the bus stop, was to go and find a girl he could "fuck senseless."

After that, well, whatever came his way, he would roll with it.

CHAPTER 2

KYLE HAD WHAT he called "half-baked" plans as he broke from those ward-of-the-state chains holding him down. Just out and free to do what he wanted, Kyle thought about going to college, studying, maybe taking up a career of some sort. That thought came and went rather quickly, however, as Kyle realized he first had to find some money to live off. Moreover, a lifelong dream of his to become a published writer would have to take a backseat to surviving on his own.

"My main concern was filling out the Social Security paperwork and getting that going," he said. "I had already been approved for it."

Odd, the government had approved him for mental disability—and there were funds set up and headed his way, come December—yet he was "sane" enough to leave the institution and fend for himself on his own.

It didn't make sense.

Kyle said he was told by the state: "Because of your mental health, you are going to have a hard time holding down a job."

It was the reason why they approved him.

"They had already seen how I handled jobs in the past," Kyle explained. "I got fired from each job I ever had."

There was not a doctor or therapist whom Kyle had spoken to over the years who did not know that demons whispered to

Kyle, that he saw things "others couldn't or wouldn't," and that the world spinning out of control inside Kyle Hulbert's head was not a place where "happily ever after" resided. Kyle had talked about having "dreams or visions of the apocalypse." Those "voices" inside his head would eventually (in totality) go by the name of "the 6."

A lot of this, Kyle realized, sounded foolish. Imaginary. Something from a person who should be locked up. Most would respond by saying he was crazy. But as a five-year-old kid, this sort of make-believe world he lived in became an everyday part of his life. It continued as Kyle grew into his teens. For Kyle Hulbert, he believed it was as real as the pet dragon he saw regularly and explained was as genuine as "one of my cats."

"I cannot identify the first [memory]," he said many years later, talking about that moment in childhood when these different visions and thoughts inside his head began, "and you must understand that one of the aspects of psychosis is an inability to distinguish 'reality' from 'fantasy.'"

To him, that chaos going on inside his adolescent mind—the dreams, hallucinations, and voices—were his absolute reality. It all seemed "perfectly natural . . . even if they weren't."

It did not take long for Kyle to become aware that he thought differently than the other kids around him and "there was something wrong" inside him. He knew that if he approached the other kids, talked to them about what he saw and heard, he would be shunned and ostracized, bullied, and likely beaten up, definitely laughed at. So he kept most of these things to himself, at least at first.

The voices and visions did not scare him, he said later. Some kids might be frightened by what he saw; but to him it was a world he embraced. A secret he came to love.

There was one day—Kyle was six years old—when he had what he recalled was his first "hallucination." It is a term Kyle needed to put in quotes, he said later, because "hallucination" was not the best way to describe what he saw. Hallucination was merely "the quickest and most efficient way" of explaining what happened. People could comprehend what a hallucination is—yet he considered what happened to him to be real—even to this day.

Another way to describe it, he reconciled, was to use the word "magic."

Inside his head, Kyle lived within a world of his own, literally. This was *his* world. He didn't create it, he claimed. Or ask for it to appear before him. It wasn't like that at all. It just happened. One day it wasn't there, and then the next, well, it was—and the most important part of this for Kyle as he talked through it years later was that to him it wasn't a fantasy or some type of dream. It wasn't something that came and went: the bogeyman underneath the bed, the monster in the closet, the imaginary friend you sit with and share tea as a child.

This was his life. His world.

There was one—of many that would begin to accumulate—major issue with all of this for Kyle Hulbert as he sat years later and looked back on everything that happened.

"The biggest problem I have encountered—and one we will have to address—is that I have a great deal of memory that conflicts with things I *know* to be true. . . . Consider everything I tell you to be as 'true' as I 'know' it all to be, and any inconsistencies are entirely unintended."

This statement, so incredibly honest and sincere, would come back to haunt Kyle Hulbert as he grew into an adult, and some of what he "saw" and "heard" would indeed become reality—however interspersed with brutal violence, blood, murder, and carnage as it would soon be.

CHAPTER 3

IN OCTOBER 2001, after a month of not doing much of anything, with the exception, he explained, "of spending a lot of time alone with my girlfriend," Kyle Hulbert got an invitation to the Maryland Renaissance Festival. Accepting this invitation would change Kyle's life.

The Maryland version of what is a nationwide celebration, generally called the Renaissance Faire or Festival, runs every August through October. It is set up to re-create "a sixteenth-century English village, with crafts, food, live perform-ances . . . a jousting arena, and lots of games," according to a PR description of the activities. It's billed as a "fun family event" and held at a location about thirty miles outside of Washington, DC. The festival attracts people from all over the world, all walks of life. For sixteenth-century history buffs, it's the ideal occasion. Families can go and have a blast. Same as what the Civil War reenactment events and festivals do for Civil War enthusiasts, the Renaissance Festival does for fans of knights in shining armor, maidens, belly dancers, fire-eaters, acrobats, and musicians. The allure for Kyle was that it fit with the chosen era of fantasy and the role-playing games (RPG) he had fallen into and embraced when growing up. Here was a chance to dress up, wear a costume, and be somebody else, live out some of those epic fantasies Kyle had had all his life.

Kyle wore a cat mask made of latex that covered the top half of his face, which he had painted completely black underneath. He wore black clothes.

As he walked around the festival, Kyle noticed he was getting lots of looks from the girls.

"I liked that," he said.

What eighteen-year-old boy, cooped up all his life inside one institution after the other, moving from one foster home to the next when not institutionalized, wouldn't enjoy all the attention? Kyle had a girlfriend (whom he did not bring with him to the festival). Being noticed by others felt good now. It fed his ego—his enormous sense of self. For Kyle, he had to be somebody all the time. Mostly, it was because he was so uncomfortable in his own skin or, more important, in his own mind. Being someone else, or something else, allowed him to develop and satisfy his fantasies. It allowed Kyle the opportunity to express those strange feelings he had—not to mention the visions and hallucinations—and live them out in the physical world around him. At the festival, the type of people Kyle met and hung around stayed in character throughout most of the day. Something caught Kyle's attention as he walked around. There were dozens of various types of booths spread throughout the festival. Vendors were selling food, clothing, weapons, props, all sorts of items connected to the Renaissance that might be appealing to festivalgoers. So Kyle walked up to one particular tent. There was a girl behind the booth. She was a pretty girl—young, nice figure—and she smiled at him.

"Brandy," the girl said after he asked her name.

"Nice name," Kyle responded.

They chatted. Small talk mostly. She seemed interested. They had things in common. They seemed to like each other.

"Can I get your number?" Kyle asked.

Brandy didn't hesitate, Kyle said later. She got a piece of paper and wrote it down.

"Call me soon," Brandy said. They'd hang now, but she was working.

From there, Kyle found his way into the weapons tent on the grounds of the festival. If there was one subject within the era that Kyle was infatuated with the most, it had to be weapons. He collected knives and swords. He fancied himself an expert knife and sword handler. He knew all there was to know about medieval weapons, especially knives and swords. And wherever Kyle Hulbert landed, he rarely went anywhere without his trusty twenty-seven-inch ninja-style sword he liked to keep as sharp as a razor blade.

CHAPTER 4

"I LOVE THE medieval period," Kyle Hulbert explained. "And I love all things fantasy, so these swords and weapons inside the shop there at the festival were just a natural extension for me."

Odd choice of words—"a natural extension for me"—but there you have it.

Standing inside this weapons tent, Kyle looked around and felt at home. All of the weapons around him spoke to him on so many different levels.

Kyle had met someone his age just before being "locked up," as he called it, earlier that year, in March 2001. Kyle and Joey (pseudonym) had hit it off. Joey lived near a friend of Kyle's. When Kyle was emancipated that September, post–hatching day, he had nowhere to go, so he rented a room from an old friend, an older man he described as a Vietnam veteran. Candice (pseudonym), who was a girl Kyle knew, lived right around the corner from the vet.

"She's a pagan," Kyle said.

They threw a party for Kyle one day in early October to celebrate the fact that he was back—and now free.

To Kyle and his friends, being pagan meant that "they were practitioners of witchcraft, Wicca." Kyle had even described himself as Wiccan at the time, he admitted. Later he would step away from calling himself Wiccan. "Primarily," Kyle explained, "because I hate hypocrisy. And years later, I realized that not only did I not believe in the tenets of Wicca, I did not follow them."

Kyle, however, would still—to this day—describe himself as a pagan, but what he means by that is rather complex, like most of what Kyle Hulbert says.

"I believe in multiple gods and goddesses," he clarified. "But I also believe that all gods and goddesses are manifestations and aspects of the one true source—one God, so to speak."

That one God, though, would not be the popular God of the Bible.

"All faiths," Kyle commented, ". . . are all aspects of one God—we believe it. Think about it, we've got seven billion people in the world with seven billion cultural histories. Seven billion different points of view. It is impossible for everyone to see God the exact same way. We're all looking for something. We're all looking to understand something greater than ourselves."

At this party celebrating his emancipation, Joey introduced Kyle to Brittany (pseudonym), one of Joey's close friends. Joey and Kyle had just met earlier that year, but by October they had become close friends. Maybe even best friends.

"Joey liked my extensive knowledge in weaponry and the fact that I played the game Magic," Kyle said.

ONE OF THE first times Kyle and Joey were together, Kyle was at a friend's house near the foster home he was living in at the time. They were doing something Kyle enjoyed: knife tossing. Joey happened to stop by. He watched for a moment.

"How good is your aim?" Joey asked.

"Pretty damn good," Kyle had answered. "I generally hit what I'm aiming at."

Joey thought for a moment. "Well, if I stood over there"— Kyle was throwing at a wooden backboard twenty-five feet away—"do you think you could hit a target around my head?"

Kyle was stunned. "You *trust* me to do that?"

They had just met.

The thing about Joey, Kyle said later, was that when he trusted someone, after he made that decision, he was all in.

"Well, you had better wear a blindfold," Kyle said, "because if you twitch or something, that could mean disaster. You're going to wind up with a hole in your head."

"Nope," Joey said. "I'm good."

Joey then walked over and stood in front of the board.

Kyle stared at his target.

"And I planted that knife about two inches to the left of his ear!"

IN LATE SEPTEMBER, after Joey had introduced Kyle to Brittany at that party in Kyle's honor, Joey pulled Kyle aside. Joey explained that he had been dating Brittany.

"I need your help," Joey said to Kyle.

"Name it."

"Are you doing anything tonight?"

"I'm up for it—what's going on?"

"Listen, Britt's ex-boyfriend has been giving her some problems. I am going to be gone tonight. I want you to come over to the apartment and hang out with Britt just in case the dumb-ass decides to show up. I want someone there with her."

"No problem," Kyle said.

Kyle found Brittany. He wanted to tell her about himself, where he came from, what he did. They really didn't know each other. He and Joey had told her what was going to happen that night, and Kyle wanted her to feel comfortable with him.

"Look, if Joey trusts you implicitly, so do I," she told Kyle. She didn't need any rundown of Kyle's accomplishments.

Kyle wasn't much of a fighter. Sizewise, he was below average weight for his height. He didn't see himself as a combatant in any way, per se. "Scrapper," he liked to label himself. "Grappling a little . . . but fighting, hand to hand, I had no technique."

So how was this lanky, underweight kid going to protect this young woman if her overly aggressive ex-boyfriend started banging at the door?

"Weapons," Kyle explained. "I brought my sword with me that night."

Kyle also brought along a nightstick. "Because, let's be honest, killing the dude might have caused me a few logistical problems at the time."

He hung out. They ate pizza. Kyle slept on the couch. The ex-boyfriend never showed.

That night led to Kyle staying there as October came to pass. He had worn out his welcome, he thought, at the Vietnam vet's apartment. The guy was letting him stay for free. Kyle's Social Security wasn't slated to kick in until December, so he was cash strapped. He had nothing, really.

For the most part, from then on, Kyle started hopping from one friend's flat to the other, never overstaying his welcome. He also had a tent he lived in, pitching it in the woods near a friend's apartment, or anywhere he thought he wouldn't be bothered.

And then the Renaissance Festival came and he met Brandy.

CHAPTER 5

TO UNDERSTAND THE life of Kyle Hulbert is to look back at where he came from and understand how he wound up sleeping in a tent, staying with any friend who would allow him to crash on the couch in those days after he was emancipated. If you ask Kyle, this period—between his emancipation in September 2001 and that fateful day in October when he attended the Renaissance Festival and met Brandy—is the most precarious time of his life. It was when Kyle, who truly had lived within a fantasy world that had been kept pretty much stabilized by medication and treatment, allowed himself to begin to explore that realm out in the real world, without mind-altering prescribed medication infiltrating what was happening inside his head.

Since he was a kindergartener, Kyle said, he had lived with foster families. This life was no "ideal family" situation all the time. Not to mention the fact that discipline was sometimes wielded out in the form of the foster child being sent away. It was March 2001, for example, when Kyle found himself in trouble with the foster family he had been living with then. He was soon locked up and staring at the walls of Poplar Springs Hospital, a behavioral-care specialist facility with twenty-five acres of "natural setting" and a host of other amenities. If one had to be institutionalized, this was basically a palace.

The mission of the hospital, in part, has been to "improve the lives of those in our community who are experiencing psychiatric and addictive-disease concerns." This was a far cry from the institutions of the 1950s and 1960s that many might recall images of; places like Poplar would be country clubs compared to these mental wards of the past. Forget about the Hollywood scenarios that conjure up bouts of electroshock therapy and Nurse Mildred Ratched types who rule over "crazy" people confined in the hospital, walking that paper-slipper shuffle down shiny waxed hallways, zoned out on enough meds to put down an elephant. Poplar aims to give tools to its patients in order to live as normally as they can. That was something Kyle Hulbert wanted desperately: to walk out one day and be free from those mental chains that had held him in bondage, he claimed, since he was six years old.

That last time Kyle had been committed to Poplar, in early spring 2001, his foster family claimed he was "manic" and suffering from "delusional thinking, delusions of grandeur, psychosis," as Kyle put it, "and a whole host of other things.

"They said there had been a steady decline in my behavior," Kyle remarked. "This culminated in what they said was a threat by me then to blow up my school."

Serious accusations.

Kyle was seventeen. He was "gearing up," he said, for his eighteenth hatching day and looking forward to walking out of whatever facility, whatever foster home he was in, able and ready to go out and do what he wanted in life.

According to Kyle, the bomb threat, or blowing up a school, was an entire "misunderstanding. I really mean that."

Kyle had missed the bus to school on the day before it happened. So he decided he wasn't going to school that day. He had been up all night, anyway. Tired, grumpy, a bit impatient, that chaos of his mind swirling and running all together, he was in no condition to walk to school or call for a ride or deal with anyone who was going to question him about showing up late for the bus. The next day, determined not to miss the bus, Kyle arrived at the bus stop a half hour early, somewhere near 6:15 A.M. But the bus never showed up, Kyle claimed.

So he walked back home.

"I'll drive you," his foster mother said.

This particular family Kyle was living with, the Moores (pseudonym), were the type of people "not to give up on a child," according to Kyle's counselor who described them before Kyle moved in. They stayed the course, generally. They weren't going to toss him out because he acted up a few times. Kyle was an old veteran of living within the foster family system; he knew that this was rare—finding a family willing to love him, yes, but, maybe more than that, also put up with him. Kyle Hulbert knew he wasn't easy to get along with, that he probably talked too much, too manic, often repeated himself, and said things most people found disturbing or at least offensive. But Miss Moore was going to help him. She was a woman in her early sixties when Kyle moved in. She had been a foster parent for decades. She knew the way the system worked; she was invested in helping children.

"[Miss Moore] is dedicated to making sure this works," Kyle's counselor told him.

"And I trusted that counselor," Kyle said. "She was the first person to actually reach me—the problem was, she didn't reach me until I was fifteen. Still, she's the only reason I am still functional." Additionally, Miss Moore, Kyle said, "was a great woman. She fought for me. She loved me. She took me in and made me feel like I was one of the family right away."

At home now after missing the bus for a second day, Kyle told Miss Moore: "Mom, it's not your job to drive me to school." This sort of thing was important to Kyle. Rules, regulations, and procedures—they meant something to him. Kyle adhered to and took to the idea of a structured life. He had lived most of his life under the rule of an institution or in foster care: schedules, routines, and planning. He took organization seriously. He was used to being told what to do, following the rules, and expected others to do the same.

"I am not going to have you drive a half hour out of your way because the bus company screwed up," Kyle told Miss Moore as he felt his adrenaline rising. He was getting himself going. "Screw it . . . I'll go in on Monday." It was a Friday. He was taking a long weekend.

To put this incident into perspective, Kyle had been involved with the revolving door of the institution for as far back as he could recall. "I had been in and out consistently," he commented. He'd live with a foster family, do something bizarre, act out aggressively, or say something that scared the people in his life and around him, and he'd be committed. "By 1999, a few years before this bus incident, I was so tired of living with foster families. I'd get to like a family, get used to them . . . feel comfortable . . . and they'd kick me out for some reason. And then I am left with that whole abandonment-issue thing."

In this situation, wherein Kyle was such a volatile person, the relationships he had with his foster families were often forged and shattered on a series, or culmination, of incidents and words, not on one event in particular or one fight between Kyle and a foster family member.

Nonetheless, this lifestyle wore Kyle down, he said later.

So heading toward the end of the school year (2001), when he missed the bus one morning and it didn't show up the following morning, Kyle had had enough. He was finished with adhering to the "law of the land." He was making a decision on his own and sticking by it.

There was no way he was going to allow his foster mother to drive him to school. Yet, to put this event into even a more cogent perspective, Kyle had gone off his medication by the spring of 2001. He said in one breath that it wasn't "a complete and deliberate choice"; yet, in another, he went on to explain he was in charge of taking his medications by then. So it was his decision to stop. Miss Moore would ask, keeping tabs on him, reminding Kyle, and he would always lie, answering, "Yes, sure, done deal. Did it." Kyle wanted to take it, he claimed, but he would get "focused on something" and totally forget to take it and "miss a couple of doses." And because of those missed doses, his "psychoses would begin to set in," he explained. The demons, the dragons, the voices, the rage, and the sheer chaos going on inside his mind would come back and he would unwittingly, perhaps, enter into that inevitable Catch-22 we all hear about. When he was on his meds, he knew he needed them and he understood how good it was for him to take them; off his meds, he didn't realize their value and thought he didn't need them.

"I get into a manic phase and I just stop thinking about the missed doses anymore and then I stop altogether. My mind ends up in an entirely different place—and you can see, as I explain it to you, how this exacerbates itself."

Kyle was extremely protective of Miss Moore. He did not like a lot of what was going on inside her house. There were other foster kids living there besides him, and some took advantage of Miss Moore, he said. This was why, when she offered to drive him to school, he was adamant: *"No way."*

"You're not going out of your way when it's the bus company's responsibility to get me to school," Kyle said. "They get paid to do that."

"Well, your guidance counselor is talking about truancy," Miss Moore explained.

"Let me call them and explain what happened," Kyle insisted.

Miss Moore seemed unsure. She thought about it. Love was about trust. Trust was about responsibility and honoring your word.

"Okay," Miss Moore said. And she took off for work.

Kyle rode his bicycle over to a friend's that morning after

Miss Moore cleared out. While there, he called the school. He expressed his feelings and his predicament to the guidance counselor. Kyle was not one to hide how he felt. And there was a time in his life when he needed to be right. He liked to tell things the way he saw them. Good, bad, indifferent. Didn't matter to Kyle. *"This is how it is!"*

"Well, you are not showing up for school, and that is truancy, and you are going to get into trouble," the guidance counselor said.

It was one thing to clarify a situation for Kyle Hulbert; it was quite another to tell him what he didn't want to hear. Here was an unpredictable, ready-to-explode young adult off his meds—meds that he needed desperately just to function, maybe not on an even keel, but somewhat normally. To begin with, the school Kyle attended was an alternative establishment. He wasn't allowed to attend the local community high school because of his unpredictable and explosive behavior. His guidance counselor at the alternative school also worked for the foster care service—so the counselor was quite clear about whom he was dealing with on the telephone.

Kyle sat and listened to the guidance counselor "chewing" him "out," he later claimed. According to Kyle's version, the guy was saying, "Your behavior over the past few months has been becoming more and more erratic and degrading. You need to straighten your ass out. Now you get your ass into this school. . . ."

Seems unlikely a guidance counselor would speak to a foster child with issues in this manner, but Kyle swore by it.

With that, Kyle felt threatened. He called it a "slip comment" later on when he retold this story. But in a day and age of guns and schools and violence and impulsive, on-edge students, no comment, however off-kilter, would be taken for granted.

"Coming to school right now is not a good idea," Kyle said to his guidance counselor. "I am feeling very much too volatile and I don't want to make a big hole in the ground." Kyle later claimed he didn't even know or realize what he was saying, only that he responded the way he thought he needed. He reacted to the counselor's yelling. He was telling his counselor that going to school would not be a good idea—that he was *not* in a good state of mind.

Kyle hung up and went to the mall.

The guidance counselor called the police and explained that a student had threatened to blow up the school and was talking strangely, wanting to hurt himself and others.

On his way back from the mall, Kyle was riding his bicycle down the block when he saw a cop car. The officer driving slammed on the brakes and pulled up in front of him.

"Kyle Hulbert?" the cop asked.

"Uh, yeah . . . ," Kyle said, surprised.

The cop had an emergency detention order, which generally was handed out along with a court-ordered isolation order for a person with a communicable disease, like tuberculosis or bubonic plague. But in Kyle's case, it meant that he was headed back to an institution, a familiar-enough place to him by that point in his life.

CHAPTER 6

RENAISSANCE WAS ALL Kyle needed to hear. That era spanning a time period from the fourteenth to the seventeenth centuries, arguably born in Italy and spreading throughout Europe, gave Kyle a warm and fuzzy feeling, as if he'd been back to that society and reincarnated into the twenty-first century. Renaissance, much in line with Kyle and his philosophy of life, means "rebirth." Historians say the Renaissance was about "classical learning and values." It was a time of discovery, new thought, and artistic exploration. All of this was something Kyle could relate to. As he walked through the weapons shop on the grounds of the festival on that crisp, cool, windy October afternoon, Kyle spotted several kids his age hanging around. There was a bounce to Kyle's step on this day. He'd just met Brandy and had gotten her number. He was feeling empowered. He devoured the attention the cat costume had given him all day long. People were constantly stopping him and admiring the costume and complimenting him for it.

"Hey, hot girls want to come up and pet you behind the ears," Kyle said later with a laugh. "I'm ready and willing to purr."

Kyle had stepped away from those friends he had gone to the festival with and told them he'd meet up with them at the weapons shop. As he searched the weapons shop tent for his mates, something else caught Kyle's eye.

One of the girls in the weapons shop had her back to him. He walked up stealthily. The guy behind the counter, who turned out to be the proprietor of the shop, grinned. He picked up on what Kyle (the cat) was doing, and he decided to play along with the gag. Kyle wanted to scare the girl. Not in a Jason from *Friday the 13th* way, but rather in a startling break-the-ice manner to introduce himself. The cat costume had been receiving positive comments for how real it was. He had become quite the attraction at the festival—or at least he felt he was—and now he was playing the role of the cat quite zealously.

The guy behind the counter kept the girl's attention as Kyle walked up stealthily from behind.

"And by the way, I'd like to introduce you to a friend of mine," the proprietor said to the girl as he gestured for her to turn around.

Kyle was right behind her. She turned at that moment and, with her eyes meeting Kyle's chest (she was so short), she took one look at him and screamed.

"I was laughing and trying to apologize at the same time," Kyle remarked later. It was one of those moments.

They introduced themselves. With the girl screaming, several of her friends came running to her side. They had been in another section of the shop, browsing around, and hadn't seen what had happened. As they approached, everyone had a good laugh.

"I'm Mike," one of the kids said to Kyle, introducing himself. "Great costume."

"Katie," said another girl, nodding. "And that is," she added, pointing to the third wheel in the group, "Clara."

Clara, Kyle thought. He liked the name. He'd seen her before, too.

But where?

It had been earlier that same day. Clara had approached

Kyle. She introduced herself. She said how much she appreciated Kyle's look, the black clothes, the mask, and especially the long sword strapped to his back as if he were a Ninja Turtle. She had looked him over that first time they met as if sizing him up for a role in a movie.

"Everybody, this is Kyle," Clara said aloud as they stood inside the weapons tent. "He's an assassin!"

Kyle liked that.

They were role-playing already.

Clara smiled at Kyle. There was an energy between them, a moment of pure poise. Not necessarily romantic, but as though they were connected spiritually.

Katie laughed. She stood there, thinking for a moment, recalling how Clara had, earlier that day, pointed Kyle out as Katie, Mike, and Clara walked around. "Check him out . . . ," Clara had said. "You know, I think I may know that guy from the Underworld."

Katie looked at Clara. She knew what Clara was talking about.

And now here they were, being formally introduced, hanging out together inside the weapons tent. The meeting seemed so random, yet Clara knew it was inevitable. She felt as though she and Kyle were destined to meet, and here they were, running into each other at last.

Kyle could tell immediately that Clara was different from the other kids. There was something about her. Clara was dressed in a long gray cloak, her everyday clothing underneath. She stood with a long wooden shaft in her hand, giving her that Gandalf look, like a leader from *The Lord of the Rings*. She had a magnetic quality about her, Kyle considered, however dark it was, and he could tell the others looked at Clara, to a certain extent, for guidance and direction.

The other male, Mike Pfohl, had an unkempt look about him. He wore a scraggly mustache, not fully grown in, and a bit of a goatee. Mike sported thick, dark, bushy eyebrows and long, stringy hippie hair. He had a 1970s rock-and-roll look, like a member of Grand Funk Railroad or Led Zeppelin.

Quiet, Kyle thought while sizing up Mike. Though he would soon learn that Mike's silence wasn't a shyness necessarily, but it stemmed more from curiosity. Kyle considered that he had fallen in with his kind of people.

Mike was also checking out Kyle in his own way. Kyle came across as boisterous and loud, and he talked speedily. He had a full-on personality. Kyle wanted people to like him and notice him—right away.

"Mike was generally fascinated by the people around him," Kyle said later.

Kyle didn't know it yet, but Mike had a dark past. He wasn't all right, or quiet for quiet's sake. Back in December 2000, Mike cut himself badly. Not by accident, but with a razor blade, an X-Acto knife. He'd self-inflicted several wounds: arms, chest, and stomach. A friend had caught him in time and Mike was taken in and saved. Four weeks after that, one report claimed, Mike tried swallowing a bottle of pills, but his mother stopped him before he could complete the job. He wound up in a mental hospital. Since getting out, he was sleeping in the basement of his parents' house.

The way Kyle acted, as they all stood around that tent talking and introducing themselves, Mike latched onto his personality. Mike liked the idea, Kyle later observed, of this new kid being assertive and loud and talkative. Kyle was original and unlike anyone this group knew. He had a leadership quality about him, but not to the degree of being bossy or brassy. Although Clara might have come across as the group's architect, she was far from it. Kyle was now with a group of followers. Kyle was unlike anyone within Mike's world whom the kid had been accustomed to meeting.

Mike was "very reserved," Kyle said. He kept to himself. The greasy hair, long and flowing over his shoulders, the round silver-dollar-size thick glasses, were all features that personified who Mike was. Mike looked a lot older than his age. He had reticence to his gate, as though he would just about go along with whatever anyone in the group wanted to do, and would not ask too many questions. Mike, who had been working at Walmart, had one shining testament to his life (beyond Katie, whom he adored). It was his black Honda Civic, a car he had purchased with money his grandmother had lent him. The car was all his. It allowed him the opportunity to come and go as he pleased. He wasn't cemented to the basement of his parents' house, living in a dungeon without much light. The car gave him mobility, freedom. He could pop in a head-crunching CD of metal and bang his head while driving.

"Mike was very prone to black moods," Kyle explained, "but he loved that car. Man, did he love his car."

The entire group, Kyle soon realized, was like this: dark, gloomy, and sad. Listening to Mike talk, after they hit it off and started walking around the festival, Kyle thought: *His life is boring in a lot of ways.* The guy was existing, Kyle felt. Just going about life, not knowing what he was going to do next, where he was headed. Mike also stayed at a rental property with Katie and several other friends at times. His prize possession in life was his shitty car. Mike did not have much.

"He was used to dealing with a bunch of people," Kyle said, "who weren't caring a whole lot in their lives about achieving things."

Mike wanted success; his only hang-up was that he didn't know what he wanted to do. He yearned to "achieve something great out of his life," Kyle added. "He just didn't know what that was."

As he got to know Mike, Kyle believed Mike saw him as a larger-than-life figure who did not belong, as Kyle put it, in "the right and ordered world" that all of them—Mike, Katie, Clara, and some others—existed in at the time. Kyle had no reservations about showing people who he was, telling people how he felt, and he did not care what people thought about him. Kyle was over being bullied and picked on and talked about, which had become a perpetual part of his life as a child.

"There's that crazy kid . . . ," Kyle would hear as he walked down the hallways of his school. "He's on meds!" He was used to being "that kid," the one everyone else talked about and steered clear of. Making his way through school, Kyle's life had become such a litany of paranoid delusions that he kept a knife on him at all times—and carried the weapon with pride, knowing he would use it if he needed. He sometimes even traveled with that sword, a weapon so sharp and powerful that one swipe could sever the head off a human being in an instant. Kyle believed there were people out in the world after him. He was constantly running, constantly looking over his shoulder, waiting for the day he would have to do battle with someone. Yet, he didn't know who, where, or when that was going to happen.

"Back then," Kyle explained, "I was constantly under the belief that 'someone was after me.' The paranoia fluctuated from day to day. Sometimes I believed demons were hunting me. Other times it was rival vampires."

A lot of the time, there was no "specific 'them,'" Kyle added. "Just the sure knowledge that some . . . 'other' was out to get me to do me harm."

As he walked around the festival, getting to know Mike, Clara, and Katie, Kyle thought maybe he wouldn't share with them just yet the voices ringing in his head and the fact that, he said later, "often this paranoia I experienced dovetailed with my desire to be protective of those I called my friends." Kyle felt this already about these three and he'd just met them. He could sense a bond immediately. For Kyle, this meant something. Because "if 'the other' was out to hurt me, then it would hurt my friends to get to me. . . ."

Here was a group of wayward kids going nowhere, doing nothing, living in a bubble of melancholy and darkness, and Kyle, an exact match, had found a place to fit in just weeks after walking out of court an emancipated man. They got up in the morning, called each other, hung out, walked through the local malls, and basically shifted from one place to the next, complaining about life, embracing the dark moods overtaking their days.

Then, quite unexpectedly, as though he fell from the sky, along came this animated, over-the-top, eccentric kid. He was dressed from head to toe like a black cat (Kyle wore only black and generally a trench coat), living out the life of that costume. He was talking and talking and talking about everything he could think of, immediately relating to what these three kids were feeling regarding how society had not understood who they were. For Mike, Clara, and Katie, they had found their Gandalf, their spiritual leader.

"The word you're looking for is 'emo,'" Kyle explained, describing this group that he was now an intricate part of—that is, he added, if a label needed to be put on who they were.

Most people believe that being emo is equivalent to being lonely, depressed, isolated, and dark. Perhaps being emo is partly living within that framed, profiled, labeled structure. But those who actually live it claim it is a way to express their inner artistic creativity: through music, poetry, reading, writing, and art, all of which can influence the way they present themselves to the world. The safe truth of the matter is that emo—like the label "hipster"—can mean different things to different people.

But emo, alt, goth—all those brands people put on kids these days—Kyle Hulbert noted, did not best describe who he was when he ran into this group randomly and became a central part of their inner circle. Nor had it described or labeled who Mike, Katie, and Clara were. At this time of his life, Kyle said, as he got to know Katie, Mike, and Clara, there was one word that best defined who he was—or, rather, who he *believed* he was.

"Vampire."

CHAPTER 7

KATIE INGLIS HAD a wired look about her, more frenzied than natural. She looked like the girl next door; though when she spoke, you immediately knew she wasn't the girl next door. Her brown eyes were wide and globelike, as though she was whacked out on mind meds. Katie also wore big-framed glasses, which gave her the look of a cross between a modest librarian and a chick on the run from something. Her blond hair was straight and flat like seaweed. She didn't say much of anything, except maybe after being asked. Katie had this weird way of coming across as a girl who could pass for fourteen (and you'd believe it) or a woman of twenty (and you'd believe that, too). In other words, she could pull off either look, if she had to.

"What are you into?" Katie asked Kyle as they wandered round the festival. They had broken away from the others. In fact, Mike was so concerned after not seeing Katie for some time that he had gotten everyone he could muster together to form a search party to find her. But Katie was off with Kyle, whom she was totally infatuated with the moment she met him. According to one account, Katie thought Kyle, or what she could tell of him through his costume, reminded her of Joe Perry from Aerosmith, her favorite band.

"Katie was just loose," Kyle said later.

Kyle knew what she meant when Katie asked what he was into: "Dungeons and Dragons," he answered.

The way Kyle told it, he said Katie then asked him if he wanted to "check out" her "regimentality."

Kyle presumed that meant her vagina, and he smiled at that thought.

According to what Kyle told me, Katie took his hand and moved it underneath her dress. She wasn't wearing any panties.

They kissed.

Kyle, greatly aroused, began to finger Katie, he later claimed.

She moaned, getting into it.

Her promiscuity was bizarre, Kyle later said. As they walked around the festival, for example, and he and Katie broke off from the others, she was all over him aggressively. They had just met. Later, Mike would explain to Kyle that he had met Katie and they slept together just a few days later.

"It's something I regret now," Katie said later, confirming that she had gone to the festival with her boyfriend, Mike, but had snuck off with this new kid, Kyle.

"She was Mike's girl," Kyle said. He was clear to point out that this hindsight image of Katie he now had was terribly biased because of what would happen within the group in the coming months and the division that grew among them after that. "But she didn't care."

As Kyle got to know the group more personally, he viewed Katie as someone "who was just there." She was part of the crowd, no doubt, but there was no vitality to her character. She never had anything of value to add to a conversation, Kyle said. She didn't have her own ideas. She didn't speak up. She was always spoken to, told what to do, where to go, and how to think. She didn't do anything for herself, Kyle felt—with the exception, perhaps, of cheating on Mike.

"You know, she's with Mike," Kyle said, "but here she has this loose sense of fidelity." Kyle had no idea that Katie and

Mike were an item until the days following the festival, when Kyle and Mike started hanging out. "You'd never have known it that day." And even then, Kyle found out that Mike was a guy who really didn't care.

"His concept behind him and Katie was different," Kyle explained. Kyle had asked Mike about Katie one day, how long they had been dating, how serious the relationship was.

"I don't *own* her," Mike said. "She's her own woman."

"Look, man, I respect that. She's just a girl. We're *friends*. I'm not going to be sleeping with her—even though I could."

And Mike, Kyle said, was cool with that remark. It didn't bother him.

After he felt comfortable enough, Kyle told Mike and Katie he was a vampire—a genuine, blood-drinking, night-prowling, sword-carrying, *Twilight*-type vampire. No one in the group had known an actual blood-drinking vampire, Kyle soon found out. In this respect, he came across as an intriguing figure, a bizarre display for them to be curious about and in awe of.

That was something Kyle absolutely adored.

CLARA SCHWARTZ WAS the different one out of the bunch—and Kyle began to see this as the four of them—Kyle, Mike, Katie, and Clara—talked and opened up to one another. The first thing about Clara that Kyle noticed was her gaze. Clara could look him in the eyes and not look away. Her stare was arresting, important, and fascinating. Her gaze was determined, definite, and confident. She was the quiet one, yes—the one who stood off to the side and checked you out from top to bottom before trusting you and allowing you into her strange, desolate world. But Clara also had an aura of self-reliance that Kyle picked up on right away. He appreciated it.

Back at the festival, Kyle remembered, while they walked around, as everyone else talked and joked and mingled, Clara flanked the group silently, like a leopard surveying her prey, not saying much of anything. Everyone was in character that day. And for the most part, they talked in character and referenced the era as well.

"She's on the fringes of the group, just watching, being very quiet," Kyle explained. "She had this intense stare. Never forget that."

This intensity that Clara displayed spoke to Kyle. It told him a lot about who she was. He was attracted to this about her, more psychologically than anything else. Kyle wanted to know more about Clara, her philosophies on life, her thoughts about the world.

"A lot of people," Kyle remarked, "if you look them in the eyes and you keep their gaze, they'll turn away. Or look down. They won't keep your gaze. It's a self-conscious thing most people have. Not Clara. She did not flinch. That *intrigued* me."

Clara was kind of frumpy (a description that Kyle later said he unquestionably agreed with). She had these chubby, infant-like cheeks that drooped like hanging pink water balloons. Clear, porcelain skin, chalky white, Clara carried an atmosphere of weightiness in her stride, and played up what was a total secrecy about her. When one studied Clara, it wasn't hard to determine that had she put a little bit of time and effort into her makeup and hygiene and looks, she would have been a beautiful young woman. But she chose to look natural, idle, like a girl who shopped at thrift stores and wore no cosmetics.

Clara came across as depressed, with a blue cloud hovering over her. Yet, at the same rate, Clara wasn't a depressed person, once you got to know her. She enjoyed the attention this dark milieu gave her—or simply didn't care what people thought. She wanted others to feel sorry for her, certainly. Although she never admitted it, she yearned for those around her to feel the pain she was going through. All of that was clear to Kyle as he got to talking to Clara in the days, weeks, and months following the festival. On several occasions, in writing, during instant messaging, and in person, Clara had even referred to her life in general as "living in a hellhole." When Kyle met her, Clara was attending James Madison University (JMU), in Harrisonburg, Virginia. She was in her sophomore year. JMU was not an easy school to get into, tuition alone coming in at around $25,000 a year. Not bad for a girl who didn't claim to have any prospects going on in a life she categorically loathed.

As Kyle would learn, the unhappiness Clara carried—however transparent he would come to see it—might have stemmed from losing her mother years ago. As it were, when Clara wasn't living at school in her dorm and attending classes, she stayed with her dad, fifty-seven-year-old Dr. Robert Schwartz, who worked long hours as a respected DNA biophysicist, researcher, and scientist. Clara made it clear that she didn't get along with him at all. In fact, there was a good indication—and Kyle picked up on it immediately—that Clara hated this man with a passion rarely seen within the father-daughter relationship.

There was one time in the tenth grade when Clara sat in class and realized how smart she was and that the work was easy for her. In this way, she took after her intelligent father. Yet, being smart was not enough, she realized after having an epiphany on that day: *I wonder sometimes if life's this easy,* she wrote in one of her journals, *and I'm that smart, why do I wanna die so much?*

This occurred in 1998, when Clara was still trying to figure out her role in life without a mother. She claimed then that all her father ever did was yell at her and put her down for "knowing nothing." She wrote that being "rich" was "synonymous" with being "well-brought-up" and a "loving family"—though there was no evidence to prove that Clara and her family were rich, whatever that term means in this day and age. According to her writing, she yearned for normalcy, but then she did everything she could to come across as abnormal and to lead an anomalous lifestyle. She claimed to have an IQ of 196 and wrote that she still got *yelled @ for doing homework.* If only, she concluded in her writing, *I had a loving home, my life'd be perfect.*

Clara wore baggy men's clothes, for the most part. She had dark brunette hair, stringy and fraying in sections, parting it unequivocally down the middle, the remainder curling down past her modest breasts. Clara had an intellectual quality to her, right from the get-go, which Kyle noticed and took note of. She came across as a shy recluse, sure; but by talking to her, Kyle could tell Clara Schwartz knew exactly what she was doing.

As their friendship blossomed, Kyle would come to see that Clara's introverted nature was born out of being a girl who had been severely bullied in high school. She was an outcast. Made to feel like she didn't belong—less than others. Of course, Kyle nestled up to this feeling, as if they had been split at birth.

"Kids hated me," Clara told Kyle that day at the festival.

Kyle laughed. "I know how you feel!"

She's quiet and shy because she doesn't have a lot of self-worth, Kyle thought. *Yet, I like her. . . . She's cool. My kind of people—intelligent, perceptive.* He knew right away they were going to connect.

Along with a brother and sister, Clara grew up on a property that her family, which had owned it for more than six decades, called "The Stone House," near Mount Gilead Road, just outside Leesburg, Virginia. Set back from the main thoroughfare, very secluded, this creepy-looking property, which would work nicely in any 1970s-era drive-in horror film, had been the base for Clara's family on her mother's side. The yellowed, stone-face-textured home was covered with overgrown brush and unclipped tree limbs in desperate need of an arborist. There was a smaller addition attached to the main home. It appeared to be so run-down and weak, it might fall over with the slightest touch. Clara and her dad kept several horses on the property. From the outside, the place appeared to have been badly neglected, in need of a total makeover and some serious reconstruction. Inside was no different: the walls were shoddy and poorly maintained; the wooden floors were dirty and in great need of sanding and refinishing; the cabinets in the kitchen were old, rickety, and falling apart. The entire house, from top to bottom, could benefit from a bulldozer and a new beginning.

If we are to take as family gospel what Clara's aunt (Clara's mother's sister) later wrote to the court, *My story in this house parallels Clara's. There are patterns of isolation and abuse that are family secrets.*

With regard to Clara's mother, the aunt had always been told that she was "prettier" than Clara's mother; yet, the aunt always felt "inferior" to her sister, Joan (Clara's mother), because the kids were often told that Joan might not have been given the looks, but she was smarter than the rest of them—and a mind would go a hell of a lot further than a body.

If true, one story, which depicted how neglected the kids were, was frightening and spoke to what Clara would later detail in her own journals and diaries. According to Clara's aunt, her and Joan's brother once went missing. He was gone overnight. He had gotten lost in the woods. He screamed and cried out, he later told the family, walking around, trying to find his way out of the forest. Eventually he slept under a tree when no one came to find him. The following morning, the child found his way back home, only to find out that nobody had even noticed he was gone. He was eight years old at the time.

CHAPTER 8

EVERYONE IN THE group knew Darcy (pseudonym), the girl whom Kyle had come upon and scared with his cat costume inside the weapons tent on the day they met at the festival. Kyle had felt that these new friends were his kind of people, which was why he walked over in the first place and introduced himself, however sneakily, to Darcy. He knew they'd all click on certain levels. Never once had he thought that as they got to know each other and chatted during those days following the festival, he and Clara would connect on more violent and fantastical planes than Kyle could have imagined.

"I make friends easily," Kyle explained to me during our twenty-plus hours of interviews in 2013 and 2014. "I'm quick to engage people. I laugh. I joke. I am always grinning ear to ear. That's me. So when I get around people who I think are actually interesting, I can have a *really* good time."

At the end of that festival day, Kyle and Mike had a chat. Along with Darcy, there was another guy who came to meet up with them, who was actually Clara's boyfriend, Patrick House, Kyle learned later. It had been Patrick who introduced Mike to Katie. Mike and Patrick had met inside the office waiting room of a psychiatrist one day the previous year, according to one report. When Mike started working at Walmart in July 2001, he ran into Patrick again and they started hanging out. Clara would tag along at times. Mike found Patrick a bit on the odd side, he later told one reporter, but he liked him. According to Jason Cherkis, who wrote a *Washington City Paper* article about Mike, Patrick often talked of how he once "cast a spell that killed thirteen people who were trying to kill him."

"I wanna kill Clara's father," Patrick told Mike one day. It was the summer of 2001. Clara had filled Patrick's head with so many ideas about her father by then. She talked about the nasty things her father did to her so often, Mike was tired of hearing it. "I don't like her dad," Patrick concluded.

When Patrick talked like that, Mike told Cherkis, he "just listened."

THE RENAISSANCE FESTIVAL had been a fun day all around. Kyle met a half-dozen new friends—Patrick, Mike, Katie, and Clara, among them—and got a girl's phone number. He was stoked to hang out with Katie, Mike, and Clara, especially in those days following the festival. They had exchanged numbers, e-mail addresses, and instant-messaging tags.

"Let's chill," Mike Pfohl suggested. "Call me, Kyle."

"Yeah, man, no doubt. Definitely."

One did not have to twist Kyle's arm to get him to hang out, suffice it to say, if he liked your company. Kyle was always ready and willing. On top of that, Kyle still hadn't found a place to call home. He essentially was bouncing from friend to friend, even staying at a shelter or in the woods inside that tent he carried with him inside a backpack. With more friends in the mix, that meant more places to crash.

Speaking with writer Jason Cherkis, Mike later recalled a different version of how Clara and Kyle had met. Mike did not think Clara was there at the festival that day. Mike told Cherkis that when Katie and Kyle took off, Katie had told

Kyle, "You need to meet my friend Clara," and so they made plans to meet and hang out after the festival.

Kyle had said sure.

The foremost truth in all of this is that Kyle and Clara eventually did become very good friends, with shared interests and tremendously similar ways of looking at the world. Within Kyle, Clara saw something—something she could use to her advantage in the near future.

CHAPTER 9

CLARA, KATIE, AND Patrick had birthdays coming up. It was mid-September.

"Applebee's in Leesburg," Clara suggested.

They were pumped.

Mike picked everyone up (as usual he was the driver). Clara had just turned nineteen, so had Katie. Patrick's nineteenth birthday was in a few weeks.

This was a rare occasion for Clara these days, to leave the dorm and actually show herself in public.

The waitress asked what they wanted.

"Steaks," Clara said, smiling and raising her eyebrows.

They toasted to themselves as they waited to eat. This was nice. Four friends, double-dating, celebrating their birthdays. Clara had been drilling Patrick with the idea that she wanted him to do her a major favor that involved violence against her father. She hadn't given up on this. Patrick was playing along like the sly, slick tough guy he had built himself to be in the world he and Mike shared. All of it fell under the banner of a fantasy game Clara had created. Clara hated Christians. She believed they would take over the world. She was planning a war in which she and all of her warriors would revolt and fight against them. It would start when Clara, the leader of this fantasy world, died.

"Katie is to be my successor," Clara said. "She will take the world's throne."

With a shake of his head and a roll of his eyes, Mike would always watch and listen. Katie bought into it all, following along with Clara—whether serious or not—all the way.

The waitress soon brought the food. As she placed it down on the table, Katie thought she heard Clara say something to Patrick.

"When are you going to help do something about my father?"

"I need to see him once more," Patrick said. "Before Christmas . . ."

Clara cut into her steak while the waitress stood by.

"This is rare! Fucking raw," Clara barked bitterly. There was a sense of entitlement in her voice, as there always had been. Many later agreed with this observation: Clara believed she was owed something from the world, due to her tortured life at home. Her family, she had always said, had loads of money and she wanted—shit, she *deserved*!—her rightful share of it. How dare someone serve her a raw steak!

"Ma'am, would you like me to take it back?" the waitress asked.

"Uh . . . yeah!"

The waitress brought back a second steak.

"This is not what I ordered," Clara said again. "It's fucking rare!"

The steak went back and the waitress brought a third. She placed it in front of Clara and waited for her response.

Clara cut a piece, took a bite, and spit it out on the table.

"This is bullshit."

The waitress walked away, likely shaking her head in disgust.

Clara slid her plate across to Patrick.

"Taste it."

"What?"

"Cut a piece and eat it."

Patrick did as he was told.

"Nasty," he said. "Something's wrong with it. I think it's a drug specifically targeted to assassins."

"This steak has been poisoned," Clara whispered to Mike, Katie, and Patrick, leaning over the booth table, gathering them around.

Mike tried a piece. He didn't find anything wrong with it.

"Yeah . . . and what I need to find out is how my father got in touch with this cook and was able to pull it off."

After the others finished eating—Clara had not touched her steak again—Clara explained that she believed assassins or demons had somehow gotten inside the kitchen and poisoned her steak. Her father, of course, was one of them.

"We should go now," Clara said.

"What about dessert?" someone asked.

Clara suggested the TGI Fridays across the street for dessert.

It's important to note that at no time that night were any of them in character or involved in any narrative revolving around that "world" Clara had created. It was a night out, talking and being kids.

Clara tugged at Patrick's arm as they made their way across the street. She said: "When do you plan on killing my father?"

Patrick didn't know how to respond to this. He wanted to placate Clara, play along with her and her little fantasy game. According to Patrick later, he never intended to carry out any of Clara's so-called "plans."

There had to come a point where Patrick asked himself how serious Clara was. Clara certainly sounded on this night as though her request was not part of the game; she truly wanted Patrick to kill her father.

"Look," he said, the others unable to hear him, "when the time is right, it will happen."

Patrick longed for her to forget about it. He hoped she was kidding around.

CHAPTER 10

THAT WEEK AFTER the festival, Kyle called Mike—and, according to Kyle's recollection, a best friendship was born. They hung out at Mike's place. Katie was there. Kyle suggested that he, Katie, and Mike meet up with Brandy, the girl Kyle had met at the festival. Kyle had called Brandy and made a date with her. Kyle said he needed to blow off some steam. He had a court appearance coming up on October 8.

"Shit yeah," Mike said.

Katie agreed.

They drove up to Maryland, where Brandy lived. Along the way, Mike told Kyle a story about Clara browsing through a weapons catalogue one day at his place. Clara was fascinated with knives, Mike told Kyle. She had picked out several. One, in fact, she told Mike she was buying specifically for Patrick as a gift.

Kyle smiled. The more he heard about Clara, the more he liked the way she thought.

Brandy was the "cheerleader type," Kyle said. Very cleancut. A nice girl. She had a bird, an African gray parrot named Bizzy, or, as Kyle called him, a "malicious fucker." That first time Kyle showed up at Brandy's house, she and her mother went into the kitchen to fetch some soft drinks while he and

Katie and Mike waited in the living room. Kyle walked over to Bizzy.

The bird looked up at Kyle and said, "Pretty bird . . . pretty bird."

"Get a load of this shit," Kyle said to the others. Then, to the bird, "You are such a pretty bird."

"Cracker?" the bird said.

Kyle saw a box of crackers on the table. He picked one up. "Cracker . . . cracker!"

He put the cracker up to the cage.

"And, shit you not," Kyle said, "he bit my finger just at the same time, like in a movie, Brandy's mother yelled from the kitchen, 'Oh, by the way, don't try to feed the bird—he bites!'"

Bizzy laughed.

They all went out that night and had a good time. But Kyle was more interested in Mike, Katie, and Clara—even though she wasn't there that night. He liked Brandy, saw a future for them, but there was something in this trio of new friends that intrigued him. More than that, they were interested in *him*—especially his vampire lifestyle. Kyle considered himself a bona fide vampire and they all found this fascinating. Kyle was the type to go off by himself to the clubs in search of "donors" (women to trade blood sucking and sex with). He walked the earth at this period in his life, Kyle said, with the absolute belief that there were good and bad vampires roaming around, some of whom were searching for him. Mike, Katie, and Clara would ask him questions about his lifestyle. This made Kyle feel important, looked up to.

A force.

A protector.

A role, effectively, he adored.

CLARA WAS EXTREMELY adept at "not being noticed," Kyle realized as he got to know her more intimately over the course of that fall. She never spoke very loud, talking almost in a whisper. She also had a bit of a lisp or speech impediment, where she had trouble pronouncing the letter *R*. All of this, however, fascinated Kyle, who observed, "She was very direct in her mannerisms."

"I ever tell you about September eleventh," Clara told Kyle one night.

Kyle knew all he needed to know about that devastating day. He never thought too much about it.

"I did that," Clara told Kyle.

He was confused. "Um, you did what, exactly?"

"I have a list of the chemicals used in making the planes crash. Lord Chaos might have been responsible."

It seemed Clara was taking responsibility for the terror attacks of 9/11.

"You'll have to tell me more about this Lord Chaos," Kyle responded, ignoring the absolutely ignorant comment Clara had made about 9/11.

"All I knew then," Kyle said later, "was that 'Lord Chaos' was Clara's nickname."

Assertive. That was Clara. No, she was not the *leader* of the group, but Clara was the focus, the center, and the core. Hence the "Lord" and not "Lady" of her title.

Or at least she *believed* she was.

"I'm an outcast at home, and a prisoner," Clara told Kyle. Immediately, in those days after the festival, as soon as Kyle started hanging out with Mike, Katie, and Clara, Clara opened up about her home life to Kyle, telling him any chance she got how much she despised her father. On this day, she and Kyle were alone at Mike's parents' house, hanging out, talking. Mike and Katie were off by themselves having sex.

"They liked to have sex in front of us," Kyle said. "And when they did, we just walked away."

Kyle wanted to know more about Clara. "How so?" he asked, referring to Clara's home life and how much of an outcast she felt within the family unit. So far, Clara was hitting all the right bells for Kyle. It seemed she could be talking about his life.

"Well, even my brother and sister blame me for my mom's death."

"That's horrible."

"This is why I like staying at JMU. It keeps me away from home. Allows me to escape that place. It keeps me free."

This, Kyle said, hit him the hardest. As he heard the details of what Clara described as blatant "abuse by her father," Kyle was appalled by what Clara had experienced, but he could also relate to how sheltered and overly burdened she felt living there, as though she didn't belong. Kyle had never felt like he fit anywhere. Roaming from foster home to foster home, psych hospital to lockup, Kyle was a kid who had never found his roots or a foundation—same as Clara was now suggesting she had gone through most of her life. They clicked immediately. A bond was being forged between them.

"Like at school," Clara said, talking about how hard high school was for her, "I felt like a troll. Kids gnawed at me."

Kyle found himself in an awkward position within this new group of friends. "I didn't try to be the leader," he later recalled. "But when it came to Mike and me, especially, he was always looking to me for *'Where do we go from here?'* type of advice. You know, *'What do we do today?'* With Clara, it was almost as if as we were getting to know each other, she knew so much about me already."

Whereas Clara was a bit more curious and self-reliant, not ever needing to be led or told what to do or how to think, she was trying to figure out Kyle as much as he was trying to figure her out and what she wanted from him.

There was a difference, however: If the inch-thick psychological reports of his life from this time period were accurate, Kyle was a paranoid schizophrenic, suffering from delusions of grandeur and severe, animated, and genuine (to him) visions (hallucinations). Whereas Clara came across as a spoiled, smart little girl who had an overbearing father and a problematic home life of abuse and emotional attacks (if we believe her)—issues she belabored without backing them up with any tangible evidence other than her own words and accusations.

Clara understood her situation, could deal with it, and showed no signs, gave no warnings, of being mentally incapacitated. Furthermore, Clara knew how to arrive at a common ground and to build a rapport with Kyle, using his mental instabilities to her advantage. This was never clearer than in the way she began to associate with Kyle and go to him with issues about her home and problems with her father. And it's important to say here: There was not one report ever written about this so-called abuse Clara would talk about routinely.

When they went off on those walks as Katie and Mike had sex, Clara would hold Kyle's hand. Make like she was interested in him sexually *and* emotionally.

It all gave Kyle a false sense of power—a position that Kyle had grown accustomed to. Inside those hospitals and facilities, and even some of the foster homes he had lived in, kids would go to him, Kyle explained, because he didn't care so much about image or what people thought. He was his own person, and people accepted and gravitated toward that strong personality.

"Example? When I was in school—I mean like seven or eight years old. There was this bubble around me. When people came around me, they quieted down. Took notice. Then the whispers would begin. 'There's that crazy kid who threw the desk at the teacher.' It was so stupid. Because I was on medication and placed in hospitals, I must be sick!"

Those were the times when no one wanted to hang around Kyle. He had a terrible go of making friends. But then one day, it all clicked for him. Kids flocked to him. They wanted to be near him. But it wasn't genuine, Kyle felt. It seemed rooted in a keep-your-enemies-close thing and more of an interest in his psychosis than actual friendship.

"I said, 'Fuck all of you!' I stopped caring what people thought. And the damnedest thing happened—they all wanted to be my friends."

And now, within a few weeks of knowing her, Kyle had a new best friend, Clara Jane Schwartz, who basically acted the same way those kids back in his childhood had. Clara, who seemed to be a lonely, old-fashioned, goth girl, asked all the right questions of Kyle to keep him interested, to keep him thinking they had this core connection between them.

Clara had plans for Kyle Hulbert, however—only he didn't know it just yet.

CHAPTER 11

ONE AFTERNOON, KYLE took a call from Mike. Kyle was staying with a friend and would alternate his welcome there with shelters and living in his tent in the woods. The one thing Kyle always kept close by was his cell phone, now a direct line to his new group of friends.

"I got a letter from my shrink," Mike explained.

"What's up?"

"He says he thinks 'I'm vulnerable to psychosis that could develop into schizophrenia,' among other things. He claims there are 'aspects' of my 'thinking that are not based in reality.'"

"No kidding," Kyle said. He was very familiar with that sort of analysis. He had heard it himself all his life. "What are you gonna do?"

Mike said he didn't care.

"I never heard about that letter again," Kyle said.

That afternoon, Kyle rode his bike, which a friend had given him, to the Potomac Mills shopping center in Woodbridge, Virginia, your typical suburban-American corporate mall. He was hanging out by himself, waiting for Clara and his new group of friends to meet him later on that night. Mike, who had become Kyle's taxi just about everywhere Kyle wanted to go, said he couldn't get away until the evening. That was fine with Kyle. If there was one thing Kyle didn't have trouble with, it was finding something to do or making new acquaintances. It was a quiet day. The mall would be fun.

Or so Kyle thought.

As Kyle walked around in a common area of the mall, a security guard approached Kyle on his left side. Kyle had a knife strapped to his side on the right. He was wearing sunglasses and his signature black trench coat—a look he would become known for, along with his Kikwear "Extreme" pants, those over-the-top baggy jeans that funnel out and are double in size at the bottom of the leg, with lots of pockets and places to stash things. The emo and alt kids liked to wear these types of clothes; though Kyle said, "Look, I liked wearing black pants. I liked Kikwear. I liked my trench coat. I didn't wear this stuff to be emo or alt, or even a vampire. It was just how *I* dressed." Save for the shotgun, Kyle looked like he belonged on the set of the *Matrix* films. He even wore his dark sunglasses during the day and at night. ("My eyes are very sensitive to light," he claimed later, seemingly having an answer for everything.) "That's why I wore sunglasses all the time. Looking good in them was a plus!" he added, not bashful about flexing his inability to express a smidgen of humility.

Kyle also had a backpack over his shoulder. So he was likely being profiled, as were others walking around that mall on that day, based solely on appearance. Security watched kids. Security guards in malls profiled. It is, as they say, what it is.

"Excuse me," the security guard said, walking up on Kyle, staring at the knife Kyle had strapped to his belt.

"Yeah?"

"That's a concealed weapon."

"Come on," Kyle said. "No, it's not concealed."

Security called police and Kyle was arrested.

Kyle said he had made a point to make sure his coat did not cover the weapon: "I know it's a Virginia state law."

Still, why even carry a knife?

"I liked it," Kyle reckoned. "I carried a sword, too, but I did not have it that day."

During his knife- and sword-carrying days, Kyle believed there were "people" after him—"the others," he called them. He needed to be armed, in case that day came when he had to confront those rival vampires. And the idea that they were out there—even though they were not—was as real to Kyle Hulbert as the sky above, he later explained—same as the pet dragon that followed Kyle around wherever he went.

There was nobody who could have ever convinced him otherwise.

"And those weapons, I needed them," Kyle explained. "They were out there. 'The others.' They were going to get me and anyone with me if I didn't protect myself. I knew they were close by, too."

How?

Why, Kyle said he could smell them, of course.

CHAPTER 12

HALLUCINATIONS ARE A major part of where Kyle Hulbert fits into the story of Clara Schwartz, Mike Pfohl, and Katie Inglis. Not drug-induced apparitions, as in an acid trip bringing about streetlamps that drip like a leaky faucet, plants that move on their own and speak, or the street rolling as you walk. The way Kyle explained it, the "hallucinations" he experienced—a word he claimed he was forced to use because it's the only way most people will understand—weren't anything like a scene from *The Song Remains the Same,* Led Zeppelin's classic 1970s film that featured "trips" the boys in the band had gone on. No, Kyle said his trips were his reality.

"If only it were that simple," Kyle said later, explaining how he wished his visions and hallucinations could be clarified by saying he took LSD. "Believe it or not, contrary to popular belief, I am not a fan of drugs. I don't have anything morally against them. . . . My life and my mind, I realized, were screwed up enough without me adding to it with drugs."

Here's where a difficult part of Kyle's story begins, however. Kyle Hulbert feels strongly that these hallucinations are genuine visions of *real* beings and *actual* events—for him, they are *not* illusions or delusions. He believes there were times in his life when he would enter into a world of cartoons and exist with certain characters and then exit and enter into another world, where faeries flew and sprinkled magic dust.

It sounds dramatic, unreal, and even surreal. Maybe not worth the time to explore. You want to brush it off by shooing your hands, saying, *"That's crazy, dude!"* Yet, for the person experiencing it, if we are to believe Kyle Hulbert and what he now says, it is as real as any memory any human being has had.

Kyle said that as a child, before he even knew that Seelie Court, a fantasy world where faeries invite humans to help along their fantastical quests, existed, he was going there, visiting with Seelie Court characters. He was part of this world.

Seelie Court is an online sensation, same as Magic and Dungeons & Dragons. It's a mythical place with good guys and gals, as well as bad guys and gals. It's that age-old narrative of good versus evil, repackaged another way, set in a fantasy world where Fae (faeries) have existed "since the beginning of time."[1]

Kyle said he knew of this place since he was five years old. When he later found books about Seelie Court and those other worlds like it, he realized, "Oh, my God, I've been through this. It's not like I had been exposed to folklore and mythology and just came up with it. My own experience reinforced stories I had read later. This is why I think it was real."

[1] In lieu of me writing long paragraphs explaining this world of Fae and Seelie Court, bogging down my narrative, if you wish to learn more about this fantasy game and world, please Google *Seelie Court,* whereupon you will have more information about it than you will have time to read.

CHAPTER 13

WITHIN KYLE'S MAGICAL worlds of faeries and gods, goddesses, good and bad people (including vampires out to get him), Clara Schwartz saw an opening. Though they had not known each other long by this point, Clara did not have to work hard to get Kyle on her side. Every time she opened her mouth and talked about her life, her beliefs, her past, Kyle took it in as though following along as Clara spread crumbs over the forest floor behind her. Clara spoke; Kyle inhaled.

Clara realized this reaction almost immediately.

"Clara was intelligent enough and perceptive enough to see my flaws," Kyle observed years later, "to see that she could exploit them to her advantage, and she was egotistical enough to not only try, but try, succeed, and then believe she'd get away with it. . . ."

Kyle's feelings regarding violence toward women began to play a role in his life with Clara. Because on the one hand, Kyle stated emphatically with a rather stoic, reserved tone, "I don't like it (violence toward females)." And it was clear he thought about his answer before uttering a word. On the other side, however, he added, there needed to be some clarification about something that was important to him: "If, for example, I was ever attacked by a woman, and I felt like my life was in danger, I would treat a woman no different than I would treat a man [in a fight]. Aside from that, speaking of the actual concept (men hurting women), I don't like it."

One of the reasons, Kyle went on to note, revolved around the idea that "most people who perpetrate violence against women, their egos tell them that they are superior. And to show they are superior, they physically abuse a woman."

This was a vital part of Kyle's life: having an advantage—the absolute pecking order of there always being a king or queen and his/her minions; there had to be a leader and his/her followers. Kyle was quick to claim that he had weighed in on this at different levels at different times of his life. He maintained that he was in no way a born leader (king), but that the mandate of it all was something he respected greatly.

Which was right where Clara fit.

It was not long after they met that nineteen-year-old Clara Schwartz, this new and fascinating friend Kyle had buddied up to, began opening up to him more personally, describing intimate details about her life she claimed to have not shared with anyone else. Kyle and Clara weren't lovers. For Kyle and Clara, the connection went much deeper.

Part of Kyle's empathy for a woman in peril, or anyone being abused by a person in a superior position—an authority figure—stemmed from the fact that Kyle claimed to have been "sexually abused when [he] was twelve." He had a strong need to explain this.

This abuse, according to Kyle, had a monumental effect on the rest of his life (as one might expect) and how it eventually played out. Kyle also claimed he shared this secret with Clara very early into their friendship. He said that it just came out one day while they were sitting and talking. He sensed that Clara had issues with people violating her, not necessarily in the same way, though. Kyle felt as he spoke about his past that Clara wanted to say something, share a heavy burden with him that she had been living with. Even more than that, Kyle made it clear to Clara that he had strong feelings against people who sexually abused others.

"I've had a rough childhood," Kyle said one day. He liked to share this about himself with people he cared for. There was a sense of freedom in just stating it, allowing the words to leave his mind and body.

Clara nodded. "Tell me."

He wasn't prepared to open up and talk details about the sexual abuse just yet, but Kyle told Clara how he had been savagely bullied in school.

Clara could relate to that, of course. Back in high school, where her daily life centered on people making fun of her and calling her names, Kyle explained, Clara had been bullied because of the way she dressed, looked, and acted—everything about her.

"I don't even like the idea of people like that," Kyle told Clara. They were still on the topic of bullying.

For Kyle, his memories, a lot of them (he said), have been heavily influenced by him looking back at his life later on, viewed in hindsight. As a caveat, he added, memory was something for him that has become one of the key pieces of his story, of his history, really. He has memories, to this day, he said, he cannot explain.

"Pre-2000 through 2001," Kyle commented, "before meeting Clara and Mike and Katie, I can recall only because I read about it later, or someone has told me. My psychiatrist says I suffer from post-traumatic stress disorder."

As they talked, Kyle was incensed to hear something else from Clara.

"Death threats," she explained.

"Death threats?" Kyle asked. "What do you mean?"

"Yeah . . . and you'll never guess who!"

CHAPTER 14

CLARA WAS LATHERING it on heavily as the end of October approached. Leaning on her new friend, Kyle Hulbert, sharing with him the supposed "abuse" she claimed to be subjected to at home on an almost-daily basis. In Kyle, Clara had found someone who seemed to understand what she was going through. Mike and Katie had heard a lot of this from Clara already. Mike usually shook his head and told himself, *Here we go again;* Katie listened because she and Clara were BFFs. Kyle now was a fresh set of ears for Clara.

"My honest analysis of Clara and that abuse," Kyle said later, "was that there was *some* form of abuse going on. . . . I mean it could be as minor as he smacked her across the face because he was irritated with her, or whatever." Yet, "smacking" your daughter across the face would hardly be considered "minor."

Whatever type of abuse—if any—was going on inside Clara's house, Kyle noticed that within Clara's mostly protected, small world at JMU and home, it mainly affected Clara's "magnificent ego" more than anything else that he could see. She wasn't necessarily touched by it all in a declaration of *"My life is ruined."* She hadn't turned to drugs or alcohol to cope. She seemed to accept it—and yet she couldn't let it go and wanted something for having gone through it.

Revenge.

"And this is coming from someone," Kyle recalled, "who will admit to . . . Look, I am a narcissist. I love myself. And so for me to tell you that Clara Schwartz had an ego that rivaled mine, that should say something."

There was an attraction there for Kyle with regard to Clara. It was more intellectual than sexual, although Kyle admitted later that he and Clara gave the sexual aspect of their relationship a go of it. They'd kiss and "do things," but it just wasn't there, Kyle said. He was attracted to a certain type of female—and Clara did not fit into that mold.

"At the time, I was not the person I am today," Kyle said later, trying to explain his relationship with Clara and his overall outlook on females during those days, including his new girlfriend, Brandy, of whom he was seeing more and more. "I had a girlfriend and I was unfaithful. I never went all the way with Clara. It was there for us if we wanted to take it—and this sounds superficial—but it was halfhearted, at best. I was never pursuing Clara romantically. No, I had no interest in that realm with her."

Kyle said his expectations and attitude toward females in general back then was "very shallow. I had a very specific ideal in what I wanted out of a relationship and a girl. Usually petite, hourglass figure, C cup, and a really nice ass." He laughed. "I was very superficial."

Clara was beginning to lay out for Kyle a fantasy world she had created. She took her time with this. It was a lot to absorb—even for someone like Kyle, who was very familiar with it all, to begin with. Within her circle of friends, including her boyfriend, Patrick House (and several others), Clara very carefully had constructed a make-believe world, with characters and rules and intricate plot lines she developed and instructed in person, in her journals, and online. It was, essentially, an RPG that they were all involved in. Now Clara had a new character in Kyle, someone, she could tell almost immediately, who took this stuff more seriously than anyone else she knew.

Kyle had spent some time with Patrick House, but not until many years later did he have an idea that Patrick and Clara were even dating. (Clara never talked about Patrick to Kyle in that manner.) Kyle liked Patrick. He found him to be "very well-versed in Renaissance culture." Patrick was about six feet tall, with shoulder-length brown (reddish) hair. He filled the role of Renaissance musketeer to a tee, Kyle explained, as far as his haircut and "that little goatee" he kept. "He fit right in at the fair. He belonged there." What's more, Patrick, like Clara and the others, had a solid background in RPG.

Clara called her creation the "Underworld," and her role as leader within that world was known as "Lord Chaos." She'd sometimes go by the "Priestess of High Chaos." The first time Kyle heard about it was a conversation he had with Clara during the first weekend he and the others all hung out with Clara at her JMU dorm. Columbus Day was coming up on Monday, October 8. Kyle, Katie, and Mike showed up at Clara's dorm on October 6, a Saturday. Kyle had a court date on Tuesday to answer to that knife incident at the mall.[2]

"The Springtime War," Clara explained to Kyle. They were heading toward the rec hall to get some dinner.

"Springtime *what*?" Kyle asked.

Clara explained. She detailed how she was the "embodiment of the Lord Chaos and wanted dead by all of the opposing factions." Apparently, within the Underworld, Clara possessed special powers. There were "witch hunters" out to get her because the only way they could gain the power she had would be to kill Lord Chaos.

Generally, the way it worked: From her computer at JMU (a place she sometimes sat for hours and hours, day after day),

---

[2]This date is disputed by Clara and some of the others with whom they hung around. Clara claimed that the first time Kyle ever came to her dorm was a few days before Thanksgiving that year. This seems entirely false. Moreover, Kyle and Clara were hanging around quite regularly from October, after the festival, and onward from there—another fact Clara later disputed.

Clara spoke to everyone in the game, initiating the plot line, facilitating a narrative of the Underworld through instant messaging that she had written out in a journal or talked over with them in person beforehand.

A chunk from a conversation she had with Patrick one night went like this:

I am the only one who has seen Death's face, Clara instant messaged.

That is fine, as long as you can prove who you are . . . , Patrick responded. (Both of them were entirely in character.)

OK . . . the dragon's claw?

Yup, let him hold it, he knows the imp that is inside it.

The only other thing that would prove it is . . . the Elder stone necklace I have.

He won't accept that, the only reason he will accept the pendant, is because I gave it to you.

While they were playing the Underworld game, it was always clear and specific. There was hardly ever fluctuation between the Underworld and the real world, as the exchange between Patrick and Clara shows.

"Her goal was to gather a group of allies, so that when the Springtime War came, she could use her group to prevail," Kyle said.

In prevailing, Lord Chaos could implement a new system of the way things were run. A new order, if you will.[3]

---

[3]Now, if you ask Mike, Patrick, Katie, and likely even Clara about this Underworld, you are going to get four different versions of the same game Clara constructed. In all of the accounts available, there is no firm narrative line. Each player had his or her own way of describing the game and rules and the narratives. I am going with Kyle Hulbert's version and several documents that exist about the game that seem to somewhat back up Kyle's version.

There was one issue here within all of this that perhaps nobody observed or talked about, with maybe the exception of Clara: Patrick, Mike, Clara, and Katie were perfectly capable of walking a fine line between fantasy and reality and stepping in and out of the Underworld. To them, it was an RPG, a way to kill time and postpone adulthood for as long as they possibly could. Maybe even an escape from their mundane, boring lives of being underachievers in a world that expected them to do great things with their lives. Clara probably used the game as a way to escape from the realities of home and the clear, unquestionable problems she had with her father.

For Kyle, however, as he listened to Clara, she spoke a language he not only understood and embraced, but he comprehended as truth. He honestly believed that parts of this world were real—and he could actually relate to what Clara described because he was then living inside it. Kyle, a vampire—the "good kind"—felt he knew exactly what Clara was going through.

"My own father," Kyle explained later, "had said I never knew where the fantasy world ended and the real world began. I, at the time, was obsessed with my own apocalyptic visions, and her talk united perfectly with that, which made it so much easier for me to fall right into it—it was ideology."

Clara had lifted elements from Norse mythology, particularly an age-old Norse word, "Ragnarök," a term depicting a series of events from the future that include a "great battle," where several major characters meet catastrophic death.

"Later, when I went back and studied Ragnarök," Kyle said, "I realized that Clara had bastardized the Norse mythology and took elements from other things and tried to make it her own."

Part of creating and scripting the Underworld for Clara was that it made her feel important. She was the center of the "faction." If Clara died in real life or in the Underworld, the Underworld ended; and a new world, one that she also created, might be born out of the afterlife. That made her life on earth—her survival—more important than anyone else's. In Kyle, his role in the Underworld became that of the protector, of course. Clara needed someone strong and powerful and mentally ready to take on the challenge of defending the most important player in the Underworld, Lord Chaos. Mike, Katie, even Patrick, none of them could take on this job the way Clara had long desired. Patrick, especially, routinely let Clara down and rarely had fulfilled his duties in the game. Clara was growing increasingly impatient with Patrick.

But here now was Kyle Hulbert. The prince had arrived to protect the princess. And Clara knew that Kyle, a kid who carried a 27-inch *Shinobi* (ninja) sword in a scabbard on his hip (or back), was the right man for the job she had in mind.

CHAPTER 15

KYLE SAID HE didn't like to impose on people. He had an issue with people buying him things, doing favors for him out of the kindness of their hearts. It was born out of a life growing up in foster care. Within that environment, you learn to survive on your own and not count on others. It's a survival mechanism. This produces within you a preconceived judgment about people, however. When someone steps forward to show a bit of kindness, for example, you question it. *What do they want from me?* you ponder.

Kyle had been dating Brandy since they had met back at the Renaissance Festival. They liked each other. Brandy was good for Kyle. She was grounded and had somewhat of a plan for life. Kyle never brought her along when he went to hang out with Clara, Mike, and Katie—only because Brandy didn't know them all that well, lived in another state, and had other friends and another lifestyle altogether.

"Listen, this is great," Kyle said to Brandy one day. "Our relationship is going well." Kyle was concerned that he lived in Virginia (or, rather, that was where he chose to be homeless). Brandy and her mom lived in Maryland. "I like you and I like where this is going . . . but . . . I'm not sure how often I'll be able to see you or when." Kyle went on to explain that he was living, mostly, in a tent he carried with him and stayed with friends when they'd have him. He had no place in particular to call home at the moment. "I literally have my tent . . . [on me] right now as we stand here, Brandy." He was embarrassed. But Kyle said he was not someone who minced words or cared what people thought about him. He delivered his truth. You take it and do what you want with it, but the truth (as he believed it to be) was all Kyle had to his name.

"I don't know when I'll be able to see you, but I will try to get up to Maryland as much as possible," Kyle explained. It was his way of telling Brandy it wasn't going to work out any longer. Kyle knew that the relationship was doomed. There was no way for it to last through big gaps of time between seeing each other.

Brandy was working at the time. Kyle left and told her he'd be back.

That night, when he returned, Brandy's mother was there.

"Apparently," Kyle said later, "Brandy went and told her mother what I had told Brandy regarding my living conditions."

Brandy's mom approached Kyle: "What's this I hear you're living in a tent?"

"Yeah. . . ." Kyle didn't want to explain, but he liked Brandy's mother. She was real, as he later put it. Down-to-earth. She accepted people for who they were—not for what the world expected them to be. "I live in a tent. I don't have a real job, to speak of. I'm trying."

Inside, Kyle was telling himself: *Please, no charity here. Please, please, please don't offer me anything.*

"I'm really big on self-sufficiency," Kyle added. He didn't want a handout.

Brandy's mom said, "Look, Kyle, I believe everyone deserves a chance. And you, clearly, if anybody needs a chance, you clearly do. So you are going to come live with me!"

She wasn't taking no for an answer.

"Okay . . . I guess if you want to give me a place next to your heater, I can toss a blanket on the floor for a few days. I don't want to be in a position to rely on anyone. I don't want to be a burden. I do not want to be a freeloader."

Kyle knew he could take care of himself. Sleeping in a tent was not a big deal.

"That's fine, but you will sleep on the couch. . . . I am going to help you get a job. And you are going to make something of yourself!"

Kyle moved in.

CHAPTER 16

"WHAT DO YOU WANT?" Clara asked. Kyle was standing in the cafeteria at JMU, looking at the menu board. It was Tuesday, October 9, 2001. Kyle, Mike, and Katie had just come from Kyle's court date. Clara had invited them to her dorm and said they could stay the night if they wanted. Kyle was feeling particularly manic and impulsive after court. He wasn't telling anyone, but he had sensed that "the others," who were out to get him—the bad vamps—were close by. It was one of the reasons why he'd made sure not to leave that morning without strapping his sword to his side; and why he definitely didn't want to go back to Brandy's house for the night. The last thing Kyle ever wanted was for Brandy and her mother to be put in harm's way.

"Nothing, I'm good," Kyle said.

"Kyle, come on, what do you want?"

"Nothing." Kyle had looked at the menu board and craved a steak. But since he didn't have the money for it, he said he wasn't hungry.

"I'm buying, Kyle," Clara said. "It's okay. What do you want?"

He thought about it.

Clara picked up on Kyle's indecision. "You like steak?"

"Yeah, I like steak."

"Well, how do you want it?" Clara asked.

Kyle looked at her and laughed. "Bloody, of course!"

"I should have known."

Clara bought it for him.

By now, Kyle had met the "OG" a few times. ("OG" translated to Old Guy or Old Geezer, depending on who you asked, which was how Clara described her father to her friends and in her journals—"OG" was also one of the main bad guys in the Underworld.) There was one time when Kyle and Clara decided the night before that they were going to hang out with Mike and Katie the following day. So Kyle stayed at Mike's and got Mike to drive him over and pick up Clara at the secluded Schwartz farmhouse.

Kyle knocked on the door.

The OG answered.

"Ah, is Clara home?" Kyle asked. He sensed the trepidation ("and judgment") on the OG's face. Kyle didn't like the look of this guy. He'd had a biased opinion of the OG to begin with, based on all the details Clara had shared about her life inside the house. By now, Kyle believed Clara was being abused (psychologically and sexually) by the OG. Clara continuously shared the details whenever they talked. "He gave me a really dirty look after he opened the door. It was a look I was used to by then."

In all fairness, Dr. Robert Schwartz didn't approve of what he saw. Here was another one of Clara's friends dressed in all black, that gaze of despair in his eyes, on his face, along with a feeling of guile that oozed from his pores. Back then, Kyle took on the persona of a vampire rather effortlessly: ashen, chalk-white skin, cheekbones visible and pointed, as if he were malnourished (one psychological report claimed Kyle had an eating disorder on top of everything else), the long black trench coat, black shirt (sometimes a pentagon symbol on the front), and black pants. These were the only clothes Kyle had to his name then, and thus his hygiene suffered greatly. Based on appearances alone (and come on, what father would not judge a book?), Kyle was not the boy you wanted to see at your door, picking up your daughter.

"I knew he was a guy who was telling himself, after looking at me, 'Grab your children and finger your cross, because he's here to steal your kid's soul,'" Kyle said about the OG.

THE REALITY OF the situation was that the polar opposite was true: Clara was working on Kyle's soul, stealing from him the last bit of sanity—if any—the boy had left. And as far as Dr. Schwartz being some sort of hateful, bitter man who walked around with an angry chip on his shoulder waiting to explode on anyone who crossed him (a picture that Clara had spent years painting rather studiously), not everyone saw the guy under this light. Schwartz's son, Jesse (Clara's older brother), later said his father was a "confidante" whom Jesse could go to and "talk to" about his life and where it was going. Jesse described him as a good man, a great father, who was always there when *any* of the kids needed him. "He was just a person I could lean on and trust and value, not only in this father-son relationship but . . . more of a friendship as he was a close friend to me."

Jesse and Clara's sister, Michelle, viewed Dr. Schwartz as "the most important and respected person" in her life. One of the "fondest memories" she had of her childhood, she later told the Associated Press, was a time when she and her dad danced around the house to the 1980s Cyndi Lauper megahit "Girls Just Want to Have Fun." Both Jesse and Michelle would describe Schwartz in total contrast to what Clara had been saying, often noting that their father was a "simple family man," who only wanted what was best for his kids. He liked to put on his blue jeans, plaid shirt, and boots—with his trusty dog trailing behind him, tail wagging, barking—and go out and tend to his goats and horses.

Dr. Schwartz was a guy who had earned numerous awards for his work on DNA sequencing. He'd graduated cum laude from Catholic University and later earned a doctorate from Stanford, going on to work at both Georgetown University and the University of Maryland. Dr. Robert Schwartz had the distinction, in fact, of being a primary member of a team that had put together what is the national database of DNA sequencing.

CLARA CAME DOWN the stairs and walked in between the OG and the doorway, brushing the OG off with a dirty gaze.

"Let's go, Kyle."

They took off with Mike and Katie.

The second time Kyle had the opportunity to meet Dr. Schwartz, Mike had driven Kyle to the farmhouse and dropped him off. Kyle and Clara had made plans to spend the day together. Kyle, however, did not realize that it was seven o'clock in the morning when he asked Mike to drive him over (he had been up all night). But what the hell, Kyle thought, he was there. So he might as well knock on the door.

Another knock and another dirty look from the OG, who said: "Come back in an hour. She's not even up."

Kyle went for a walk in the woods surrounding the farmhouse. He found a deer hunter's tree stand and climbed up to get out of the cold and rain. After she awoke some time later, he and Clara went to one of her friends' apartments across town. It was an ordinary day—more of the same. Clara bitching about the OG, making allegations that he was plotting to kill her, talking through her Underworld and how the game was coming along—and how her new hero, Kyle Hulbert, fit into it all.

CHAPTER 17

IN COURT, KYLE had been given community service for walking through the mall with a concealed weapon. He promised to be a good boy and was cut loose.

At eighteen, Kyle was the youngest within this group of Mike (who had recently turned twenty-one), Clara, and Katie.

"Thanks for that steak," Kyle told Clara after dinner. "It was really good."

They next all walked over to a friend of Clara's dorm room and watched a movie, *The Wizard of Oz*.

After the movie, they decided to sleep in Clara's dorm. Kyle was feeling a bit antsy. He sensed something around him that he knew to be "the others." Without sharing his delusions or feelings with the group, Kyle actually felt as if the bad vamps were closing in. He believed they were surrounding him or the building, just waiting for the right time of the night to strike.

Sitting on Clara's bed, Kyle gripped his sword, making sure it was there.

Kyle later recalled what happened next as a "waking dream." For him, it was as real as anything he had experienced throughout his life. Later, when he looked back at it, he knew it to be a hallucination, although you could tell it was still hard for Kyle to say it was not a real memory.

At the moment it all occurred, however, Kyle believed it was happening.

Katie, Mike, and Clara had dozed off. Kyle could see that they were sound asleep. As he was lying down, somewhere between that moment when sleep comes and actual REM occurs, he claimed he was startled completely awake by a noise outside the dorm room. So he got up; he walked over to the door. And it was then, standing in front of this closed door into Clara's dorm room, Kyle said, he "smelled" them.

"The others."

Kyle walked outside, gripping the sword attached to his hip.

"Mike, Katie, and Clara were inside," Kyle explained. "This was going to happen. I knew it. I did not want them to end up as collateral damage."

This meant a battle between Kyle and the others. There was going to be a vampire fight. Kyle knew it was game on.

But more than that, he said, he *felt* it.

"It fluctuated between vampires, supernatural entities . . . but it always came down to the fact that something was after me," Kyle explained when I spoke to him in 2013, a time when he could look more confidently back at this moment and understand it for what it was: a hallucination, dream, or made-up memory. "It's the nature of insanity. You don't recognize these things for what they are at the time. I look back now and cannot believe what I believed at the time. I can't *believe* that was me. It's a sad fact that it was."

Still, even today, you ask Kyle about vampires and his answer is shocking: "I believe they're real."

Backing up for a moment, on that night when Mike, Katie, and Clara were sleeping, Kyle did not think he was a bona fide, actual vampire just yet. He reckoned that he was "aspiring to be an actual vampire—the undead type." He drank blood and was into bloodletting and rarely went out in the sunlight, but he did not think he was all the way there—which explained to him why he could function during the daytime in sunlight.

Perhaps it was this battle between Kyle and "the others" that would be the crowning moment, when Kyle could consider himself a true vamp.

As Kyle was outside Clara's dorm room in the fresh air of the very early-morning hours, clutching his sword, the aroma of vampires looking to kill him wafted through the crisp air. Smelling this, he knew one thing: "It was going to happen. . . ."

Then he heard a noise and knew it was time to run.

CHAPTER 18

LEESBURG, VIRGINIA—LOUDOUN COUNTY, in particular—has a history of horribly bloody violence. No, not the type of contemporary violence we see on the news these days—although the county does have its share, same as the rest of the planet. We're talking about the mortar, shell, ball-and-bayonet type of Civil War brutality pitting "brother against brother" that much of the Northeast, the South, and the East Coast endured throughout its rather brief history. Loudoun County, especially at the time of the secession, was split down the middle, literally: the eastern and southern portions of the county going primarily with the South in their political and moral beliefs, while the north and west leaned staunchly toward being pro-Union. Just about everywhere you walk within the county, you step on a battlefield or place of historical Revolutionary and/or Civil War significance. This was where the colonies began to merge into one America, with states and political bodies governing a mass of people immigrating from all around the world. Thus, it became the middle battleground of what was the bloodiest war on record, a fight for the dignity and honor of every human being, no matter the color of his or her skin. All the big names have walked the streets of Loudoun County: Grant, Lincoln, Hooker, Hill, Stonewall, and many more.

This sort of nostalgia, especially where blood had been shed, interested Kyle Hulbert—although in an entirely different way. There was one night not long before the vampire battle outside Clara's dorm that was about to get under way when Kyle got a ride into the city from a friend. Baltimore and Washington, DC, were less than an hour from Leesburg. In those cities, Kyle had learned, he could find anything his vampire heart desired.

On this night, it was late, around midnight—and Kyle needed a fix.

Not dope.

Or booze.

But blood.

Kyle took this aspect of his life intensely seriously then. He trolled "goth clubs," as he called them, carefully prowling for the right "donor."

"There were plenty of girls in those goth clubs that would allow me to drink their blood," Kyle said. "They were not hard to find."

Quality versus quantity, however, was an entirely different matter where Kyle saw it. Kyle desired clean girls. Some he had met "were smart enough to have their blood checked regularly and carry that paperwork with them."

A must for him, he claimed. He would "not feed from any" female who did not have her blood checked and could not prove it.

Kyle talked about how he had been drinking blood since late 1999, when he had been introduced to it by a woman from California he had met online. They talked about it and she exposed him to the ritualistic nature of drinking blood and how to do it properly.

Kyle was infatuated with the process and ceremonial allure of it all. He was totally taken in by the darkness of the process and how taboo it was.

So he made plans to meet the woman.

"She was going to pay for me to come out there. I was

really looking forward to it, but my girlfriend found out and"—he laughed—"screwed that up for me."

After being introduced to it, Kyle began doing his own research online. He found a few clubs close by (Baltimore and DC) and started going periodically. One was Club Orpheus in downtown Baltimore, an establishment billing itself as "one of America's oldest and wildest gothic-rock dance clubs."

Perfect.

He walked in, roamed around, checking out the place. He found himself a girl who was into drinking blood and made a move.

THE THING TO keep in mind about all of this is that when Kyle Hulbert did something (anything), he held little back. Kyle went all in or he didn't dabble. For example, he'd studied the body and the best parts of the body to extract blood from by cutting and sucking. He looked at blood charts and found a muscle group in the neck where the trapezoid meets the shoulder. When cut, this part of the body, Kyle claimed, bled perfectly for the task of sucking blood.

"That section of the neck bleeds well, but there are no real veins there. So when you bite down, or you cut it and drink while you're fucking, it's a really nice area. You need to make sure you don't hit certain veins." (He laughed after explaining this.)

The first time Kyle met a girl and swapped blood, Kyle said the experience was "very ritualistic. I used a knife. It was something leading up to sex—and was also a part of sex."

After that first time, Kyle started drinking lots and lots of blood. He enjoyed it immensely and it fit with his gothic, dark, predatory outlook on life, and certainly his belief that he was an aspiring vampire.

It also fed into his unraveling mind of visions and dreams

and belief that bad vamps were after him. Kyle was living within this world, and everything he did—all of his thoughts, for instance—focused on a culture of gloom and doom. He steered clear of the norm. He stayed away from common, everyday things most people did: post office, school, work, out to eat, a play, a movie. Every day was an adventure for Kyle. He needed constant stimulation. In one way, Kyle needed and thrived on anarchy and chaos—much like his new soul mate, Clara.

When it came to this part of what he called his "animal nature," Kyle didn't appreciate it when some of the girls made it out to be a cartoonish ceremony by saying all sorts of bizarre things that you'd expect to hear in a Hollywood film. That made it all unreal to Kyle. He didn't need the fanfare and hype. Drinking someone's blood wasn't a game. He claimed not to be in it because he was engaging in some sort of fad. It was now a part of his life.

"My psychosis presented aberrant-thought processes," Kyle said later, trying to understand his life in hindsight himself, "which I had no reason to question—because my reality was already aberrant. So it all rang with the truth in my mind."

Kyle once met a girl who liked to talk "about the spirituality aspect of drinking blood, and I have to admit it was all kind of trite . . . clichéd, tired."

She was straddling him one night, both were naked, and she started to go through this seemingly scripted language, as if she were a satanic goddess overseeing a séance. It was all so fake and contrived. Kyle could only look on and think, *I cannot believe she's saying all this shit. Are you fucking serious?*

"It was one of those things that when you hear someone say it in a situation like that, you know they're just saying it because it sounds nice."

* * *

ONCE AT ORPHEUS, Kyle had hooked up with some people whom he had never hung around before. They were not his "usual group," which wasn't around on that night.

"This group talked the talk, but didn't walk the talk, you know what I'm saying? They *portrayed* themselves as vamps."

It was really late into the night. Kyle approached one of the girls in the group he was attracted to and said: "Let's go hunting."

The term "hunting" in this context for Kyle meant he wanted to find a "donor"—i.e., another individual who could feed his/her blood to him. He explained the various names they used: "thrall," "Renfield," or "donor."

Renfield's syndrome is an actual clinical term describing someone with an obsession for drinking blood. Renfield was a character from the 1931 *Dracula* film and Bram Stoker's 1897 novel of the same title. During the Viking Age, in Scandinavia, a "thrall" was considered a "serf or unfree servant" and viewed as the lowest member (based on class) in society. You could also call a "thrall" a person being controlled by a much more powerful source than him- or herself.

Kyle preferred the "thrall" term, never saying why. Yet, it was clear that the power and control aspect of this term appealed to him. Where Kyle Hulbert was concerned, and whether he realized it, everything had to be an over-the-top situation, or else it offered no stimulation for him. He drove through life at one hundred miles per hour all the time. When it came to acting out on the thoughts they had and the things they discussed and ultimately did, Clara, Mike, and Katie were like lambs; Kyle was a lion. He did what he said he'd do—and he did it with a great, big roar.

"Why . . . are you thirsty?" the girl asked Kyle as they stood in the club, loud music blaring, the darkness enveloping them.

"Yeah."

"Me too."

After agreeing they were both in the mood to go hunting, the girl pulled out a lance set.

Kyle thought: *What the hell is she doing?*

Then she pricked her finger as they stood there inside the club.

Kyle rolled his eyes. *Come on, what the fuck!*

After drawing blood from a finger, the girl offered it up to Kyle so he could have a drink. Looking around, with plenty of gothic characters talking and enjoying a night out, Kyle considered that the club now had the feel of a Halloween party. There was nothing serious about it. And here was this "chick" standing in front of him, offering her finger to "feed" on.

"What's this?" Kyle asked, her bloody finger still in his face.

"Feed!" she said, sticking it closer to his mouth.

"Are you fucking *kidding* me?"

It was then that Kyle realized the types of people he was standing around inside the club. He could see through them for the first time, he realized. How they all liked the mystique of the scene and the portrayal of being a vamp. Maybe one was an accountant by day or a waiter, but then he put on his costume at night and went out to fantasize and dress up. The club suddenly felt like a getaway. An escape for these people, Kyle surmised. For him, it was a lifestyle—it embodied who he was.

"My delusions were apparent to everyone except me (of course!)," Kyle later observed. "Insanity being what it is, I thought it was all perfectly real and perfectly natural. I, at no time, gave any thought to whether it was 'really' happening or not."

That girl offering her finger "infuriated" Kyle. "I take my animal nature very seriously. I've put a lot of time into understanding it, understanding who I am. . . . For me, when I fed, there was *blood*. Lots of it. You're not going to sit here and prick your finger and feed on a drop of blood!"

He was insulted by this gesture.

Kyle looked at the girl holding out her finger and said: "Look, honey, you wouldn't enjoy a night with me."

"Yeah, right," she said smartly. Kyle could tell she didn't believe him.

"Gather your friends around," Kyle said. He addressed the entire group as they crowded around him, breaking into a soliloquy focused on the subject of all of them wearing disguises, costumes, explaining how this wasn't who they truly were.

"It's Halloween every night for you people," Kyle said. He was upset that they did not take it as seriously as he did.

"Fuck off," one of them said. The entire group didn't appreciate Kyle's frankness.

"You put on a mask, wear that shit, and go out and call yourselves vamps, goth?" Kyle laughed. He looked at each one of them. *"Please!"*

Kyle explained later: "I would never call myself 'goth.' You know, like I would never identify with saying, 'I am a goth.'"

This life was Kyle's identity. He was living out his destiny. He was a creature of the night. He believed this was what he was supposed to be doing.

Going home that night, Kyle considered his life and his new friends, Clara, Mike, and Katie. They would never pose as people they weren't, Kyle felt. That was why they didn't go with him to the club. They didn't consider themselves vamps. Why put on a show? Kyle took note of this—especially Clara, who, out of all of them, leaned toward a tendency of maybe one day becoming a vamp.

What Kyle didn't know then was that if it had become necessary for Clara to pose as a vampire to draw him deeper into her web, she would do it. But as their relationship went from friends to the puppet master controlling her puppet, Clara realized she didn't need to do any of that. She had Kyle right where she wanted him, answering her beck and call, willing and quite capable of doing anything she asked. All Clara needed to do was continue to frost the cake—add more and more saccharine to her tale of woe as the days passed. And when the right time came, simply put a bullet in the chamber and ask Kyle to take the weapon and pull the trigger.

CHAPTER 19

BETWEEN SLEEP AND being totally awake, this was a part of his day that Kyle later said he enjoyed more than any other. Katie, Mike, and Clara were still asleep. Meanwhile, Kyle had heard—felt, rather—somebody "probing" outside the door into Clara's dorm room.

And that was when he heard a voice.

"Get up. . . ."

It was subtle, but one he was used to.

"They're out there and they're looking for something— they must be looking for me," Kyle recalled feeling on that night as he walked outside Clara's dorm room to confront "the others." It was the reason why he had gotten out of bed, grabbed his sword, and headed out the door to begin with.

The Enemy, Kyle believed, had been walking around outside, looking specifically for him. Yet, Kyle understood, they would not think twice about killing whomever he was with.

I cannot be around people who will get hurt, Kyle told himself.

There was going to be a "battle," as Kyle saw it. Clara, Mike, and Katie, they didn't deserve to get involved.

They don't deserve to die.

Standing outside while most of the campus was sound

asleep, Kyle Hulbert ran stealthily through the grass, both hands planted firmly on his sword. He knew better than to be walking around the campus of JMU with his sword in his hands. Still, he had it at the ready, under his trench coat. Kyle had trained many a day and night in the woods, with this very sword; he could holster it in a flash and take a swipe with the ease and accuracy of a ninja warrior, or so he believed.

Kyle was now "tracking" *them,* he claimed. He could decipher their "scent." Not a smell, he was quick to clarify, but more of a psychic vibration—their minds. He could tell they were close by.

Telepathic energy.

The other side of this was that with Kyle's loud and robust aura, he knew they would not have any trouble tracking and following him, either.

He felt surrounded.

Then he heard something across the way, closer to a wooded area on the edge of the parking lot near Clara's dorm, a section of land and trees and brush separating the dorms from an apartment complex on the other side of the trees.

Kyle, unafraid to confront darkness, walked toward it.

There was less a chance of anyone becoming collateral damage over near where Kyle was headed, anyway. He thought about this as he sniffed his way toward the trouble. It was farther away, heading into a wooded area.

As soon as he reached the other side of the woods, near an apartment complex, "They surrounded me and the fight was immediate."

But also short-lived, Kyle said.

As the battle ensued and several bad vamps encircled Kyle and went after him, he lashed out with his sword and scared many of them away—this, however, occurred as the main vampire stayed to fight. This was the vamp that wanted Kyle's soul.

Kyle wasn't prepared to give it up, however.

They struggled, Kyle said—all of this a memory for him that was as clear and lucid as if it had happened the day before.

"If we are the accumulation of all of our experiences, and all of mine were false," Kyle observed later, "what does that make me?"

During the struggle, Kyle lost control of his sword and so he reached down toward the ground in search of it. They were fighting inside what was a small construction site on the grounds of the apartment complex.

Reaching around like a blind man searching for his fallen cane, Kyle came up with a dowel, some sort of wooden stake.

(How convenient.)

So he picked it up and broke it in half, as he held off the vamp with his other hand.

"And then . . . I staked him."

Kyle said he drove the dowel directly through the vamp's heart. Then he stood over the vampire, with that stake burrowed into the ground through his heart like a skewer, as "the others," standing around in shock, scurried off.

"I looked down at him and said, 'Fuck it. You ruined my sleep. Now you can stay out here for the sun to find you in the morning.'"

According to Kyle, the danger, that deadly threat, was now over. He'd killed the main vamp. Sent a direct message to the rest of them that he meant business. He was a force to be reckoned with. There'd be a price if any one of them decided to come after Kyle Hulbert.

Satisfied the others had fled, he walked back to the dorm and found Clara, Mike, and Katie still sound asleep.

So Kyle joined them.

"Look, to me this was real," he said later. "I was there. It happened. I saw it as this—those vampires learned a valuable lesson that night. They cannot fuck with me. Coming around me when I am with friends is *not* the best idea."

Morning came. The sun was up. Kyle and Clara awoke first.

"Let's take a walk down to the store, Kyle," Clara suggested. "We'll get some food and something to drink."

"Yeah, sure."

Kyle thought back to the previous night, about how he had killed that vampire, as genuine a memory as that juicy steak Clara had bought him inside the JMU cafeteria.

As soon as they got outside and started walking, Kyle said, "that was when we saw the fire trucks."

Which was where reality had always seemed to find a way to reinforce the paranoid delusions Kyle was experiencing during those days.

They trekked through the wooded area. The fire trucks were parked, fighting a small fire, exactly where Kyle had recalled having that battle with the vampires the previous night.

Shit, he thought as they came upon the scene, *I left him out here.*

"What I thought was, obviously the sun came up, he burned up, and his body caught the damn apartment building on fire," Kyle said later.

"Listen, Clara, I have to be straight with you," Kyle said, turning to Clara as they stood watching the fire being put out.

"What is it?"

Kyle explained the situation from the night before, how he had staked a vampire and he was now afraid that the vampire's body had caught fire from the sun's rays and ignited the building.

Clara didn't flinch.

"I staked that fucker right there," Kyle said, pointing. He was certain of it.

"You were protecting *me,* Kyle," Clara said, immediately falling into the role of damsel in distress. She'd seen an opportunity and grabbed hold of it.

"Yeah. I brought the fight out here because I didn't want you guys involved."

Clara blushed. She was beside herself. Kyle had protected her, just like she had thought he would.

"My dad," Clara said, "he once tried to poison a lemon and give it to me."

"No shit."

"Meat too. He's tried to poison meat and give it to me."

Clara took the drink she had in her hand and told Kyle she wanted to show him something. They were almost back to the dorm. Here were two people, both of whom dressed like characters out of a late-1800s English Dickensian scene. Black cloaks and capes, wooden walking staffs and wide-brimmed hats. It was as if they were on the set of the film *Dr. Jekyll and Mr. Hyde*. Kyle even said later that kids would heckle them, scream out of the windows as they walked by: "Freaks!"

"What?" Kyle asked Clara.

Clara placed her hand above the rim of the drink. She said something to herself with her eyes closed while waving her hand over the drink.

"Take a sip," she said to Kyle after coming out of what seemed to be a spell.

Kyle did what he was told.

It tasted like blood.

"I'll teach you someday how I did that," Clara said.

She's a witch, Kyle thought. *She cast a spell over the drink and turned it into blood.*

"And I'll protect you," Kyle answered.

CHAPTER 20

AS CLARA BEGAN to get to know Kyle and consider him a major player within the Underworld, she figured she had found the perfect weapon. Clara started to phone Kyle every day now. Each time, she would ladle on, heavier and heavier, her "feel sorry for me" rhetoric.

"Clara would call the house where he lived in Maryland [Brandy's] almost daily to speak with him," said one law enforcement source. "Clara and Kyle started to talk all the time."

There was even some sexual interaction between them now, whenever they got together, yet it never went very far.

With Kyle and Patrick, Clara had options. This was important to her. Yet, she had found in Kyle someone entirely dedicated and focused on her fantasies. That tale Kyle had told Clara about the vampire and the fire certainly fed into Clara's belief that she'd found the right candidate for the job she'd had in mind. Kyle was smart, she knew, but not quite as smart as she was. By now, Clara was plying Kyle with the right amount of stories regarding her supposed tortured life at home. She felt that a rage-fueled intensity already present within Kyle increased with each tale she told him—all of which now aimed directly at the OG.

"We got close very quickly," Kyle later said. "I considered her my most dear friend and sister as well."

"I ever tell you about the blisters on his tongue," Clara told Kyle one night over the phone.

"The what?"

She explained, saying how she and the OG were sitting down to dinner one night back a year or so ago. She had eaten more than he had that night. So she asked what was going on. Why didn't he want to touch his food?

The OG stuck out his tongue. It was covered with large boils or blisters.

"What the hell?" she asked.

The OG became enraged: "I have an infection!" The way he said it came out in a tone that meant Clara should have known this already.

"How did you get that?"

"You enacted a downfall curse on me," Clara claimed the OG said to her.

"I thought he was going insane," Clara explained to Kyle.

It was precedence: Clara was establishing a character for her father within the context of her relationship with Kyle. Building the OG up, brick by brick, to be a monster.

It was the death threats that began to bother Kyle more than anything. The thought of Clara's father hovering over her while she slept, maybe contemplating killing her, or preparing to sexually abuse her (as Clara had told him many times), ate at Kyle like acid bubbling on steel. He could literally sit back and see (in visions) the OG standing inside the kitchen preparing Clara's food and putting poison into it.

Kyle went to a friend one day, an older gentleman he knew and sometimes stayed with, looking for guidance.

"Is it possible?" Kyle asked him, referring to the notion that Dr. Schwartz, a well-respected scientist, could do such a thing.

"Hell yeah, it's possible. If he's a scientist, he has access to all sorts of chemicals that he could use to kill her."

"Shit . . ."

"But listen, Kyle, if this is true, what she says, you need to go to the police and explain to them what's happening inside that home. That's the only way to handle this."

"Thanks, man."

When he left his friend's home, Kyle thought, *If I do that, I tip off the OG to what we're doing . . . and then he kills Clara sooner.*

No cops, Kyle decided.

"The voices were telling me to handle it myself," Kyle recalled.

Clara had no idea who she was twisting and turning and shaping by what she was telling him: Kyle was more volatile than anyone around him knew. These memories and/or "delusions" (whatever we want to call them) were controlling Kyle's every move, every thought. There lived a little, tortured and conflicted boy inside his head. Kyle later explained that he had memories, like that vampire fight, of violently murdering "regular" people. They were so real and vivid, he believed he had committed these crimes; at the time, there was nothing anyone could do to convince him otherwise. (Even today, you can hear it in his voice as he explains it all, that he still believes some of the events took place, even if he knows they did not.)

"Some would later call Clara psychotic," Kyle said, chuckling respectfully. "I never believed any of that. I *lived* it. I grew up with those kinds of people around me in psychiatric hospitals and group homes. I did not see *any* of that in her."

Clara had an uncanny way of getting people—classmates at JMU, friends and acquaintances—to "project a forlorn kindness that one can pick up on," Kyle figured out many years later, when he had time to reflect on all that had happened. "It's the type of thing that provokes a primitive reaction within a person and the desire to reach out and help and comfort."

People around Clara generally felt sorry for her. She was

able to draw that emotion out of some, massage it and truly work it to her advantage. Mike and—possibly—Katie had heard it all before. In some ways, they were tired of it; and now, with Katie living in Mike's bedroom at his parents' house, they were focused on themselves, anyway.

Kyle, though, was a different story. Clara realized quickly that she didn't have to work as hard at it as she had with the others to convince him of her fantasies. Kyle was easy. All she had to do was tell him a story.

"I want my dad dead," Clara said to Kyle. ("Look, she could have said, 'I want him gone,'" Kyle recalled later, but it was clear to him what she meant and what she was asking, regardless of the words she chose to use.)

Kyle and Clara were sitting outside her dorm. Kyle could see his "gods" nearby, hovering around him and Clara.

"Yeah . . . ," he said. "I'm not so sure. That's like this *big* thing—not sure I am able to do that for you."

"Well, file it away for a later time, then," Kyle recalled Clara saying.

"Sure, later. . . ."

The seed had been planted.

CHAPTER 21

AS FAR AS her boyfriend, Patrick House, was concerned, Clara was growing increasingly less confident that he could help her in any way—although, she still wasn't giving up on the possibility that Patrick could do the job. After all, having two candidates was a hell of a lot better than one.

Clara had met Patrick at the Celtic Festival in Leesburg back on June 9, 2001, four months before the Renaissance Festival (where she met Kyle).[4] Patrick was friends with Mike, Katie, and another friend, and they introduced Patrick to Clara. By August, Clara and Patrick were officially dating.

In Patrick, Clara saw the shell of a boy she might be able to manipulate and mold into what she wanted, the only difference being, Patrick wasn't as psychologically imbalanced as Kyle.

"I'm going to call you 'Path,'" Clara had told Patrick soon after they met. She was referring to his character and role in the Underworld.

"Okay," Patrick answered, playing along.

"And 'Rowan, the bard'!" Clara added.

In the world of Magic, bards are lore-keepers and "great magic workers." Some refer to them as "soul singers of

---

[4]There are several differing accounts of how they met. This account was taken from Patrick's trial testimony.

healing." From Clara's authorial perspective, Patrick, an otherwise quiet and engaging boy, out for a good time perhaps, not taking things too seriously in life (nothing more), fit both of those roles rather soundly.

"What about Path?" Patrick asked. "What does Path do?"

"Path . . . ," Clara said, explaining his role in the Underworld, "Path is an assassin."

The way she explained it to Patrick, Clara was the DM, or dungeon master, of the Underworld. "She creates the game and decides the rules," Patrick explained.

The characters in Clara's make-believe world were created by the players and the DM. "And those characters created by the players are personalities that come and go. The ones created by the DM are personalities that are used when needed," Patrick said. "CJ"—Clara Jane, as she liked to be referred to when not in her Lord Chaos role—"called the shots."

"Lord Chaos's father," Clara told Patrick, "is named OG."

Biophysicist Dr. Robert Schwartz, the founder of the Virginia Biotechnology Association, a man who had created the first online DNA database, had been boiled down into the Old Guy both within the Underworld and outside it. The guy had received a lifetime achievement award from his peers and Clara rarely even called him "father." This was the epitome of disrespect.

As early as August, right after they started dating, CJ, in her Lord Chaos role, went to Path and gave him his first assignment. It's clear here that Clara felt as though it was time to test Patrick—to see how far she was going to be able to take things with him.

"I need you to 'tay' OG," Lord Chaos ordered.

"'Tay'?"

"It's a word I've developed for 'kill.'"

Lord Chaos needed to have the OG killed. He was trying to strip her of her powers. He was after her soul.

This language CJ used within the Underworld, Patrick explained, was not something Clara used only during the times when they played the game. "It was more something that she used on a general basis." Many others agreed with this statement.

Clara's life was the Underworld; the Underworld was her life. She knew the difference between reality and fantasy, but she chose to exist (live) within the play world all the time. It was an easy escape for Clara and whatever she was hiding from, either within herself or out in the real world.

"And why does OG need to be killed?" Path asked.

Lord Chaos explained how the OG was trying to poison her. ("Among other things," Patrick added later.)

Path thought about his orders.

"No," Path said. He couldn't do it at this time.

Weeks went by. Clara continued to push Path, explaining that his role in the Underworld was that of an assassin. If he didn't kill the bad entities, well, he was not fulfilling his role very well. Path needed to do his job. He needed to protect Lord Chaos from the OG.

Patrick began to sense from Clara, his girlfriend, that this Underworld was something she was taking too far. There seemed to be no separation for Clara. Patrick was feeling a bit uneasy about it all. He understood the way RPG worked and enjoyed it. Clara, however, took it to another level entirely. She hardly ever broke character. She was always inside Lord Chaos's world. As Patrick saw it then, Mike and Katie didn't really have large roles in the game. Katie's was a secondary character, "Auriel." It was more about Path and Lord Chaos—and the OG's demise, of course.

"I've come up with something," Lord Chaos explained to Path one day. She sensed his trepidation.

"Yes?" Patrick said. He was in character.

"When you have met the OG the equivalent amount of times as the OG has attempted to kill me, you can then tay him."

"What number is that?" Path asked.

"Eight," Lord Chaos said.

After Lord Chaos had made this decision, Clara started to

show Patrick journal entries she had written. Most of these writings were focused on the game, Patrick later said, and others pertained to Clara's life in general. Yet, both had a way of juxtaposing with one another. There was a perpetual blurry line where the two met, as if Clara didn't want anyone to know the difference. It was obvious this was her outlet, her release. The journals doubled as a diary in one respect, and her master plan for the Underworld in another. Clara wrote all the time. Maybe not daily, but there were hundreds upon hundreds of pages, from as far back as 1997 to her days at JMU. In one entry, undated, she talked about those friends in her life that were "annoying" her. She didn't name them. She also hated with an intense zeal the friends that tried "to change" her. There was one girl who attempted to stop Clara from, she wrote, *doing things I normally do & do things I don't like.* One of those "things" included hugging. This friend would hug Clara whenever she ran into her. Clara despised it, which probably said something about intimacy for Clara. Her "response" to her friend constantly trying to fix her was to do the opposite in order to piss off the girl. It showed, if only in a subtle way, how Clara rejected any type of criticism about her character and certainly despised anyone trying to get personally close to her. She wanted nothing to do with either.

One day with Path, Clara sat him down and took out her journal. She pointed to an entry involving an attempt on her life by the OG.

"It was a sexual reference," Patrick later said. "It was a sexual attempt on her. . . ." It was one that Clara had fought off and won, apparently. And it was after that, she explained further, that the OG had tried to poison her.

"Wait a minute," Patrick said. "Lord Chaos or Clara?" He wondered which entity the journal entry had been written about.

Clara looked down. She put on that somber face she was so good at: the pity, the sullen persona she had mastered.

Then, speaking about herself in the third person, she said: "CJ."

As time went on, Clara opened up to Patrick, he later claimed, about other things going on inside her home.

Patrick drove her home after a day out. They were pulling up to the farmhouse when Clara brought something up. They had been discussing getting their own apartment or house with Katie and Mike and another friend.

"Money," Patrick said. "A place is going to cost money." He knew none of them had much. And money was the main reason why they couldn't all move in together at that time.

"I'll get an inheritance, you know, when the OG dies."

"No kidding?"

"Yup. And I'll be able to purchase property with that money."

Patrick didn't think much of this. Her father wasn't old at fifty-seven years. What in the hell was she talking about?

Clara grew quiet. A look of total desolation came over her.

"What's wrong?" Patrick asked. He had stopped the vehicle. They were sitting in the driveway of Clara's home. She stared at the door to her house.

"I'm concerned . . . ," she said.

"About what?"

"The OG is trying to cut me out of his will. I'm *certain* of it."

Clara would express this concern to Patrick "two or three times," he later recalled, over the course of that late summer and into early fall. She had a fear that when the OG died, she was going to be left holding an empty bag. As it stood, Clara had made a point to tell Katie and Mike and Patrick that if the inheritance was split fairly, she would receive a sum in the neighborhood of $400,000.

DURING THAT FALL semester at JMU, for the first time in all of her schooling, Clara's grades took a free fall. Schoolwork had always come easy to Clara. In fact, when she was young, she'd "steal," as she referred to it, her sister's books (Clara was the youngest of the three Schwartz children) and study them, taking the tests at the end of each chapter. Her sister soon found out and corrected the tests. They realized that Clara, who was always "bored" with school because it was too easy, had been acing the tests.

As that summer ended, her journal entries from the past few years depict a girl who claimed not to have any direction within an adult world closing in around her; thus, she was obviously distracted enough to give up on her studies. What that distraction became, entirely, was utterly clear to everyone around her: Lord Chaos and the Underworld game.

Clara wrote in one entry, *I hate society. I hate life.* One of her reasons for this was that life, she wrote, *hates me back with bitter passion.*

She referred to "mankind" as being, by and large, "so fucking stupid."

The game took her out of all that. She could create the perfect world. Clara's attitude was dark and gloomy, an end-of-times view. She hated people (society) in an antisocial manner; yet she never saw herself as someone who should get help for those feelings. Clara didn't see any point to engaging with people, with the exception of those within her circle.

One of Clara's main reasons for hating life was that within the past seven-and-a-half years, she'd seen seventeen deaths. She broke them down in her journal, although her math didn't add up: *11 friends, 3 family & friends, & 4 relatives.* She was beside herself over the sad notion that two of her friends in recent years, she'd just found out, had "tumors as kids." She mentioned how the "betrayal rate" among her friends was about eighty percent. Then she broke into a "why me?" rant. She wondered what was "so special" about her that she'd been subjected to "all these bad things." She was upset that four of her "closest friends" had committed suicide over the past few years. She wondered what it all meant.

On top of this depressive outlook, as Clara's grades slid during her first few months at JMU, the OG stepped in and asked what was going on. He was concerned.

"I see no reason for this!" Dr. Schwartz said to his youngest one night, according to Clara's recollection of the conversation.

"I don't know. . . ."

"You're failing this for a *second* time—how is that possible?"

"I need to take the semester off."

She later told Patrick that what she really wanted was to "relax." School was too much. She wanted to rest and just enjoy doing nothing for a while.

Nothing but play her games, in other words.

"As long as you live in this house and I pay for your tuition," the OG said, "you will have to continue going."

"She had been wishing to take a semester off the entire time I knew her," Patrick said later. Clara had told him about this conversation between her and her father, how it had bothered her. She felt her father wasn't on her side, supporting her.

Whenever Clara talked to Patrick about the OG and taying him, she was serious, Patrick later believed. It seemed to Patrick that she had thought long and hard about all of this. It wasn't something she had just come up with during a time when she was plotting out a narrative thread for the Underworld. This was something on CJ's mind—not only Lord Chaos's—all the time.

"But it cannot trace back to me," Clara told Patrick one night.

He was beginning to worry about her. "What can't trace back to you?"

"It cannot trace back to me and it has to appear to be natural."

"Natural?" Patrick now knew what she was referring to and grew concerned about how serious his girlfriend sounded about having her father killed.

"Yup, a heart attack or natural causes," Clara clarified.

That first semester, when Clara left home for JMU and began spending more time away from family and friends, she communicated with Patrick, Mike, Katie, and Kyle via cell phone and Internet instant messaging. Whenever Clara went online and instant messaged, she went by MYGMU, her screen name. Patrick used DRASGON666. They would chat on the phone or on the Internet no fewer than two times a day at one point, Patrick remembered. And on many of those occasions, all Clara Jane wanted to talk about was the OG and taying. How and when was the OG going to meet his Maker? And how and when was Path going to fulfill his job within the Underworld and take care of what Lord Chaos had ordered him to do?

CHAPTER 22

SHE WALKED OVER. Took it out. And showed it to him.

"I'm throwing it away," he said.

"No." She grabbed it.

Then she walked over to another friend and showed it to him.

"It's aloe," he said. "Totally harmless."

"Okay," she said.

And then: *I ate it all,* Clara wrote in her journal of a suicide attempt she made one day while in high school.

Within a few moments, Clara claimed, she "felt dizzy" and couldn't "walk well." She had trouble swallowing. She told her friends—two of whom sat in the front of her classroom and two in the back—and explained what was happening.

"That can't be good," one of them said.

Class had started. Clara's friend kept looking at her, waiting, apparently, to see what was going to happen next.

He looked concerned, Clara wrote.

Then, as her friend watched, Clara stared at the ceiling and, she wrote, it was "dripping." She was now freaking out: *I became a spectacle for everyone to watch.* She wrote that she was *shaking so hard you could see my pen move visibly.* She was cold. She gave everyone "quizzical looks." She was "changing colors" and losing "focus."

Clara was scared. She went to her teacher. Asked him a question.

He blew up in my face, she wrote. She recalled him saying (which is very hard to believe in this situation), *"You cannot do anything right!"*

As she stood in front of her teacher, all Clara could think was: *The OG said he'd ground me and probably send me to Oklahoma if I got an F.*

She explained this situation to a friend after walking away from the teacher and her friend, she wrote, had a "mental breakdown."

Clara had ingested what she described as "arrowhead poison," which is actually nephthytis (arrowhead vine), a small-leafed plant similar to poison ivy with "heart-shaped leaves" and "distinctive light-colored veins." The clinical signs of poisoning include oral irritation, excessive drooling, vomiting, intense burning and irritation of mouth, tongue, and lips, and difficulty swallowing.

She must not have taken enough to warrant a trip to the nurse or the ER, because Clara never wrote about what happened next, other than saying how sick she felt. Her next entry was dated two days later. She talked about getting yelled at for not taking care of her horse. She also mentioned that she'd slept well as it rained and the weather became "really foggy" outside her window. Her general feeling on this day? She said she was "happy."

As Clara made her way through those tiring and seemingly endless latter years of high school and into her first few semesters at JMU, she wrote seriously about ending her life. It had become an obsession to write about the thought of suicide; however, her attempts were clear indications that she wanted nothing to do with dying—that it was all just one more way for Clara Schwartz—a budding narcissist and sociopath, scheming and plotting and planning so many devious and menacing things—to keep the focus always on her. Because whether Clara was playing her Underworld game or walking through what she'd said was her torturous, tumultuous life with the OG, the most obvious suggestion she put out into the world was that it all revolved around her. She cared little for anybody else or how they felt, showed very little compassion or empathy for anyone or anything, and only worried and cared about what was going on in her life.

This is a blood book, Clara wrote in her journal. She then talked about how she hoped to have dreams of a boy that night and that she was "banishing" a friend of hers from the Secret Society, simply because the friend had made a suggestion that Clara did not like. Clara concluded that she "hated" her.

A few days later, Clara was bashing Christians, writing how she "looked" at them and saw "infestations of evil." She had been forced to go to church that weekend with a family member: *I look at Satanic cults and see the future—bright and promising.*

She called Jesus' disciples "extreme followers" and felt that because they had drunk "his blood" and eaten "his flesh" during Communion, they were all "vampires and cannibals."

She wondered how satanic people worshiped and claimed she was going to look into it soon.

The traitor, [Judas], was the only cool one, she wrote of Jesus' followers.

Clara hated God and became increasingly interested in the occult, noting in her journal: *I have now started to turn satanic.*

CHAPTER 23

HELLO, LOVE . . . DRASGON666 instant messaged his girlfriend, MYGMU.

Hello, Clara tapped back.

Clara rarely left her dorm room now. Her antisocial behavior was evident to her sister, Michelle, who spoke to Clara about it on several occasions. Michelle lived on campus, too, at Rockingham Hall, an old Howard Johnson motel that had been converted into dorms. Highway 81 separated where she lived from Clara (who also lived in Rockingham Hall, but another facility), yet the locations were close. "Maybe a five-minute walk," Michelle said once.

Michelle tried to keep tabs on her little sister, but it was difficult, she later admitted. Clara wasn't interested in what Michelle did on campus, at parties, and during get-togethers, along with any number of "normal" college activities. And meeting new people, especially friends of her sister's, was totally out of the question for Clara.

"She was rather difficult to get hold of," Michelle later said. On top of that, maybe more important to their schedules, Clara "kept rather odd hours," her sister added. Clara liked to stay up all night long, instant messaging and playing Underworld.

As Michelle saw it, Clara "was mostly interested in her

computer and staying in." Michelle would frequently say, "Clara, get out, enjoy the school and campus. . . . It would be a good idea for you to be more social and interact with students, establish some friendships." Clara would blow these suggestions off as unimportant within the structure of the life she led.

That computer, as Clara integrated herself at JMU during the early days of November, became not only Clara's outlet and friend while in the dorm, but her way to communicate with the minions she'd collected to take part in the Underworld.

How are you? DRASGON666 (Patrick) asked.

Don't ask, Clara tapped back.

Clara went on to explain that she was not in the best mood. She was debating at that moment "whether or not to cut off everyone" because she said she couldn't "handle this world."

Here was Clara again using that manipulative skill she was beginning to master: drawing the people around her into her depressive web of "poor me." Clara was an expert at getting the people in her life to sympathize with her feelings and emotions (if they were actually real). In doing that, she was able to use the sympathetic nature most people had against them—or at least to her advantage. Only the best sociopaths can maneuver this ground as perfectly as Clara was able. It takes getting into a person's head, essentially, and mimicking his or her every move. You see, even if Clara did not experience empathy—as most sociopaths don't—she made it appear as if she did by taking on the emotional mask of those around her.

One of her best Internet buddies had been banned, Clara went on and explained to Patrick during their instant-messaging encounter that night. The girl couldn't talk anymore via instant messaging, and this deeply troubled Clara. She had no control over the situation, which was far more corrosive to Clara's intellect than the simple act of the friend not being able to instant message.

Patrick explained that his car was not running well and he didn't know when it would be fixed. He felt bad (so he claimed) because this was why he hadn't been around the dorm lately.

This was disappointing to Clara. And again she used this little fact of life—a broken-down vehicle—against Patrick, trying to gain control over him.

OG thinks you're cheating on me using the excuse of "I'm fixing my car...." I told him he's wrong, she tapped.

Patrick was likely stepping back, trying to figure out his next move: Should he carry out Clara's request of killing the OG or dump her?

They got to talking about a friend of Clara's who wanted to borrow some money. Then they moved onto the subject of poison, which was a topic these days Clara was interested in more than mostly anything else. At one point, she asked: If a guy puts hemlock in a drink and drinks it, will police think it's suicide or murder?

She paused.

Patrick didn't answer right away.

Odd question ... not sure whether I was imagining something or whether it was a vision.... Clara added.

Well ... [according] to modern law, suicide is murder 1, does it make a difference? Patrick wrote back.

But suicide you can't prosecute, Clara keyed.

This instant-messaging session then took on an odd tone. Unmistakably, here, at this moment, Clara was not talking about the Underworld or a specific thread within any RPG they might have been involved in playing. She and Patrick were talking about life in general, their day, and then Clara brought up this idea of making a murder appear to be a suicide. Sometimes their conversations fluctuated between the Underworld and reality, and it was apparent that Clara enjoyed the process of being Lord Chaos, the mastermind, far more than she enjoyed being herself. She felt empowered by the fact that she could sit in her dorm room and pull the strings of so many people by simply tapping out orders onto a computer screen.

This was very stimulating to a girl whose life was essentially melancholic and boring and uneventful, otherwise. It was as if she'd created her own turmoil and dysfunction to enrich her days. Still, during this particular instant message, Clara initiated a conversation about murder and how to cover it up. She was not talking about a game.

Clara continued, asking: **If OG died and I had no way to get home, would your parents let you take the van down to get me?**

Yes, I think they might let me do that, Patrick answered.

Then she asked, if the OG was dead, could she count on Patrick and his parents for a place to stay?

He said he wasn't sure about "that one."

Clara went on to tell Patrick she thought his parents would likely allow it if she had "exhausted all other options." Then she asked: **If the police got involved and they discovered a guy dead b/c of hemlock ingested, would they immediately suspect murder or suicide?**

With no immediate reaction from Patrick, Clara made a few inconsequential comments and then, changing the subject, wondered about Katie not being loyal to them, adding how Katie was better friends with another girl she "probably favors" over them.

Patrick answered both questions: **As long as there is no trace of hemlock, murder, but if there are traces with his fingerprints, suicide . . . and she favors us.**

Then came what sounded like a murder plan truly taking shape. Clara talked about the OG committing suicide one night in "mid-December" and her family (siblings) being "left to sort it out" after he left a note the night before stating what he was doing.

Then she followed up with the message: **Well, it was dated the night before.**

You could almost hear Clara laughing that same sort of villainous laugh of Dr. Evil's from *Austin Powers* as she wrote this. To Clara, it seemed so perfect. She had figured it out. Here was her RPG and her life standing up, side by side, becoming one.

For a kid who later said he didn't want to get involved in the murder of his girlfriend's father, and later claimed to be playing only a game, Patrick sounded as though he was now, suddenly, thinking seriously about this when he tapped back his answer: That would work, and it would qualify as suicide, as long as there is no trace of anyone but him. . . .

Then Clara gave a direct order in the form of an Underworld narrative she'd created by saying how she thought maybe that Path or someone [should] put a gun to him . . . [tell] him to write the note . . . then . . . put it in the drawer of the desk and point a gun at him while he poured the vial in his milk and drank it . . . watched him die and then left.

They signed off.

Clara shut off her computer.

Today was a day where I'd die if I had a gun, Clara once wrote in her diary. She had a strange way of interweaving these writings with bizarre drawings of triangles, lines running through them, circles, upside-down crosses, and words that made little sense, but only to her. Later, in that same entry: *I'm a mascist [sic], sadist, vampire, atheist, Satanist and cannibalist [sic]. . . .*

CHAPTER 24

NO ONE IN her life could later explain where Clara might have developed such a dark, cold outlook. There was a touch of gloom in everything Clara wrote, everything she did. She rarely—if ever—penned an entry about sunshine, blue clouds, a nice day, a beautiful sunset she witnessed, or a boy she might have had a crush on. All those common, schoolgirl fantasies that kids consume their days with never interested Clara Jane Schwartz. For her, the world was a shadowy canvas of darkness; the people around her were mostly all enemies if they did not adhere to her set of standards, beliefs, wants, and wishes.

Back on February 1, 1998, during the early evening, an incident occurred (according to Clara) that explained a lot about why she viewed the world in such a dark, petty window of gloom and doom. She wrote about it in her journal, a terrible memory (if true) of a very frightening, real moment.

I'm so scared, Clara wrote while sitting in her room. The door was locked. It was 7:30 P.M. She was in bed already. *What happened . . . was a living hell.*

Clara and the OG had sat down for dinner, she claimed. Her brother was "working late again." She hated those nights when her brother worked late because that meant Clara would be alone with the OG. Her brother, back then, lived at the house.

"Clara?" Robert Schwartz called out. (This was according to Clara's recollection.)

Clara came out of her room and went down the stairs. "Yes?"

"Set the table."

The OG had a white-and-brown cotton throw rug (blanket) that, as Clara told the story, he "insists" on having on the back of the brown chair, a piece of furniture that sat "parallel" to the television. This was the OG's personal space in the house, apparently. No one messed with it. In constant disagreement with her father, Clara did not like the throw rug being placed there, so she always put it somewhere else. It bothered her to have it on the chair. She had a unique, albeit straightforward way of recounting this in her diary—same as a lot of things she would outline and discuss over the years, in what was a terse, stale written language she'd occasionally use: *pillow => throw=> footstool.*

Order. Class. Clarification. That was Clara's way. Everything had its place. There was a place for everything. It all had to be with her approval, to her satisfaction. All centered on only her thoughts, feelings, and life. By contrast, Clara's things (personal belongings, her dorm room, room at home) were left scattered and filthy. She was a slob, in that respect.

Clara took the throw rug off the chair and moved it before setting the table.

When the OG walked into the room, the first thing he noticed, she later claimed, was that the throw rug was missing from its proper place on the chair. Clara gave no reason why she would antagonize the guy, knowing what she knew—especially since placing the rug where she had was a big no-no.

As soon as the OG realized what she'd done, he "rushed" (ran up to) her and stated rather sharply: "Put that thing back where it belongs!" According to Clara, Robert Schwartz was enraged. In fact, within Clara's description, one would assume the OG spoke through clenched teeth, seething with resentment and hatred at her outright insubordination.

Rules were rules. You live in my house—you abide by its rubrics.

"It doesn't belong there," Clara challenged. "It belongs in the blanket chest."

"If you put it there," she claimed the OG yelled, "I'll fix you forever!"

"But—"

"Do it, Clara. Take care of it!"

"Chill out. Can't it wait until after I finish getting enough silverware for dinner?"

Clara sometimes kept her hair in a ponytail. She liked the easy care of it. On this night, she claimed in her diary, that ponytail became a leash the OG grabbed and, she wrote, *yanked . . . hard enough until my back is backwards curved.* She was in severe pain, struggling to right herself, trying desperately to break free from his firm grasp.

All over the placement of a rug?

They struggled a bit, back and forth, and Clara got away. She ran into the living room and wound up inside the kitchen, where the OG was now waiting.

He was pacing, on the verge of blowing a gasket.

"I am going to call the police and report abuse," Clara claimed she yelled.

"Yeah, right. This isn't *abuse*. Call the fucking police! See what they consider child abuse. This isn't abuse. Call the police. Call. The. Fucking. Police." The OG was now insisting that she phone law enforcement, since she had warned him she would. The message was clear: If she was going to threaten him, she had better be damned sure to follow through on it.

Clara didn't move.

The OG walked over to the phone, picked it up, and held

it in front of her, as if handing the phone to Clara. "Go ahead. Call the fucking police."

"No," Clara said. Inside her head, she thought: *He's going to fucking kill me.*

"No? Oh yeah, I knew you wouldn't," the OG said, placing the phone back into its cradle. "I knew you were fucking chicken."

"Look, if you don't watch out, my friend will fucking kill you," Clara blurted out.

After she said those words, Clara wrote: *He lost it.*

Screaming, the OG ranted, "Yeah . . . yeah . . . *I* am gonna now call the police! You'll be arrested on the count that your friends told you they were gonna kill me, and you are the only reason I am still alive."

Clara stood stunned.

"After dinner, I am calling the fucking police. Now you sit down and you explain it to me what they said, because you'll have to do the same when the police get here."

After all that, Clara claimed, she and the OG sat and ate together. Later on that night, Clara wrote in her diary that at some point during dinner she confronted the OG about what he "did to me when I was nine" (sexual abuse, the suggestion seemed to be) and how her mother had explained it to her before she died. Clara concluded her soliloquy to the OG by saying, "I still trust what Mom said."

"Mom didn't know what she was talking about!" Clara claimed the OG screamed. "She was an asshole, an idiot."

Intimidation. Manipulation. Contortion. That is the way Clara Schwartz later described her father and the life they shared together—that is, if what Clara wrote was truthful in any respect. Yet the question one might have was: Had all of this been part of Clara's fantastical role-playing game? Did she create this sort of villainous character in her dad because she needed an enemy for her Underworld? Was he not the most loving guy who put a lot of pressure on his youngest daughter because he believed she was screwing up her life, so she then took it upon herself to turn him into a monster?

At this time (1998), during what became a pivotal year in her life at home, Clara was going through a witchcraft stage. Her world was all black—everything—clothes, moods, and writings. Clara and some of her friends would cut each other and taste the blood. Her life at home became an extension of this unwelcoming world she craved—a journey of living with a man whom she viewed as a tyrannical disciplinarian who was out to get her in any way he could: *Fuck him. I'm so fucking scared . . . so fucking scared. He'll kill me. He's over the edge. He took a suicidal jump over the cliff. He's gonna murder me. . . .*

Clara was sixteen years old then, obviously confused, and viewed her situation at home as an abusive prison. Her mother had died. Her siblings were not there for her. Her friends were disappointing and disloyal; they routinely let her down. She felt terribly alone and even desperate. In that same diary, near this period, she concluded one section, writing: *Help me. I hit a valley and I wanna die. Is there no end to this hell I am in? . . .*

"My wife and I had long discussions about what we were observing," Clara's uncle, one of Robert's brothers, later commented. He was referring to that period just after Clara's mother died. "But what we were seeing was somebody who at least confused us most of the time when she talked. . . ." Clara, he went on to note, exhibited "multiple levels of conversations" where she would try to explain herself and break off into "as many as ten topics at the same time, so much so that we were totally confused as to what she was trying to get across to us."

Her uncle would question Clara in the form of: *"What are you talking about?"*

"Oh, that?" Clara would respond. "That's fantasy."

All of it left the uncle and aunt "questioning . . . what she was talking about in terms of what she perceived to be reality and what she perceived to be fantasy."

There was a part of Clara she had not shared with anyone—an even crueler side that spoke of a girl who had not cared less about the death of her mother. According to Clara's sister, it was Clara who found her mother dead at home when she got up for school one morning and everyone else had left for the day. But instead of calling 911, or dialing up the OG and telling him his wife had died, Clara took a look at her mother's corpse, made herself lunch, and left for school without telling anyone.

"She went to school . . . to leave my father to find my mother," Clara's sister later said in court.

This behavior from a girl who claimed her mother's death was the catapulting, emotional moment when her life began to spiral downward!

AFTER THAT JOURNAL entry of *I wanna die,* Clara talked about entering "Phase 4," which was where, she claimed, "the demons" took over.

When speaking with those demons, while lying in bed at seven-thirty at night, allegedly scared for her life as the OG was downstairs raging and mumbling anger-fueled rants she could not comprehend, Clara confided in those demons, whom she saw as her only true friends.

She didn't record what they said to her, but her response told a tale of its own: *They said I was fine.* Moments later: *Make it stop. . . . Make the torture, torment, make it stop now. Help me.*

ON THAT VERY night when Patrick House and Clara Schwartz discussed poisoning her father and how to get away with it, five minutes later, Clara turned her computer back on and signed in, again looking for Patrick.

And there he was.

They talked about menial things for the next half hour and then moved on to the subject of their relationship. Clara was plying this boy with all the right words, spooning him just enough information to keep him satisfied but also wanting more—this all occurred at a time when, Patrick later said, he was thinking of backing off.

Although Patrick might have said in hindsight that he was considering walking away, unsure whether Clara was kidding about killing the OG or just ramping up the Underworld game, he was not sharing any of that trepidation with her.

I love you, Clara said after telling Patrick she needed to get some sleep. But we knew this, right?

Yup, yup, but it can never be said too many times.

Hey, this is the only relationship in which I was being honest about love this early into it, Clara concluded before signing off.

Patrick said he liked hearing that.

CHAPTER 25

CLARA WAS SITTING at her desk inside her dorm at JMU several days later. The computer monitor brightly illuminated the messy room around her. Garbage was strewn all about the floor: food wrappers, empty cans and bottles, balled-up papers, and other trash. She tapped away, hoping Patrick was online.

After a few minutes, there was that familiar greeting glowing across the screen: Hello, love.

Clara said meeting Patrick online was the "happiest" part of her day, besides talking to him over the phone. On this day, she seemed content, in a good mood. This was a rare moment for Clara.

Within a few keystrokes, however, it was obvious that Clara's fleeting moment of happiness was only the bait. After saying how nice it was to talk to Patrick, Clara wrote: Just a horrid night. Then she explained (after Patrick prompted her) that she'd had another fight with the OG. It had to do with a friend of the OG's: His brother died ~ grins evilly ~ not sure how.

Patrick warned her to be "nice."

Clara talked about a theory she had involving mental fury. She referenced a "thought transference" that she personally had projected, ten days previously, proffering a guess that it was that mental fury that was responsible for killing the guy.

You arnt spose to kill people. . . . That's my job, Patrick wrote.

Was Patrick back in? Was he sending mixed messages? Or was Patrick simply playing the game, hoping to stay in the good graces of his girlfriend?

Patrick soon moved on and talked about something else.

But Clara brought him back around, writing, Now for OG . . . or is that your job? She sounded confused, as if Patrick was saying that Path had handed over his responsibility of killing the OG to another character.

Clara was nervous, as though lost in the conversation— Was Patrick referring to the Underworld or the real world? She brought up that mental fury, mind transference again, and Patrick made light of it, thinking, of course, it was all part of the Underworld game. He suggested that with her mental fury, Clara could make the death of the OG look natural. Therefore, she didn't need him.

Make what look natural? Clara asked, the eagerness she harbored to hear Patrick's answer nearly jumped through the screen.

Fury, Patrick clarified.

Compared to? Clara wondered. Then: Somewhat confused?

Don't worry, it's still my job, Patrick cleared up.

To tackle OG?

My job.

Okay . . . have you found a natural way?

I may have.

~interested~ go on.

No, I am not going to tell you how, until of course for sure, anyway.

Okay . . . any hints?

It will kill a person.

Beyond that . . . herbal, what?

Nope.

?

There?

I am here, and no, I am not going to tell you.

Okay, guess it's better that I not know. . . . I just wish he'd go away. . . . [I'm] so sick of fighting.

I understand. . . .

If taken in context, this last exchange certainly sounded like a plan to kill Robert Schwartz. The back-and-forth. The feeling Clara projected of running out of patience and not wanting to fight with her father any longer—the idea that there *was* a stealthy way available to get rid of him. In no way—if we take into account other conversations when they were clearly discussing the Underworld narrative—had Clara or Patrick alluded to being "in character." A concerted plan, brought up by Clara, to kill her father seemed to be taking shape.

They talked about money next. Clara was upset because the OG wouldn't give her any money to buy the things she wanted, such as a stereo and VCR. She said she was "so sick" of him looking at "her finances," as if the OG was going into her bank account and questioning her about every dollar she spent.

Then they talked about how Katie was possibly cheating on Mike because Clara said she'd seen ads online that Katie had posted where she was looking for dates.

Clara forwarded Patrick several e-mails she'd recently seen that had been in her school account from the previous girl who'd had her same "box number." The girl had apparently not deleted her account. Clara and Patrick had a nice laugh for a time, going back and forth, talking about the strange e-mails between the girl and several guys she was seeing.

As they continued instant messaging, it was clear when they both became totally immersed in the Underworld. There was no chance of confusing this part of the conversation with reality. It was hard to follow and made little sense, except to the two of them. They were deeply absorbed in the game. Here, at the end of the conversation, while talking specifically about the Underworld, the OG did not come up. Not once. The talk was focused on goddesses and gods, characters, and the narrative of the game.

This observation said one thing: Clara and Patrick were both totally aware of the difference. She and Patrick understood it. Clara, perhaps more than Patrick, worked it. And she made damn sure that when she spoke about the OG's life coming to an end, she meant Robert Schwartz—not some sort of evil, made-up villain in her wacky, largely plagiarized RPG.

CHAPTER 26

WITH HIS CAR now fixed, Patrick showed up at JMU one afternoon just after that last instant-messaging conversation. He spent the weekend with Clara. The exact date was a little sketchy for Patrick, but it was during this key period—October/November—when Kyle, Mike, Patrick, and Katie were all in the picture.

Clara had been doing research, but not for a school project. Rather, it was for something she had been speaking to Patrick—*ahem* . . . Path—about for the past few weeks now.

"What is it?" Patrick asked.

Clara was lying on her bed. She had a book in her hands, opened to a specific chapter.

"It's a book of herbal medications," Clara explained.

"Of *what*?"

"Herbal medications."

Clara pointed to a chapter she'd bookmarked; then she handed it to Patrick.

The theme of the chapter was plants and poisoning—a subject they had discussed at length during one of their last instant-messaging sessions.

Robert Schwartz was now "the target," as Patrick (and Clara) began referring to him. Clara even made it clear during this conversation inside her dorm room that she was speaking specifically about "my father." There was no separation between the Underworld (OG) and the real OG for Clara on this day. No blurry line, according to Patrick's recollection. Clara was *not* Lord Chaos asking Path to fulfill his role in the game and take out a threat. She was the girlfriend asking the boyfriend to kill her father. It was a direct request. One she hoped her boyfriend would take care of sooner rather than later—because Clara was growing incredibly impatient with Patrick. And here, now, in her hands, Clara had a recipe to get the job done.

"She no longer appeared to be inside the game—it appeared to be all reality to her then," Patrick commented later. In contrast, Patrick added, whenever they'd discuss poisoning the OG, whether they were locked inside the game or not, Patrick always considered the murder to be *part* of the game. Never a genuine request he felt serious about pursuing. Sure, Clara took things a little too far, he thought, and she came across as being into it more than anyone else, but Patrick always assumed she was role-playing.

Yet, on that day, inside her dorm, when she leaned over and handed him that book, pointing out a recipe for poisoning another human being, Patrick got a cold chill of reality and believed—for the first time, he later claimed—that Clara was unabashedly, seriously requesting that he actually murder her father.

And that scared the shit out of him.

But he left it alone. He didn't say anything. Or, rather, nothing he recalled later on. Instead, Patrick closed the book and changed the subject.

Then he told Clara he had to go.

As Patrick drove home from JMU, he was thinking about Clara's request to poison her father, and how she subsequently handed him a formula to get the job done. He began to reconsider the relationship. This was no longer a game, a fantasy.

It was real.

* * *

SOME TIME LATER, as Patrick weighed his options of staying in the relationship and murdering his girl's father, or breaking it off with her, he drove Clara out to West Virginia, where his parents lived. He would often talk himself back into being with her after a spell of thinking she was crazy and seriously wanting her father dead. It was easy to do: *No way! She cannot be serious?* Clara had spoken ill about her father so often, for so long, it was hard to tell how serious she was at any given moment.

What Patrick didn't know until later, though, was that with the holiday break at JMU quickly coming up, Clara was going to ratchet things up a notch. Clara had repeatedly told everyone that she dreaded going home for the holidays and spending all that downtime with the OG. So, in many ways, Clara was up against a clock here. She needed something done before the Christmas break.

Going out to his parents' house was a long ride. Patrick had wanted his parents to meet his girlfriend. Clara, he understood, was not right. She'd had a tough life at home. She and her father fought. He believed that she'd get over it and get on with her life at JMU at some point. Maybe it was a stage Clara was going through? Some sort of growing pains. She had been drifting away from home, anyway. Sooner, rather than later, the OG would be out of her life altogether and Clara would be on her own. Clara, Katie, Mike, and Patrick were talking about getting a place together. There were days when Patrick thought perhaps they had a future.

They pulled into the driveway of Patrick's parents' house. He went to grab the door handle to hop out, but Clara clutched his arm, stopping him.

"Wait," she said.

"Yeah, what is it?"

Clara was somber. She sounded "very frustrated," Patrick later recalled (in court). She said plainly, calmly, but with petulant commitment: "When are you gonna kill my father?"

There it was—a direct request. It was as serious as Clara had ever sounded.

Patrick felt now that his girlfriend was sick and tired of asking him to fulfill this wish.

"When, Patrick?" Clara said again.

CHAPTER 27

KYLE HULBERT'S LOT in life had been chosen for him as far back as the late 1980s, he claimed, when he was a child without any clue as to how mixed-up his mind would become. In his earliest memory of childhood, Kyle recalled a storm. Lightning and thunder were flashing and crashing, booming outside the window of his home. He was living with his biological mother and father then. He was "between two and five" years of age, he later said, adding that they were living in "Kansas or Missouri." He was not sure exactly where. Kyle had been born in California. In between a later move to Virginia, where he would grow into adolescence and spend a majority of his life within the foster care system, he and his parents lived in the Midwest.

That storm was loud and dramatic, and little Kyle wanted to see it close-up. So he opened the door and stared out. Motionless, speechless, enamored with the power and might of the lightning, Kyle was mesmerized.

"That's what I remember the most—bright tongues of light in the night," Kyle said.

It was wondrous and alarming and exciting—all at the same time. Kyle was struck by the sheer awe and force of nature. It was as if this was the first time he realized and felt the power of weather.

But then something happened, he said, with a caveat that the incident could be stained with "my mind twisting the memory, distorting it."

As little Kyle stood staring out the apartment's glass door, he saw a massive flash of lightning burst wide open, almost as if it happened in slow motion. Kyle recalled seeing "a tunnel of lightning, a concentric ring of jagged light" inside the flash.

It was inviting and alluring and altogether magnificent. Kyle wanted to jump inside the storm and get swept away.

He cannot explain it. He can only say that it "might have been a tunnel, or a ball of lightning, or the distortion of the . . . moment in a child's life [that has] endured the passage of years, a random memory of no more significance than any other."

It is a description that explains a lot about Kyle Hulbert's life and what was about to happen in the coming days as he and Clara got closer and began to talk more intimately about the OG: cloudy memories of real or imagined events.

Maybe a combination of the two.

CHAPTER 28

CLARA WAS FREAKING OUT. She realized Patrick was slipping away. He'd stopped calling as often. He found every excuse he could not to drive out and see her at JMU. He sounded different when she did get him on the phone. She needed to speak with Kyle. He was with Katie and Mike. Clara tapped out a message:

You there?

Yes.

This isn't Kyle? Clara wrote.
She had good instincts. There was something up with the screen name KEIYORAVEN82 (it was actually Katie Inglis's screen name) writing back to her on this night. Clara could sense it wasn't Kyle, who sometimes used Katie's screen name when he slept at Mike's.

Maybe.

Kate @ keyboard? Clara asked, clearly disappointed.
I'm here, yes, Katie said. Kyle was on the phone talking to his girlfriend, Katie explained, before asking Clara what

was up. What did she want? Was Clara interested in talking about anything, such as Kyle being an ass . . .

Not Kyle but Pat . . . Clara answered. Then she explained how upset she was that everyone (including Kyle) had been, in fact, "drawn into" her "hellhole," and Patrick was just not there for her when she needed him the most.

Katie and Clara went all the way back to the sixth grade. They had gone to the same school. Had just about all the same classes and became close friends during their senior year of high school. According to Katie, it was during their senior year when Clara amped up the rhetoric about her father, beginning with how their relationship "was not the greatest," Katie recalled later, and "he was continually doing stuff to her, like trying to poison her."

"The meat he feeds me, it's poisoned," Clara routinely told Katie.

"Him hitting her on occasion," Katie later said. "Other things, like pulling her under the water in their pool while everyone was watching and nobody would help."

The problem with what Clara had been saying throughout the years was that Clara had been the only one reporting it. No one else saw any of this so-called abuse. Even Katie, who spent the night at Clara's several times, later said: "I had dinner there. . . . It was perfectly fine."

The one major problem Katie—and others—had regarding the physical abuse Clara claimed she suffered at the hands of her father was that no one ever saw any "signs" of it. No bruises, Katie explained. No scratches. No red marks. Nothing. Katie had seen Clara naked many times, either changing inside the dorm or in the locker room when they went swimming at JMU, and never once saw "any signs" of the OG having hit (or even having grabbed) her.

"I just wish he'd leave me alone and let me live my own life," Clara told Katie one night. (This statement here is extremely telling. Clara was upset that the OG would not allow her to live as an adult—that she could not do whatever she wanted—while he paid all the bills.) "You know, Katie, I wish he was dead!" Clara said.

There was another occasion when Katie and Clara were talking. The guys weren't around. Clara brought up the OG and the money her family had.

"I stand to inherit a third of a million dollars," Clara bragged to Katie.

"That's a lot of money, CJ."

"Damn straight . . . but I can only get it after he's dead."

Katie believed Clara was being sarcastic whenever she mentioned the OG being killed, so she responded, most times, in the same manner: "We'll have a damn party!"

AS THEY CHATTED online that night, Clara explained to Katie how she was losing her patience with Patrick and was more interested in what Kyle was up to. Clara asked Katie about dinner and what she and Mike and Kyle were planning. She wanted them to visit her at JMU.

Except Patrick—she didn't want him around. (Patrick had already told her, however, that he wasn't coming!)

Is Kyle a master of staff and sword? Clara asked. The comment seemed random.

Katie didn't respond directly. Instead, they talked about the size (very small) of a friend's penis and laughed about it.

Then Clara asked again: **Is Kyle a master of sword & staff?** Adding, **I get the impression he is, especially if he's teaching people.**

Kyle was taking some people from the group into the woods and, using wooden dowels, was teaching them how to spar with swords. He liked to tell the others he was a master swordsman and had trained with various masters throughout the East Coast. No one ever knew if it was bullshit or the truth, but they only believed half of whatever Kyle said, because he came across as such a blowhard sometimes. His stories sounded overly dramatic and fictional. It was hard to believe him at face value. Still, no one ever challenged Kyle.

Clara was intensely interested in the fact that Kyle claimed to be great at wielding a sword.

Katie wrote back: **Kyle won't tell me. He's too wrapped up in his little Canadian.**

Clara was confused. She asked what a little Canadian was.

Katie said it was the girl Kyle was on the phone with, Brandy.

Clara didn't like to hear this. She didn't think Kyle was at all serious with Brandy. After all, he never brought Brandy around, hardly talked about her much when they were together, and he held Clara's hand and even kissed her sometimes. Clara liked the idea that Kyle was totally into her—even if they weren't "lovers."

Katie and Clara talked for five additional minutes and Katie said she had to go. Kyle wasn't quite finished with his phone call, so Clara would have to ring him up later if she wanted to talk.

Clara said okay. She'd do that.

Clara sat in her dorm room. She had her journals spread out before her. She had been thinking about sharing some of her writings with Kyle the next time she saw him. This was her proof, Clara surmised, that she lived a "shitty life." It was all right there before her in black and white.

She opened one of her old journals from high school. It was the day before the start of her junior year: *OG woke me up @ 11:30.* (He told her to go feed the horse.) *He slapped me on the right cheek hard enough to leave it red. . . .*

That was a good entry for her to show Kyle.

[OG] yelled at me . . . thinks I'm a Satanist.

Another good one.

She described how bad her day had started off, having written, *OG said if I set my alarm to go off 2X in 1 morning, he'd kill me.*

Clara liked that one, too.

At the time, Clara had been upset because the OG was dating a woman and Clara feared that they'd marry. If that happened, Clara wrote in her journal, she was not going to listen to her stepmom because the woman had "no place." Clara believed the OG's girlfriend was "trying to fill in" for her mother—a rather common, normal reaction from a high-school student whose mother had just died: *She can go to Hell and I don't care.*

Earlier that week, Clara had tried cutting her "arteries," as she explained the incident in her diary. However, in typical Clara fashion, the knife was too dull and she couldn't complete the job. Apparently, there was not a sharper knife around.

I scare myself, she wrote back then.

One particular entry stuck out to Clara as she sat, reading through the best excerpts to share with Kyle. It involved the beginning of that new school year. She'd been a junior for a week. She hated her life. She despised her brother and her sister. Definitely her father and his girlfriend. And just about everyone and everything else. Within these pages, there was nothing during this whole period that Clara had found any solace in whatsoever.

She'd had a bad day. She was in her room, after fighting again with the OG, trying to have some alone time. She had the music turned up, *waiting for [him] to turn off my tape.*

Sure enough, antagonizing the guy once again, he came upstairs and walked into her room and shut the stereo off.

OG made a blunt death threat . . . , she had written. Clara smiled at this entry; it was perfect for Kyle to see.

"I'm pretty sure you won't last till your birthday and you won't be here to celebrate," Clara claimed her father screamed at her during that afternoon.

It was the second time by then, she wrote, that OG had

threatened her life. She concluded the entry: *I'm positive I'm going insane.*

THE NEXT TIME Clara and Kyle got together with Katie and Mike a few days later, she laid it all out for Kyle, pulling him aside and getting him alone. She showed him the diary entries she'd carefully chosen, explaining how badly her father wanted her dead.

"She . . . [told] Kyle how her father had abused her and poisoned her, and [she] pulled out some of her journals and showed them to him," Katie explained in court later. "I ignored them because it was a regular thing to hear complaining about her father."

Kyle listened closely, turning the pages of Clara's journal, reading through each entry slowly, taking it all in.

"This is incredible," Kyle said.

"It is," Clara responded.

They were alone. Mike and Katie had gone off somewhere on campus. Mike had a friend there whom he'd stop and see once in a while, which gave Kyle and Clara the opportunity to spend time together without anyone else around.

"I'm sorry, Clara," Kyle said. "I'll protect you."

"He sexually abuses me, too," she said, breaking into a graphic explanation of what had happened.

"She told me that he used his fingers on her sometimes," Kyle said. "That he didn't have intercourse with her, but would go into her room when she was home and finger her."

Kyle didn't get visibly angry when Clara showed him her journals or told him stories about the abuse, but he would internalize the information.

"Not like aggravated . . . or anything," Katie later explained. "Kyle was just quiet. And Kyle is not often quiet."

"I was thinking," Kyle later explained. "Thinking of how I could help her."

CHAPTER 29

KYLE HULBERT WAS not sleeping well. Not because of the medication he wasn't taking, or that he was drinking too much caffeine, or from the noise inside wherever it was he spent the night. No, for Kyle, as he put his head to the pillow on most nights these days, all he ever saw was Robert Schwartz.

"I could no longer sleep without seeing him (the OG) doing something to Clara," Kyle explained.

Kyle would lie down, pull the covers over his body, fluff up his pillow, maybe roll over to one side and try to get comfortable, and then came an explosion of images: There was the OG, standing in the kitchen inside Clara's farmhouse, cooking her dinner, looking over his shoulder evilly, making sure Clara wasn't sneaking up on him, "poisoning a lemon or a pork chop."

Kyle could see the man doing it. Clara had implanted these pictures so firmly inside Kyle's mind that he was now having visions of what she had told him.

Soon, after the stories from Clara became more of a daily occurrence ("We talked every day on the phone or online, and every day she told me different things regarding her father trying to kill her"), it became more than simple mind games at night while Kyle was trying to fall asleep. Kyle would get up. He'd walk from one room to another, maybe to use the toilet in the middle of the night or to go play a video game, and he'd be struck by a lucid, extremely realistic "hallucination." He'd open the door to the bathroom inside the house he was sleeping in and walk directly into Clara's house, as if through some sort of time warp or wormhole. He'd be invisible to the people around him inside the vision. From Kyle's point of view, it was like watching a film of what was happening while being inside the film itself.

One night in particular, Kyle walked from where he slept inside Brandy's mother's house to Brandy's bedroom to go play a video game. Yet, when he opened the door to Brandy's bedroom and stepped in, he wasn't inside Brandy's bedroom. Instead, Kyle found himself standing inside Clara's bedroom, watching an ongoing scene from Clara's life taking place in front of him.

The OG opened the door to Clara's room. He shouted angrily, "Get up. . . ."

Kyle stood by, looking back and forth, listening. Clara could not see or hear him. He was invisible to both Clara and the OG.

"Get your ass up . . . you worthless piece of shit. You're nothing," Kyle heard the OG shout.

Clara jumped out of bed.

Then the OG left the room, closed the door behind him.

Clara? Kyle said. *Clara?*

Clara stared at the door; she had tears streaming down her cheeks.

Kyle stood there, speechless. These scenes tore him apart as he watched Clara sit in her room, crying and shaking. Kyle felt helpless; he couldn't do anything to help her at that moment. He was part of the scene, but he was unable to react to what was happening before him.

"I think that's what did it most for me—seeing Clara cry," Kyle said later. "I could not bear the sight of that."

Then, within a flash, Kyle would be out of the scene and back in his reality.

"What the hell just happened?"

Clara would call, too, and cry on the phone to Kyle. She'd

claim the OG had touched her again, or threatened to kill her. Or slapped her.

Lying in bed, Kyle thought about his latest vision. It was over. But now he needed to converse with his gods, those voices, he said, that controlled everything he did and did not do; his allies and imagined friends. Kyle always discussed his thoughts with Nicodemus, Saba, Ordog, and Sarin, but he couldn't shut them out (or off) if he wanted. They were always there, "arguing" with him over the things he wanted to do.

It'll be easy, Kyle told himself on this night. He was fixing to kill the OG. He couldn't take it anymore—and now he was watching the OG abuse Clara. A witness to the sickness.

Eyes wide open, staring at the ceiling, Kyle waited for a response.

"To just kill him would be a violation of your desideratum," Kyle heard one of the gods say to him.

Still, as part of that desideratum, Kyle felt it was essential that he do something to the OG. He felt it was his duty to protect Clara with whatever means he had possible. The more he heard about her being abused, the more he heard about how she was being poisoned, and the more he heard about how Clara's life was a living hell, the more Kyle Hulbert understood that this was no RPG. It was life or death for Clara Schwartz. And Lord Chaos, he knew, counted on him.

"The times I had met him, he was very hostile toward me . . . ," Kyle explained, referring to the OG.

In his mind, Kyle plotted out the scene.

Not death, though. Just scare him, Kyle convinced himself. *Intimidate him. He'll back off. He'll leave Clara alone.*

"You cannot kill him without just cause," one of the gods said. *"If you are not defending yourself or someone you love, you can never kill."*

Kyle was good with that order. All he wanted to do was make sure the OG knew that Clara had allies. She had a protector now.

And maybe—just maybe—he will back the fuck off.

CHAPTER 30

PAT SCHWARTZ E-MAILED his brother Robert. Clara's uncle was concerned about her. She had spent some time with Pat and his wife and they had noticed odd behaviors.

She really needs some analysis beyond what we can do, Pat Schwartz wrote to Robert. **She needs to be understood in a way that we cannot understand her—perhaps by a professional.**

In a roundabout way, Pat was saying that Clara needed some counseling. The girl was depressed. She lived inside her head, which had turned into, as far as he could tell, a very dark place.

There was one time when Pat had walked up to Clara, who was on a computer while inside his house. "What are you doing?" Pat had asked. He noticed Clara was inside "these chat rooms" where they were talking about "murders and all sorts of horror, and things like that," he said later in court. He couldn't tell if it was fantasy or reality. So he asked Clara what she was doing: "Is that reality, Clara?"

"Oh, this . . . no."

After not receiving an immediate response from the first, Pat asked Robert in a second e-mail, **Why in the world would you allow her to spend extended periods of time on the Internet in those grotesque chat rooms?**

A week went by and Pat didn't hear from Robert, who he knew to be an extremely private person. Robert didn't like outside people meddling in his affairs.

Soon, though, an e-mail came from Robert.

Pat was stunned to read that Robert felt Clara was "his business" and that he would "deal with her." Pat should keep his "nose out of [Robert's] business."

Clara's aunt and uncle could do no more than let it go and hope the girl got the treatment and help she needed.

CHAPTER 31

STRANGE DEATHS WERE occurring around the country during the fall of 2001, when Kyle Hulbert and Clara Schwartz began to meet regularly, talk daily, and immerse themselves deeply in the Underworld that Clara had created around the supposed reality of her father plotting to poison her. Kyle had an important role to play in this new world order that Clara had scripted.

In Kyle, Clara had found certain needs met; whereas Patrick House had proven, time and again, that he was incapable of satisfying those. Where Patrick balked when Clara mentioned uncomfortable things about the OG and how she wanted him dead, Kyle listened and innately took it all in, as though willing to do whatever Clara needed. She felt that. With Patrick, there was a clear separation between the Underworld and reality; and he and Clara hardly even entered that world now, or saw much of each other. With Kyle, though, it seemed to Clara that their entire existence, whenever together in person or online or on the phone, revolved around the fantasy. Clara understood that for Kyle there was only one world. There was no separation between life and the Underworld— and Clara made sure to keep it that way.

In those weeks after Osama bin Laden had created havoc in the world with his devastatingly violent and deadly attack on the World Trade Center Twin Towers in New York, a 260-mile, four-and-a-half-hour drive north on I-95 from Leesburg, Virginia, a death occurred that would soon cause some concern within the community that Robert Schwartz was such an integral part of then.

Sixty-one-year-old Kathy Nguyen, a Vietnamese immigrant to New York, a Bronx resident who worked for Manhattan Eye, Ear and Throat Hospital on the East Side, became very ill on Halloween night, October 31, 2001. The sickness just came out of nowhere. One minute she was okay, the next she was gasping for air, barely able to walk. Her vital signs were failing quickly.

For Nguyen, who had lived under the same routine every day, going to and from work via the subway, her life was nothing but ordinary. Yet, she was "critically ill" on that night, all of a sudden, and so she admitted herself to the ER.

Not long after walking through the doors of the emergency room, Nguyen was placed on a respirator. Within moments, she was unable to speak.

Later that night, sadly and quite tragically, Nguyen died from complications related to anthrax poisoning. It would be one of several high-profile anthrax-related deaths to send up red flags within the FBI, CDC, and other agencies looking into terrorism and the growing threat that overnight had become the new normal in the United States.

Kathy Nguyen's case, however, was particularly interesting to several in the medical and scientific community watching the situation unfold, because the next high-profile case related to this community, only a few weeks later, would involve a biologist, Dr. Benito Que, who was viciously attacked by four men wielding baseball bats. It had the earmarks of a hit—a planned and well-choreographed beat-down.

After that violent attack, a microbiologist, who had been investigating immune disorders, turned up missing. His vehicle was found by a bridge near the Mississippi River. His body was later recovered downstream, about three hundred miles away. His family had no reason to believe he was suicidal.

Then another biologist, who had once worked on biological weapons in Russia, died unexpectedly and suddenly from a massive stroke; another microbiologist died from asphyxiation related to gas in a storage shed. Scientists, some of whom were working on the same types of disorders and groundbreaking projects, appeared to be dropping (or were murdered, depending on which conspiracy theorists you spoke to) at a rate of about one a week.

Clara and her troops sat by and closely watched all of this unfold. Not that they were that interested in these strange deaths, but it was hard to ignore, since Robert Schwartz, the OG, was a renowned scientist within this same community. All considered, when push came to shove, it was a very small field. Scientists talk. They stay in touch. When they start dropping due to anthrax poisoning and other strange circumstances—anthrax being a poison that can be made in a lab by the scientist—many stop and take notice.

Who would be next?

Or, could this be used as a ruse for the OG to meet his fate in the Underworld?

CHAPTER 32

KYLE INSTANT-MESSAGED CLARA one night in late October. He was writing from Katie's computer: WWWWWAAAAASSSSSUUUUUPPPPP!!!!!!

No response.

Then: (Kyle), he tapped out and hit ENTER.

Okay, I figured as much, Clara responded.

They asked how each other had been, as though they hadn't spoken in some time. It took Clara all of twenty taps of the keyboard in front of her to bring up Patrick, who was slipping further and further away from this group. Clara was "angry" at him, she explained to Kyle.

Kyle ignored the comment and said: I miss you, CJ.

Clara wanted to know who said that: Kyle or Katie?

Kyle, who else . . . lol.

Clara needed to tell Kyle that Patrick was supposed to be there to do something for her—she never said what—but since she was angry at him and he wasn't coming, Clara wanted to know if Kyle was interested in taking his place.

There was a personality trait in Kyle that did not allow him to stand down. He needed to be that person they all looked up to: the person at the center of attention, the toughest of the bunch, the one who had seen and done things they could only dream about. When, point in fact, Katie, Mike, and Clara saw Kyle as a bullshit artist for the most part—a guy who talked a big game and made up stories in order to make himself appear bigger, stronger, and more worldly than he ever was— yet they never let on to Kyle about this. They allowed him to play the role of tough guy and protector. They enjoyed the stimulation Kyle brought into their lives by simply allowing him the space to be who he wanted to be.

Katie soon jumped in on the same conversation. Kyle and Katie were now sitting at the same computer, sharing the keyboard, both responding to Clara at different times, each noting who they were by name.

Kate, imagine Kyle knowing about ALL of my life and THAT STUFF! Clara wrote, knowing Kyle was right there, reading it.

Kyle didn't bite. He wasn't interested. He had known enough about Clara by then to know that she led a life that was screwed up, according to her, and she needed a friend like him to help her fix it.

Clara moved on and talked about an upcoming day where they were all getting together to practice "gwchyndo," a fighting style she claimed to have designed and developed. She wanted Kyle to train with them so she could personally show him her style of fighting. Clara knew Kyle was into swords and fighting a certain way; he liked to go out into the woods by himself and practices for hours.

I have studied gwchyndo briefly, CJ, told you that, Kyle wrote.

It was pronounced "gwin-chin-do," Kyle explained. "For Clara, this 'gwchyndo' was something that was unique and exotic and, most important, something that made her feel special. It's like, when she said, 'I am a practitioner of gwchyndo,' and you said, 'Well, hey, what's 'gwchyndo'?' she then had to explain it because you didn't know. It made her the center. It's the same reason why some people wear strange medallions on their chest, because they want people to ask them about it."

If you enter my world, you learn about my personal life, Clara wrote.

You will learn about mine as well, so we will be even.

Clara next broke into a rant about not wanting to live. Kyle presumed it to mean that she was figuring on ending her life. This was Clara's manipulative way—so honed and manufactured by then—of bringing the conversation back around to him (and maybe Katie) feeling sorry for her.

Is there anything I can do? Kyle asked, after allowing Clara to share how bad her life was and how much of a pain in the ass Patrick had been for dissing her lately.

Clara encouraged Kyle to meet her the following day.

He finally agreed.

Clara then asked what Kyle had meant by helping her with "anything" he could do.

Kyle said in whatever way he could, of course.

Then she talked about how she had been "driven" recently to "extreme depression" and "mental breakdowns," and "the state" she was in was not so good.

I am there for you, CJ. I will do all I can, Kyle wrote back.

Well, I am thankful I don't have weapons here ... well, weapons I can kill myself w/

Please don't say such a thing, CJ.

As the conversation continued between Kyle and Clara, Katie went away. Kyle said that Katie and Mike began to have sex in front of him, which was something they often did while he was on the computer talking to Clara.

Kyle continued speaking with Clara. They talked school.

Kyle encouraged her to "ditch it" and find some fun in life. When she asked, "Like what?" he suggested "pyrotechnics!"

Then Clara said: **How strong are you?**

How do you measure strength? Kyle asked, hoping she'd clarify.

Yes, Clara answered.

I have been up for 4 days solid, Kyle said, hoping that alone would prove to her how tough he was.

Strong enough to stop me from doing something that harms me? Clara wondered, unimpressed by the fact that Kyle didn't need a lot of sleep, apparently.

Maybe I would do whatever I deemed necessary to keep you safe.

Ok!

I found a new torture. Self-torture, Clara wrote, changing the subject.

I need to explain something before I go farther with what I would do to keep you safe, ok? Kyle had thought by now Clara understood this. They had talked about it on the phone and in person so many times, but he wanted to be clear.

Ok, go ahead.

I live by the code of the warrior. . . . I believe you already know that.

Yeah.

And therefore, I have codes I follow.

Yep.

And I follow them at all costs.

Ok.

Because that is the way my life is lived.

Go ahead....

If I need to do something in accordance with my desideratum I do it by whatever means I deem necessary.

Ok.

And is whatever works the quickest at the time.

Ok.

If you were trying to hurt yourself . . . I would first try to reason with you, which never lasts long with me.

Then?

Then if I thought it necessary . . .

You'll what?

I would probably first hold your wrists.

In some cases that wouldn't work!

Then if you got violent, I would increase my hold until you finally calmed down....

Kyle went on to say that if Clara displayed a lot of anger, he would allow Clara to take it out on him.

She said that wouldn't be a "wise idea" with her: **Especially w/ my mastery.**

This sort of talk merged with Clara specifically going into her Lord Chaos character, while it was clear that Kyle was speaking about his personal rules for the way he played the game of life. There was no distinction here for Kyle between the Underworld and the real world. He was laying it out for Clara. She could take it and put it into any type of terms—and world—she wanted.

Kyle went into "teaching" Clara how to handle a staff, how to manage it to her advantage. He wanted to end the conversation there. There was only so much he could teach through the Internet.

Sleep? Clara asked, sensing he wanted to go.

No, I have to call someone.

Okay.

**I hurt when I teach as well it is the only way to learn.
I will see you tomorrow.**

Yep.

Goodnight, CJ, sleep well. . . .

Clara turned off her computer. Although she never wrote about this particular moment, as she drifted off to sleep that night, Clara had to be considering that she now had Kyle Hulbert right where she needed him—and it was probably time to give the order.

CHAPTER 33

I FEEL THE utmost hatred for him, Clara wrote, before calling her father the *one in the world who is the biggest, greedest [sic], hypocritical, most lying shithead.* Clara wished that the OG *would rot in hell (if it exists).* . . . She wanted him to suffer greatly, *[to] understand how psychotic his actions on Earth [were],* and how much of *a fucking liar he was to everyone.*

What did she mean? Was Robert Schwartz putting on some sort of front? Was he one person at work, in front of the neighbors and family, and another, more immoral man at home with only Clara?

Clara Schwartz was sixteen when she wrote that passage. The anger, the unadulterated disdain she felt toward this man who had raised her, was palpable in every word she penned in her diary then.

Kyle had encouraged Clara to write everything down—specifically, a list of times her father had abused her.

"Keep track of it all," he said one day. "Collect the evidence."

Maybe he needed to see it in black and white more than she did?

Clara agreed; she told Kyle that she'd been doing that all along.

"I have journals and journals full of it all."

"Good!" he said.

Some of what Clara wrote in those journals—Clara's aunt on her mother's side later claimed in a letter to the court—should be taken seriously. Yet, the way the aunt described things inside the Schwartz house during those pivotal years (1996 through 1997) when all seemed to fall apart for Clara, it was Clara's deceased mother who would have been the main abuser, not Robert Schwartz. (In speaking to the police, Clara's sister would later agree.)

Clara's aunt talked about the tortured history of the family on Clara's mother's side. She mentioned how Clara's grandparents had engaged in arguments so loud, the neighbors would intervene and ask what in the hell was going on inside the house. This became shameful to the sisters (Clara's aunt and Clara's mother). They learned to live under a cloud of embarrassment, humiliation, and scandal.

One time in1966, Clara's aunt claimed, she was asked by Clara's grandfather to go and look after Clara's grandmother. The woman was in a terrible place: *Highly disturbed, unhappy and aggressive, and at one point she attacked me,* the aunt wrote. More than that, in detailing a pattern of behavior within the family, the grandmother showed signs of "hallucinations and delusions," and after "forty-eight hours of trying to calm her down" on that night, they had to admit her to the psych ward of a local hospital, where she was diagnosed as manic-depressive and placed on the psychological drug lithium carbonate, also called Eskalith, a drug designed as a treatment for "manic episodes of bipolar disorder" or "manic-depressive illness."

The grandmother never recovered from that alleged manic break. Two years later, she developed intestinal cancer and died. The aunt gave no reason for it, but "there was no funeral" for the woman. Clara's aunt never said what they did with the body or how they mourned her—only that she was dead and gone.

Looking at how the aunt defined the ebb and flow inside that Stone House where Clara's mother, Joan, her aunt, and her uncle grew up—and where Clara now lived with the OG—one would have to draw a conclusion that anyone living there was doomed to disturbing and insane behaviors. If what Clara's aunt later said is factual, there were generations of questionable and troubling behaviors going on. According to the aunt, there was cross-dressing, drug trafficking, lots of LSD use, rage-fueled arguments, tantrums, and beatings throughout the years she lived there. The mental and emotional abuse alone, she pointed out, was enough to drive even the most emotionally hardened person over the edge. It was as if the house itself was possessed, like that fictional Amityville horror story, and had caused chaos in the world of these kids, before Clara was even born and the OG ever came into the picture.

In her letter, Clara's aunt called her parents, Clara's grandparents: *emotionally unpredictable . . . distant, and unresponsible [sic]*. There was mental, emotional, and "some physical abuse" going on at any given time. And the odd thing was, no one, she claimed, ever talked about it or ever brought it up. It all became a bad dream—a nightmare—the entire family ignored. It was a white elephant they all just seemed to accept would defecate, at will, all over their lives.

"He's dressing up in my clothes," Clara's aunt told her parents one day, speaking of someone she knew.

"It's your fault!" her parents said, to her utter shock, blaming her.

Because nothing was ever done about it and the entire incident was never discussed, this person began to involve the neighborhood kids in the behavior. Soon the other parents called the house; the offender ultimately got psychiatric treatment.

Joan, Clara's mother, had her own set of problems, her sister told the court. Joan had met Robert while she was in rehabilitation. Joan had been committed because of what her sister described as having "a breakdown." Joan had been married before meeting Robert. That marriage ended in a bitter divorce and Joan had turned to drugs to deal with it, her sister claimed. That was the reason she had entered rehab.

We had been in touch over the years, the aunt wrote, speaking of her sister, *but her behavior could be problematic.*

Joan's other sibling had once spoken, the aunt wrote, of *incidences with Joan which were disturbing and indicated emotional instability as well as alcohol abuse.*

There was one time when Joan took one of the kids—not Clara—to England to see the aunt, who had seemingly moved as far away from the family as possible. The child was eight. There was a family reunion. Robert didn't attend, apparently. Walking around the party, Joan appeared to be out of it. Not necessarily drunk or high, but not in her right frame of mind.

Her thought processes were fragmented, the aunt wrote, *and her behavior was distracted.*

When she returned home after the reunion, Joan was hospitalized "immediately" and diagnosed as "manic-depressive."

Like her mother before her, Joan was put on lithium.

The cycle was complete.

Where Robert Schwartz was concerned, the aunt described him as a guy without patience. She said that during the few times Joan and "Bob," as she called him, visited her in England, she observed a man who was "easily angered" and "often belligerent."

The aunt explained in the letter to the court that she had never been back to the Stone House after moving away, likely wanting to steer as far and clear away from that dark, twisted abode as possible. Still, she talked about her and Joan's other sibling going back to the house and how, when they later chatted, he relayed stories of a couple—Robert and Joan— who were always screaming and yelling at their children and each other. It seemed that the Schwartz family epitomized the term "dysfunction," and took over the role set in place by Joan's parents before them.

Their other sibling, the uncle, "disliked Bob intensely," the aunt reported. It was no secret that visiting Bob and Joan reminded the siblings of their youth while growing up in that same house. They could not escape their past. Now Joan and Bob were perpetrating on a new set of children the very same madness that Joan had managed to live through.

It was 1997 when Joan realized that a cough she had was much more than an infection or bronchitis. Joan had developed lung cancer and was very ill by the time doctors got to it. She would die that year, 1997, not having learned how badly the family and all that chaos had affected Clara, who was fifteen.

Those . . . children were living in an isolated farmhouse with two raging parents and one dying from lung cancer, the aunt wrote.

Counseling was mentioned as something the kids should undergo, the aunt said, especially Clara, who seemed to be taking it all the hardest: *Bob refused to allow it.* He didn't want any of his kids in therapy. It meant admitting defeat. They could work things out themselves—that's how families grew stronger.

It was always a given that Joan favored Clara more than Clara's brother and sister, the aunt said. The aunt met with Clara after Joan's death. The child didn't seem right. She was terribly antisocial (especially within the family), not to mention oddly quiet. She kept to herself. She rarely smiled. She seemed perpetually depressed. Clara's aunt later wrote that the family was greatly "concerned" about Clara's well-being and her future.

Why?

Clara was living alone with her father, the aunt concluded.

CHAPTER 34

ON NOVEMBER 9, around three in the morning, as most of the world around them slept, Kyle and Clara found themselves online, chatting innocently at first about mundane issues. Clara lived alone in a dorm of about seventy kids, a decaying building behind a gas station. Her window faced the interstate. It was a dark, desolate place that kids chose to live in, in order to isolate themselves from everyone else. A saying around campus was that if a student chose to live in the dorm Clara did, he or she "wanted to be left alone." The one thing—and it happened to be her JMU major—that kept Clara busy, however, was that computer and its glowing light echoing off her face and the walls of her dorm room. Clara had found solace, anonymity, and companionship on the Internet. She could be who she wanted to be. She could project any type of persona out into the world she had created. Perhaps most important, she could control and manipulate whomever she liked.

Kyle was crashing at Mike's again, using the computer in Mike's basement bedroom inside his mother's house. For the first five or ten minutes, Kyle and Clara discussed swords and fighting styles. It was friendly, even adolescent chitchat between two goth, computer-savvy kids who liked to enter into that fantasy world the Internet facilitated and inspired. All this talk about fantasy seemed guileless and, well, pointless. But as they chatted, Clara's motive became apparent—if not to Kyle, then to anyone reading the transcript later.

Clara talked about Patrick more often than she had in the past, although she was dissing his fighting skills, perhaps hoping to feed Kyle's ego.

Kyle didn't want to discuss Patrick, however; he liked to keep the focus on himself.

Clara wondered why he wasn't sleeping (it being the middle of the night, after all), adding, I sleep so much [myself these days], my friends, what little remain, think I have mono or insomnia.

Let them think what they want. As long as they do nothing to threaten you, it is okay. For if they do, they will have to answer to me, Kyle answered back.

This was a good sign. Kyle was in his protective mode. Clara appreciated that. She replied, Okay.

Even if you kill them first, Kyle responded, hoping to bring the conversation to a place he liked to enter late at night: violent fantasy. Kyle's head was full of violent and bloody images. At times, he needed to explore it all with someone he could trust. He had realized over the past few weeks that Clara was *that* person. By now, Kyle was entirely fixated on fighting with swords and blood drinking and all things vampire-related. This world online was a godsend to him. Kyle could enter into it and feed his darkest desires—but only, Kyle began to feel, to a certain extent. It was like the guy who carries a gun around with him all the time, realizing at some point that he is going to have to use it sooner or later to justify its presence, or why even carry the damn thing?

For Kyle, his life revolved around faeries, vampires, and blood (he was cutting himself regularly). His mind was his map. He listened to the voices.

Clara clarified: I don't kill unless absolutely necessary.

Aye.

If I must defend myself, I shatter bone. . . . I lacerate throats. . . . I injure.

You are a woman after my own heart, CJ.

Why?

You injure! Kyle tapped out on the keyboard.
Yeah, Clara responded.
Sounds like my style, Kyle said.
Clara talked about how she had shattered someone's knee and someone's ankle once when she went out with her staff and actually got into a fight. It was not clear if this was game chat or a true situation.
To inflict pain is to bring joy, Kyle responded after hearing the story.
How come I can never rid myself of enemies? Clara wanted to know. She felt Kyle had some experience with this. She'd known by then that his ongoing battle with those "bad vamps" was something he had under his control.

Hhhmmmmmmmmmmm. Good question.

Bad people?

I cannot help you there, as I have not figured that one out. My advice would be to avoid them.

Here?

What?

Bad people here? Clara asked. She seemed lost.

Are you there? Kyle said next. He seemed to have lost Internet contact with her.

Clara was back. She proposed a question built around a "what-if" scenario. What would Kyle have done just then if, within the time they had been disconnected from the Internet, she hadn't returned and had instead been kidnapped by the evil demons plaguing the Underworld? How would he handle such a situation?

I would have tracked you down and killed the bastards.

You sound like Sebastyen.

Kyle asked who that was.

He trained Pat—he also has a knack for finding me, Clara answered.

They discussed potential threats Lord Chaos faced, never once mentioning Lord Chaos by name. Kyle reminded Clara that he would track any of them down, at any time, and gladly "exterminate" each one, and enjoy every moment of it.

Now he was speaking a language Clara was quite fluent in. She responded by saying, **Those whose cause is solely to hurt or kill me are killed. Or in another term I use, tayed.**

Trust me, I can see to that, Kyle answered back.

Tay means to kill or killed in Moorian native language of Gwchyndo.

Kyle knew that already, but he asked if Clara was willing to teach him the language she'd created.

She explained how she hadn't learned the language herself, specifically, but it just flowed out of her. So it would be very hard actually to teach it, but there was another way, Clara explained, for them to communicate without anyone around them knowing what they were saying. Clara called it "A.L.," or Acronym Language.

It uses English, but differently.

Teach me? Kyle asked, surely engrossed in this conversation.
This girl seemed to be everything Kyle had been in search of: She understood his mind. The voices. The worlds he'd step in and out of. She sympathized with him and his ills. She seemed to care about his thoughts. He knew of no one else whom he could relate to so intimately. Not even Brandy.
Clara explained that not all terms are acronyms, such as "death."

Death as an AL term means the same as fucking ... having sex in other words.

Hmmm . . . Now THAT is interesting . . . , Kyle said, making it clear that she had this eighteen-year-old boy's raging hormonal attention.

Meinacide is suicide. Can you guess the difference?

Kyle couldn't and wanted clarification.
Suicide is a cry for help. Meinacide is actually killing yourself ... just doing it and not warning anyone. She added that "meinacide" simply meant that the person was actually prepared and willing to do it "by any means possible."
Kyle said he understood.
This point of the conversation led them into a discussion about how fun it would be to talk A.L. in public and weigh reactions from passersby. Kyle laughed and said he couldn't wait to learn it and speak it with Clara in public—which made her ask when that would be, exactly—because Clara made it clear that she desperately wanted to see him.
Kyle told her he was going to find out soon if he could

spend the upcoming weekend with her at JMU. He needed to check on a few things first.

Clara said that might work out perfectly. Katie and Mike were planning a trip to JMU to see her. Then, as they talked about meeting up, Clara tossed out something at random to get Kyle onto the subject she had wanted to discuss from the start.

~thinking and trying to divert the shaking, Clara tapped out and sent at random.

Kyle bit hard, asking why she was shaking.

As if part of a script she had written earlier that day came to mind, Clara sent back: Around this time of night, I start remembering. . . .

He asked what.

Clara said it was the kidnapping by Bylod and Satynsts on 8/30-9/1 and 9/2.

Kyle perked up. That last date was his hatching day.

I was rescued 75 minutes before they would have executed me. And 30 minutes before they would have started raping me.

Kyle could barely get a word in now; Clara was off and running, saying how they had "starved" her, "tortured" her "twice," and "emotionally fucked" her up.

All Kyle could say was I am sorry.

Didn't actually rape, but put it this way: hands, Clara added.

This was not the first time Kyle had heard Clara talk about someone penetrating her vaginally with his hands. In fact, the only person Kyle knew to have abused Clara sexually with his hands, which he had heard several times from her, was the OG.

This set off a series of sympathetic remarks from Kyle. Clara kept ladling it on as he continued to say how sorry he was. If there was anything he could do to help her, he would do it without question.

Clara Schwartz knew exactly what she was doing when she entered into this type of rhetoric. She had brought Kyle to this place online and was now feeding him the right amount of emotional blood to ingest. Clara knew what this would do to Kyle. He was inherently a protector—a guy who would turn to violence in a heartbeat to protect a lady he considered an intimate friend. Clara was very familiar with this territory of plying the mentally unstable with raw emotion and letting them feed on it.

Clara had practiced it and even talked about it in her diary, explaining, *I think I'm not mentally well. Higher the IQ, the greater the chance that person is not mentally well. . . .* She then went on to discuss how she'd sat and spoken with a friend whose IQ was in the 170 range, but he was "schizophrenic" and she realized how she could easily twist and turn, shape and mold him with simple words.

Clara promised Kyle that if he came down to JMU by that Sunday he would be "fluent" in A.L. Then she tapped out: Give you a chilling thought . . .

Give it your best shot, Kyle responded. According to the times on the instant-messaging transcript, they had been chatting for almost ninety minutes by then.

Clara brought Patrick back into their conversation, saying she "assumed" it was okay "to play."

Play what? Kyle wondered.

Down there, Clara said, explaining that Patrick had taken Clara's "silence" as he did whatever it was he did "down there" to mean the sexual experience was pleasurable. But it wasn't, Clara said. All it did for her was bring her back to a hell she had visited when she was once violated in the same way—so Patrick, Kyle now assumed, must have been fingering Clara at the time.

That's part of my problem with Pat, she said.

Kyle fessed up and talked about a time he was sexually abused. He finally felt close enough to her to open up about it. He had been waiting for the right moment.

Clara said she had always known this about him. She had sensed it in him, which was one reason why there was a bond between them that no one else could comprehend.

Kyle felt an immediate attraction to Clara like he had not felt since meeting her. He told her how the abuse had occurred while he slept, so he guessed that was why he didn't sleep much and suffered from insomnia most of his life.

Clara explained that they would use the acronym of SMO from now on to discuss "sexually molest, as a verb."

She claimed the first time for her was when she was nine years old—by her own father.

Sorry, Kyle tapped back.

It's okay, that's probably why I am a virgin. . . . He didn't go so far as death.

"Death" meant "sexual intercourse" within the context of the A.L. language. Clara explained that the OG did it "in front" of her mother, and Clara didn't know at the time it was wrong. Her mother finally stopped it. Clara later added into the conversation that the OG was the reason she feared water.

Kyle wondered if he had tried to abuse her sexually in the water, too.

No, he tried to tay me. . . . He dragged me under so by the time everyone else came out to the pool . . . it looked like I was drowning.

Clara could sense that she had Kyle totally under her wing. She'd developed the character of the OG in Kyle's head as a completely violent and sexually abusive villain, a man who walked menacingly around the house, abusing his daughter at every given moment.

Kyle sat behind the computer clenching his fists, seething, wanting a piece of this man who was hurting his friend.

Clara next wrote: Pat wants to tay him. . . . Then, without

a response from Kyle, she tapped and sent: If you do . . . all I ask is that it not trace to me.

Kyle then made it clear that this was between him and the OG now; Clara had nothing to do with it: Let's put it this way: I don't know of anything he ever did to you. . . . I just have my own issues with him.

Kyle didn't need any longer a reason from Clara to kill the man; he had his own.

Okay. He did it every time I swam from four to eight, Clara added, giving a four-year range for that abuse.

He is most lucky.

The recent occurrences have been . . . think what happens to Snow White.

With the apple? Is that what you are talking about?

Yeah. What did her stepmother do?

Kyle thought about it. What had Clara shared with him during those times they had already been together? What was her biggest fear these days?

Kyle wrote back, Try to kill her. Lose her in the woods. . . .

Kyle was having trouble finding the word.

Then it came to him.

Tap. Tap. Tap. Tap-tap-tap.

Click.

Clara stared at the screen, waiting to see if Kyle was following.

In it came.

Poison.

They discussed where the OG spent most of his time. Just outside Leesburg, at the Stone House, Clara explained. She even gave Kyle the address, which he said he wrote down, in case he didn't know how to get there from his memory of having been there once before already.

Then Kyle came out with it: **If I was to tay him would you be mad at me?**

No. Just don't do it now.

Not now—my mind is a bit too cloudy for that at the moment. Maybe in a month?

We'll talk about it down here. . . . Take a long walk and talk . . . okay. Leave Mike and Kate. . . .

Very well.

Unless you don't want to. I just hate talking about that kind of stuff on here, Clara typed back.

Clara could say what she wanted later, but with this one instant message, written by her own hand, Clara indicated that she was certainly speaking outside of the Underworld character, Lord Chaos, whom she'd created. Because the Internet was the one true place Clara Schwartz felt most comfortable talking about the game, the idea that she didn't want to discuss killing her father online meant that it was a direct order in the real world.

I would like to talk face to face, Kyle confirmed.

Clara said she needed to look for her "little black book," and Kyle should stand by a moment. And when she returned some time later, she listed the times the OG had tried to poison her recently.

Kyle felt good. She had listened to him when he told her a while back to keep track of it all. Pen a record of the attempts on her life. Clara had even sat down and remembered other times and wrote those down, too.

Clara then explained that she was concerned Kyle would

act on his own and show up at the house to confront the OG. She didn't want this. She wanted a plan put in place and then carried out with her order, at her will. She wanted to know if Kyle understood this.

I would do nothing in your domain without your consent, Kyle wrote, indicating that he, too, understood his role in Clara's life now.

After discussing the weekend and what they were planning on doing, Kyle said he had a question.

Go ahead, Clara encouraged.

When we first met, you said that you trusted me—is that true?

Yep. Why do you ask?

I get the impression that is not something that happens every day. (Kyle meant a girl trusting a boy enough to go online and ask him to kill her father.)

They agreed Kyle was "lucky" that Clara trusted him, because when it came down to it, she didn't trust many people.

Kyle brought up the idea that they could begin a relationship "physically" at any time. Clara said she desired "friendship" first, and she thought he had a girlfriend, anyway. Kyle balked, ignored the girlfriend comment, and said he would gladly "leave" the "final decision" to her.

Clara responded by saying how it could "remain unspoken," if they both chose.

I can keep it a secret if that is what's to happen, Kyle added.

There was a debate raging in Clara's heart, she explained: whether she loved Patrick or not. She thought she might. Kyle said with regard to relationships, he would never "try to force" her into anything.

There was one guy, Clara explained in a series of back-and-forth comments, she'd known since she was four years old that she'd dated right up until March of that year. He was "the one," she told Kyle. She had dated the guy seriously for five years, on and off. In the end, he was unable to commit. He had even left the country and moved to Europe. She said how she had been "willing" to spend the rest of her life with the guy, but he was ultimately too scared. That decision truly hurt her.

They spoke for another few moments and bid "adieu," calling each other "sweetness." They made plans to see each other later that same day. Kyle said he was totally into going up to JMU to see her now. It didn't matter what he had to do. He'd get out of it.

Kyle logged off and was already trying to wake Mike up.

"I wanted to see Clara," Kyle said later. "Mike was going to take me there."

Before logging off, Clara searched the desktop of her computer for the icon named "uw people," a file she had created. Clara would save various conversations between her and those involved in the Underworld. No doubt smiling, she clicked the SAVE button inside a menu she'd opened, downloading the entire instant-messaging conversation she'd just had with Kyle, saving it inside a file named "Kyle."

CHAPTER 35

DEALING WITH KYLE, Clara had to be careful. He might have been crazier, but he was also smarter than the others she had shaped and molded into stewards to play her silly Underworld game. Clara figured this out almost immediately and would have to continue working Kyle from the inside out. Thus, as November brought the coldest weather of the season, Clara intensified her narrative with Kyle. She had Kyle where she needed him, finding that perfect balance between what she could and could not say to him. Just the previous night, while they spoke online, Clara had both committed and did not commit to perhaps beginning a romantic relationship. Effectively, she left Kyle hanging.

As for her communication abilities, Kyle said later, Clara was extremely skilled. Additionally, regarding that "abuse" she talked about, Clara "likely magnified even the slightest bit of [it] at home," which she might have been subjected to, Kyle added.

"If the only time she is around at home, there's a cause of conflict," Kyle explained to me, "that might just reinforce her delusion that she is being abused—and thus becomes a *true* delusion. *'My dad is trying to kill me.'*"

Still, Clara was smart enough to recognize when someone else was in need of proper psychiatric help and actually suffering from delusion. On her own time, she had studied mostly philosophy back in high school, and was not as introverted and antisocial as her writings indicated, giving more credence to a later theory that her journal writings were based more in Clara's fantastical thinking than in her reality. It was back in high school that the OG bought Clara her horse, Cherokee. Clara enjoyed nothing more than tending to the animal and taking it for rides when she first got him. There were times, too, when she and friends went out to any number of the Civil War memorials around the state to study the history and engage in conversations about the war.

It wasn't until Joan Schwartz began battling cancer, Clara's paternal grandfather later said, that Clara drifted into heavy metal, dark clothes, and a brooding mood of melancholy. She took to a "fringe group" of "goth kids" she found at school.

"She was very, very close to her mother," Clara's grandfather told the Associated Press, "and I think it was a rather serious thing for her [Joan's death]—and my son worked overtime trying to help her."

Clara saw Kyle's weaknesses as a window she could open and use against him. Clara had once written about a precedent within this psychological framework she'd established regarding recognizing mental handicaps in people and exploiting them for her own benefit. It was almost as if Clara prided herself on being able to find these types of people, study them, and then use them. She talked about how a boy from school had similar issues to Kyle and she had hung around the kid in order to learn about his condition in order to both understand and take advantage of him.

There was a part of Clara that believed the people around her were there "for her use," Kyle observed. "This was later clear to me."

If in choosing Kyle for a specific purpose she had in mind, by first realizing her boyfriend wasn't going to do it, Clara could not have chosen a better candidate. Because as Kyle later explained: "A man who abused me, I remember killing him. I remember it as clearly as this conversation right now. I remember killing several different bad people, in fact, who were doing . . . *very* bad things."

Another aspect of Kyle's character emerged within the psychiatric reports later made public. (It was something I spoke to Kyle about at length.) Kyle had always told me he had never used drugs, never bought drugs, and was never interested in drugs.

"Sure, I smoked some weed at a party, had a few drinks here and there, but I never pursued either at all."

Yet, in a 2001 psych report I was able to obtain, Kyle told a psychiatrist that he had been abusing "shrooms" (hallucinogenic mushrooms) "since age eight."

He has used and experimented with most drugs at some point in his life including experimentation with LSD, PCP, but has mostly focused on marijuana and "shrooms," the report said.

This was in clear contrast with what Kyle later told me.

"I was in a total cannabis haze," Kyle told one psychiatrist on July 23, 2001, "for about two weeks when a close friend of mine, a 'blood brother,' died of AIDS at twenty-three years old." What Kyle meant was that his "blood brother" had gotten the immune deficiency disease from drinking someone's blood.

"When did you last use drugs?" the doctor asked.

"March of this year."

When one looked back at Kyle's life, which had been documented in great detail, it appeared that the only evidence of him abusing or even using drugs was in his psych files. Clara, Mike, and Katie later said they never witnessed Kyle use drugs.

"Did you or did you not use shrooms or any type of drugs?" I asked Kyle after obtaining these reports, which totally contradicted his statements to me. I was concerned, of course, that he was lying to me about it. And if he lied about that, well, what else could I believe? "These reports claim you were using acid and shrooms since the age of eight. Let's figure this out. Were you or were you *not* using drugs?"

"There's nothing to figure out," Kyle began. "You have to understand. I had an uncanny awareness of myself and the people around me. I noticed things as a child no one else noticed. I knew there was something wrong with the way I was seeing the world. To me, what I saw, what I heard, the visions I had, there was nothing wrong with it. They were part of my life. They were *my* reality. They were . . . They were . . . *real*. But the people I saw had a problem with it all, as they should have."

While growing up, Kyle went on to add, he had learned about hallucinogens, acid, mushrooms, and the like. He understood that when you took those types of drugs, you would experience what he was experiencing without them. There was hardly a week that went by, Kyle added, when he wasn't sitting in front of some doctor being questioned about his visions and fantasies. Doctors were fixated on the topics, he claimed. He got tired of answering their questions about it all and trying to explain that it was real to him.

"So I told them what they wanted to hear," Kyle said.

He lied about doing drugs because in telling them that he was into hallucinogenic drugs, it answered their questions about the demons, cartoon characters, and other visions he was having.

CHAPTER 36

CLARA WAS CRYING. It had become a daily ritual, according to Kyle, as he and Clara became closer after that second weekend they spent together at JMU, along with Katie and Mike. Those "visions" of Kyle's where he now saw Clara being yelled at by her father and abused, as if he were standing in the room, were happening more frequently, Kyle said. It was near the third week of November, several days before Thanksgiving. Kyle shared the visions with Clara.

Learning this, Clara had to realize it was more fuel for the fire she was fanning.

"Kyle?"

"Yeah."

"I'm . . . I'm . . . ," Clara tried saying that night over the phone, but the tears were too much.

"What is it?" Kyle asked. He had walked somewhere private within Brandy's house. He didn't want Brandy and her mother involved in any of this.

To start off a conversation, Clara and Kyle could talk about food, relationships, staffs, swords, and the Underworld, Kyle said, but it always—every single day—steered "back to her father and the things he was doing to her."

"I'm scared of him, Kyle," Clara said.

"It'll be okay, CJ. I'll protect you."

"His fingers again, Kyle," she said, insinuating sexual abuse by her father. Clara knew this one thing (the purported sexual abuse by her father) angered Kyle furiously more than anything else. Kyle couldn't get the images out of his mind of her father sneaking into her room at night, reaching down and abusing her.

"Every day, she called me. Every day, she cried. Every day, she steered the conversation toward her father."

They hung up, telling each other that they'd stay in touch.

By now, the medication Kyle had been taking most of his life was completely out of his system. He was running on his own self-diagnosis and pure Kyle Hulbert adrenaline. "Hypomanic" is how one doctor described Kyle, which might be an indication as to how he could stay up for days without the help of drugs. "Racing thoughts and pressured speech" was how Kyle was depicted in many of the psych reports written about him. There had been twenty-eight separate psychiatric hospitalizations for Kyle over the years. Twenty-eight! A remarkable number of admissions for a kid just eighteen. He had been on lithium, clonidine, risperidone, trazodone, Tegretol, Neurontin, Depakote, Wellbutrin, Ritalin, Adderall, Vistaril, Prozac, Paxil, Zyprexa, and Seroquel.

"Kyle?"

"Yeah, CJ, what is it?"

She was calling again—third time that day.

"I'm terrified. Can you come and stay here for Thanksgiving?"

Kyle knew what she meant. Pitch his tent on her property, out of sight from the house. Clara said she needed to have Kyle there, by her side, her protector. Patrick was all but done, although Clara never said a word about this to Kyle.

"I'll see if Mike can drive me," Kyle said. He had wanted to spend the holiday with Brandy and her mom. Kyle fooled himself into thinking that this Thanksgiving would be like no other in that he would be sitting at a table with people who actually wanted him there. Cared about him. But now this dilemma: Clara or Brandy?

"Please come, Kyle. Please."

"I can, CJ," Kyle told Clara.

"Thank you. . . ."

There was something else. Kyle could tell Clara wanted to share a secret.

"What is it?" Kyle asked.

"I think he's getting ready to poison me again," Clara told Kyle.

CHAPTER 37

KYLE STOOD IN the living room of Brandy's house. No one was around. He had gotten his wish and had spent the Thanksgiving holiday itself with Brandy and her mom. It had been a nice meal, Kyle later recalled. One he won't ever forget. Sitting around friends, with a feeling of being wanted, was new to Kyle. He enjoyed it immensely.

His foot bounced nervously a million miles an hour as the phone number he had dialed buzzed in his ear.

Pick up. Pick up, damn it, Kyle said to himself.

He kept looking around the room anxiously, waiting for someone to come in and ask him what he was doing and who it was that he was calling. It felt this way for Kyle these days: as if he was constantly doing something wrong, always being watched.

"Hello?"

"Mike, what's up? Listen. I need a ride out to Clara's."

Kyle expected to have to beg or promise Mike some gas money he didn't have. But Mike said, "Sure . . . when?"

"Now."

Kyle had his tent packed and ready to go. He'd told Brandy he was taking off. He'd be back in a few days.

As he waited outside for Mike to arrive, Kyle took one more look inside his bag. He didn't want to forget the one thing he needed most, the one thing he kept with him all the time: his twenty-seven-inch ninja sword.

CHAPTER 38

THE BEAUTY, GRACE, and tranquility of the rolling hills and immaculate landscape of Loudoun County, Virginia, was not what Clara Schwartz kept focused on as she made her way through those dark November nights dealing with what she had described incessantly as an iron-fisted father, who, she had alleged, expected more out of her than she could ever deliver—that is, of course, in addition to abusing and trying to kill her. There just wasn't any middle ground between father and daughter. If what Clara said is to be believed, no matter what she did, what she said, or how she approached life, the OG pooh-poohed it all, usually with a slap and some rather spiteful words of humiliation. Robert Schwartz wanted order the way he saw it. He had been raising three kids alone—two of whom were not part of the family unit at home any longer, but would stop by from time to time—since 1997, when Joan died of lung cancer. According to Clara, Robert resented the woman for leaving him with such a task. Moreover, Robert was dedicated to his work as a scientist and how far DNA had come in just a little over ten years. DNA was finally taken seriously within the law enforcement and scientific communities. One could even hazard a guess that at work there was pressure on Robert because of his signature status as such a renowned biochemist; simultaneously the position also inflated his ego a bit, since he was such a star in his field. So when he got home and had to deal with Clara and her attitude of "I hate the world and everything in it," not to mention her personal problems—social, educational, and mental—there was friction, and perhaps even an air of bitterness and scorn. If we take the precedence set by Joan's family, Clara and Robert did not live in an environment conducive to discussing problems and difficulties like a pair of healthy adults might. Heck, Robert was apparently a proud guy with no interest in seeing his daughter get any psychological help. There's plenty of evidence to support that statement. He was the type to just as well deal with things himself, in private, inside his own home.

And so, in her own way, Clara dealt with the situation she found herself facing. She viewed her home life as a "lose-lose situation," she commented. She felt "damned if you do, damned if you don't." She couldn't win. There was no pleasing this guy. Yet, at the same rate, within all that Clara Schwartz wrote and complained about during those days after Joan died and she fell in with this group of friends, including Mike, Katie, Patrick, and Kyle, there was always a constant regarding her life with the OG: *"He never loved me"* was her continual refrain. This meant the most to her. Though she never wrote about it categorically, the lack of love she felt from her father—the fact that he rarely, according to her, told her he was proud of her and celebrated her life—became utterly clear while reading her journals. This hurt Clara horribly. She felt the blow every time she looked at him.

In regard to the lack of intimacy between Clara and her father, with no mother around, Clara reacted heatedly. She reciprocated by writing that she *HATED him; I felt & feel no love, only hatred, pure white hatred and he deserves to die. . . .*

"He deserves to die. . . ."

Clara's words. No one else's.

It became a theme in her life. She believed Robert had already tried to kill her in the past on several occasions, and that one of her siblings had also tried, never explaining exactly how. She called her home the "House of Hell," where "emotional" and "physical" abuses were "rampant."

Clara wrote that when her eulogy was written (because she believed her father was going to succeed in killing her one day, or she was going to succeed in killing herself), whoever wound up writing it, she was totally convinced, would undoubtedly say she was "not happy" (a prediction she made in her journal) or "did not find happiness." She confirmed that this would be a true statement.

Within all of this, Clara said, there was one place where she had found peace and joy: *In my art.*

She meant painting, watercolors. She was pretty good and seemed to enjoy the serenity that painting offered her soul. However, she never took it seriously or brought it to the next level.

Although she knew better, Clara dreamed that her lineage and that of the OG's would stem from different DNA: *I am NOT of his Blood, because it is the most hypocritical Blood in this Planet.* Although it seemed like an odd place to put it, she added here how she had hoped that when he did go to Hell, he would suffer.

Clara Schwartz hated her father fervently; there can be no disputing this fact. Her days were centered on loathing this man and everything about him. Not for one or two years, but just about her entire teen life. His dying would not have resulted in her feeling the least bit sorry or mournful. If this man were to vanish, or drop dead of a heart attack, Clara would sleep better. She'd rejoice. Hell, she'd probably throw a party. She made this point time and again in her diary, either implicitly or straight out.

She was also feeling pressure from her classes at school, and this short Thanksgiving break at home got her thinking about the upcoming, longer Christmas break. She just couldn't do the work anymore. Clara was smart, so she was expected to produce. But the advanced classes she was in were beginning to create a backlash, because her mind was so consumed with hating the OG and the Underworld. The stress was overwhelming, she said again and again.

In one entry, written in the form of a suicide letter, Clara spoke of how she wished her friends would understand how bad it was for her at home and school; yet there was no way they could. Even her closest friends—and she named each one of six (she was not lonely and was not being excluded)—did not know the amount of suffering she was experiencing.

Goodbye to my friends, Clara concluded one diary entry. *I wish I could work it out.*

She ended by saying how it had been seven years of her trying to get past this darkness and the sheer madness inside her home, but nothing worked. She ended the entry stating: *Nothing goes to my family.* Then she said she was off to try and commit "meinacide," totally contradicting her own meaning of the word.

Like her aunt living in England had suspected all along, Clara Schwartz was a confused and messed-up child, experiencing violent thoughts against the man raising her. Her core values and her goals were askew. She felt the walls closing in on her. She felt her father was trying to kill her. She felt her siblings did not care about her or love her. She felt her friends didn't understand her. It was either this or she was making it all up in some kind of elaborate narrative she was penning for the Underworld.

And yet, as total gloom seemed to be enveloping this young woman, here was her prince of darkness, thank goodness, about to come and rescue her. Clara Schwartz now had Kyle Hulbert on her side—and he was on his way to her house to spend what was left of the Thanksgiving holiday weekend.

CHAPTER 39

CLARA PLANNED ON spending most of the Thanksgiving weekend at home. The OG was going to be there, along with Clara's brother and sister. During an instant-messaging chat with Katie on the Wednesday night before Thanksgiving, Clara said she believed Patrick was "ignoring" her.

Katie warned Clara not to jump to conclusions with Patrick. He's "ignoring everyone," Katie said.

But Clara's tone during this instant message indicated she was done with Patrick. Finished. It was over between them. She'd found herself a new "boy" to complete the task Patrick obviously didn't have the guts to do.

Katie didn't want their relationship to end. She told Clara to relax and expect a call from Patrick to smooth things over. Katie, who had introduced Patrick to Clara, said she'd spoken to Patrick about everything and he was going to be talking to Clara soon, explaining himself. Katie claimed to know what Patrick's core issue was, but she was not going to get in the middle of it and tell Clara what was truly bugging Patrick.

After moving on from Patrick, Clara asked about Kyle. Was Mike going to be bringing him to her house on Friday? She never said that she and Kyle had made plans already to get together.

Katie said Mike didn't have enough gas money. Clara

needed to talk with Kyle and tell him to start carrying his load and come up with some money for carting him around. Mike was like Kyle's personal taxi service, and Mike was too bashful and scared to speak up for himself.

I can meet you guys and give you gas money, Clara told Katie. Clara didn't want anything to stand in the way of this weekend.

Mike and Katie were going over to Mike's dad's house on Friday, anyway, Katie said, so they might be able to pick up Kyle and drop him off.

Katie asked what time would work for Clara.

Clara suggested noon.

Katie said Kyle needed to find a place to stay for that weekend because he wasn't going to be staying with them.

It's a little cramped [with Kyle there] plus nobody . . . likes him but us and [they] don't want him here.

Well, he can't stay at my place, Clara said, adding how her siblings were home for the holiday.

Katie needed to get some rest, she said, and had to sign off so she could prepare her mind for the coming holiday with her family—all of whom she clearly did not get along with.

Mike took over the keyboard. First he explained that the people in his house were tired of Kyle. If any of them found out that Kyle had stayed in the house once in a while, they'd want money from Mike and Katie. Kyle was a handful. He was manic, wired, loud, and always telling people what was on his mind—which wasn't always what people wanted to hear. Aside from that, Kyle had overstayed his welcome with the group itself. Mike was sick of him. He was tired of driving Kyle everywhere: to his lawyer's, to court, to Clara's. It was getting to be too much. Even Mike's grandmother didn't want Kyle around.

Mike typed to Clara: [My grandmother] makes me feel stupid, criminal and subhuman for having Kyle in the house.

Why?

She thinks Kyle is taking advantage of me, particularly when it comes to money and rides.

Clara encouraged Mike to think for himself and tell people to leave him alone.

They next talked about family; Mike dissed just about everyone in his, especially his mother. He referred to her as the "bitch," who was "really good at arm-twisting" and "psychological torture."

Clara brought the conversation back to Kyle. She needed him at the house that weekend, making her plea obvious in the questions she asked Mike. Yet, when Mike turned the tables and suggested that Kyle stay at her house, Clara said that because of "the obvious," meaning the OG, there just wasn't any way.

Mike thought about having him stay at his house—again. He could sense that's where Clara was leaning. But, he pointed out, having Kyle around: **[It's] akin to keeping nitroglycerine in the back of your pickup truck—chances are an explosion will occur.**

They discussed where else Kyle could stay. Then Mike had a thought, saying how they should never "underestimate" Kyle's versatility. He'd be "quite happy to camp" in the woods near Clara's farmhouse.

Clara never shared that she and Kyle had already decided on this.

PATRICK AND CLARA had made plans long ago to spend that Thanksgiving weekend together. Clara hadn't told the others, but she was still holding on to Patrick, thinking that perhaps he was a possible Plan B. Their relationship wasn't what Patrick had in mind, however; over the past month, Clara had stepped away from asking him directly to kill her father, or since she'd picked up her rhetoric with Kyle. But there was still that itch in the back of Clara's throat to see if Patrick showed any interest in doing the job.

Patrick still wanted to give the relationship one more shot, so he called Clara at some point that Thanksgiving weekend.

They talked. It felt shallow to Patrick. They chatted about family and friends. There just didn't seem to be much there between them anymore.

Then Clara said: "You know, Path, that number of times you need to meet the OG as equal to him trying to kill me will come up over this Thanksgiving weekend and Christmas, if you met both times."

Clara obviously hadn't forgotten that deal they'd made some time ago.

Patrick didn't respond. He'd heard enough.

CHAPTER 40

"THANKS FOR THE ride, Mike," Kyle said. They were on their way to Clara's house. Katie was right beside Mike in the front; Kyle was in the back, with his tent, backpack, and twenty-seven-inch steel friend in the trunk. Mike had insisted on it.

"In case we get stopped," Mike explained.

Kyle wasn't going to argue.

There was a patch of woods near the farmhouse where Kyle could pitch his tent, and the OG would not see him.

"It was very overgrown at the time," Katie said later.

Katie had called Clara before she and Mike picked up Kyle. They said they were bringing him over, making sure that he could stay at Clara's house in the woods. The last thing they wanted was to get out there and realize Kyle couldn't stay. They'd be stuck with him.

Clara said, "Drop Kyle off, up near the power lines."

Kyle brought his camping gear. That section of the woods around the Schwartz farmhouse had become a popular place for Kyle. He felt safe out there. It was far off the beaten path—nowhere near anything. The OG would never suspect a thing. Never see him. To boot, he could keep tabs on Clara.

"Right there," Kyle said. There was a fork in the road some

distance before Clara's house. Kyle pointed to the right. "Take that way. . . ."

It had just rained. The road was "very muddy," Katie recalled. The area where Kyle pointed out was in a position where you could just make out the Schwartz home from inside the woods.

"I'll camp here," Kyle said.

"Cool," Mike answered. They shook hands. Kyle grabbed his stuff and got out of the vehicle.

"CJ's gonna bring me up to your place tomorrow," Kyle said.

Katie and Mike looked at each other. They didn't want him there, but Mike couldn't back down. "Sounds good," he said. "See you then."

At this point, Mike and Katie had no idea Kyle was the chosen one to kill Robert Schwartz. For them, any talk of killing the OG was part of Clara's Underworld game fantasies. Both claimed later that the more they heard about it from Clara, the less they believed in its validity.

CHAPTER 41

KYLE WAS MADE for spending time alone in the woods. He enjoyed the absolute silence of his surroundings. With so many voices whispering inside his head, the tranquility and stillness of the forest made Kyle feel as though he just might be able to manage the demons keeping him company.

It was Friday night. After Kyle pitched his tent, he and Clara hung out inside and talked about the same things they had discussed for the past several weeks: the OG, the abuse, and the rough spot Clara said she was in. Their relationship and topic of conversation revolved around Robert Schwartz. For Clara, there was nothing else to talk about as long as her father was still alive.

"Let's get something to eat," Clara suggested. They were sitting inside Kyle's tent. Clara said she had enough gas in her car, an old beat-up Mazda Protegé, to head into town.

"McDonald's?" Clara asked.

"Sounds good."

They took off. Kyle brought his backpack with him, including his twenty-seven-inch sword.

"This is nice," he said. It was just the two of them. Kyle found Clara intriguing and intellectually stimulating. To be in her presence was different from being around the others.

Clara understood the deepness Kyle felt. She knew how he saw the world and the things in it.

As they drove, Clara kept looking in her rearview mirror.

"What's going on?" Kyle asked at one point when it seemed Clara became nervous.

"Nothing," she said, pulling into the McDonald's parking lot.

"You sure?"

Clara parked.

"Look, I think we're being followed by a blue SUV," Clara said.

Kyle searched the parking lot with his eyes.

No blue SUV.

"What do you mean?" he asked.

"I saw him as we drove here."

"Yeah," Kyle said. "I thought the same thing." He gripped his sword.

"I'm thinking it's someone from an old Underworld alliance," Clara explained. Then she drove around to the other side of the parking lot. Luckily, there was an SUV parked there. Not so much blue, but it would do.

"See?"

"Yup," Kyle said.

Clara gunned it and drove as fast as she could out of the McDonald's parking lot. She kept looking back in her mirror.

"He's not following us."

"You lost him," Kyle said.

Kyle had no idea Clara was making up this entire episode, and that she was further messing with Kyle's head. For Kyle, every moment of an experience like this was real to him.

"You have to understand my mind-set at the time," Kyle explained later. He had a hard time recalling this particular incident; but after thinking about it, he remembered that Clara was so "determined" to get him to think they were being followed. "I am already experiencing delusions and hallucinations, to begin with. You start telling me people are following us and I am gonna *believe* you."

Clara drove back to the house. She said she had some things to do at home. Mainly, it was to feed her horse. The OG was around the property, she told Kyle, who was ready and armed. Anytime Clara wanted to put a bullet in the chamber and give the order to pull the trigger, he was prepared. But Clara did not indicate it was time for that just yet.

At some point that day, Kyle and the OG met. Clara was in the barn with Dr. Schwartz; they were tending to the horses. Michelle, Clara's sister, later recalled the meeting between the two of them—Kyle and Dr. Schwartz—as "casual." There was nothing in particular strange about it beyond Kyle's "goth" look and dark nature.

That night, Kyle packed up his tent. Clara drove him back to Brandy's.

"You going to be okay?" Kyle asked before getting out of the car.

"I'll be in touch," Clara said.

Kyle stepped out.

"Wait," Clara said as Kyle turned to walk into the house.

"Yeah?" Kyle said, leaning into her open window.

"Can you come back to the house tonight?"

"I'll get Mike to bring me."

Kyle walked into Brandy's and called Mike.

"I guess . . . ," Mike said reluctantly.

Mike showed up hours later. He and Kyle took off. They drove to Mike's parents' house first, where Katie was waiting for them.

There was a car in back of Mike's along a stretch of road near Mike's parents' house.

"You see that?" Kyle said.

"What?"

"That car has been following us."

Mike looked. It was just another car on the road. Common traffic.

"We're being followed . . . ," Kyle said.

Mike got scared.

When they pulled into Mike's parents' house, the car went another way.

"You see, this incident was residual from what I had experienced with Clara before," Kyle said later: "The idea that she put in my head that people were following me, it began to fester and build. By this point, I am degraded. I'm literally falling apart at the seams. My medication is entirely out of my system and all of the old psychoses are slowly, every day, reinserting themselves into my life."

Beyond that, Kyle said, he had what he called a "constant stressor" of Clara telling him about her father, "over and over again, every day, every day, every day." With all of that, Kyle said, his "mind started to take off." Clara had implanted in his mind that they were being followed that day on their way to McDonald's: "Okay, I am constantly looking over my shoulder now, wherever I go. I now believe I'm being followed because I am helping her."

After talking about it, Mike, Katie, and Kyle decided to hang out with Clara for the night. When they pulled up to Clara's, it appeared as if she had been waiting for them, because Clara walked out of the house in a hurry as soon as Mike parked in front of the door. She appeared wired and nervous, frantic, desperately wanting to say something.

As she approached the backseat of Mike's car, where Kyle was sitting, Clara pulled something out of her pocket.

"What the hell?" Kyle said.

It was a piece of a pork chop wrapped in a napkin. Clara had it in her hand as she sat down in the backseat next to Kyle.

"Take this," she said. "Give it a taste!"

"What?" Kyle responded, taking the pork chop.

"Taste it," Clara said again as the others looked on.

Kyle bit into it. Then he opened his door and spit out what was a mouthful of meat onto the Schwartz driveway.

"What the hell?" He said it tasted sour, bitter, and spoiled.

"It actually stung my tongue," Kyle later claimed. "It was really terrible. Not just bad, but rancid bad. I tasted it for quite a while afterward."

"Yeah, well, the OG cooked that one separately from the other pork chops," Clara said angrily. The indication was that the OG had tried to poison her. Clara ranted and raved as Mike pulled out of her driveway. She said sooner or later the OG was going to make good on his attempts to kill her.

Mike hadn't gotten completely out of the driveway yet, and Kyle yelled for Mike to move so he could get out. With a two-door car, Mike would have to get out and lift the seat forward so Kyle could step out. Kyle was fuming. "Sit up, man, get out of my way. Let me out. . . ."

Katie didn't say much. She stared back at Kyle and Clara as if dumbfounded and shocked.

"You are not getting out of my car, Kyle," Mike said. He knew what Kyle wanted to do: Run into Clara's house and have words with the OG. Get to the bottom of what he was doing to his daughter. "Look, I cannot believe the OG did that, but you are not getting out of this car." Mike started the vehicle and peeled out of the driveway to save them all some trouble.

Kyle punched the back of the seat. "Damn it."

"You have to protect me," Clara uttered quietly to Kyle.

They left Clara's house and went to JMU.

When they got to JMU, Clara and Kyle sat and talked. Mike and Katie had taken off to visit a friend Mike knew at the school. It was getting to the point, Clara explained, where she was afraid to sleep in her own bed. There was no telling what the OG was going to do next, or when he was going to do it.

"Here," she said to Kyle after reaching into a drawer and taking out a slip of paper. Later, Kyle would explain Clara's demeanor at the time she handed him this list as "unnaturally subdued." It was though she was "deliberately not making a big deal of it because that would, of course, bring *more* attention to it. So, actually doing that made a big deal of this list. '*Here, take a look, it doesn't matter to me at all.*' Obviously, if she approaches me with that attitude, which she did, I am going to pay *more* attention to it than I normally would."

Reverse psychology—Clara was a master manipulator. She had become an expert, especially where Kyle Hulbert was concerned, at mimicking his behavior and mirroring him so as to build a rapport.

"What's this?" Kyle asked.

"It's part of the list you told me to make."

By that point, Kyle had given a lot of advice to Clara; he couldn't recall right away what she was referring to. But after looking down at the paper and seeing what Clara had written, he realized it was a list of times her father had hurt her. She had each section of incidents labeled: *PA* stood for physical abuse, *EA* for emotional abuse, and *MA* for mental abuse. The list was extremely anal. It looked as if she had taken her time and put a lot of thought into it.

Clara didn't need to sell Kyle on this any longer.

"That's for you," she said, gesturing toward the list.

"Me?"

"Yeah."

Kyle looked àt it. "Crazy," he said later. "There was so much shit on that second list, I could not believe it."

Clara had written everything down in order.

Kyle folded the piece of paper and tucked it inside his wallet. "Thanks!"

One of the reasons he kept it in his wallet, Kyle later explained, was because he never went anywhere without his wallet. In fact, he called his wallet and backpack his "mobile-ready" kit—he could always, wherever he was, pick up and leave. Secondly: "At one point, I thought it might be useful to have the list as evidence . . . and yet the more I thought about it then, I didn't have *any* proof. All I had was her words and this piece of paper she had written."

CHAPTER 42

KYLE WAS AT Brandy's hanging around on December 1. By now, he was getting a bit overwhelmed by Clara's calls, the pork chop, the lists, and the incessant badgering—all built around the OG trying to kill her. It encompassed much of Kyle's fragile mind. He understood she was in a tight spot. But these calls on top of everything else? They were coming three to five times per day, sometimes in the middle of the night. Every time Clara called, she'd be hemming and hawing, hysterical over something the OG had just done or said to her. She could not stand it anymore, Kyle heard over and over. The OG had to go.

"You have to do something, Kyle" was a common phrase Clara would use. The indication being: If her life had been a hell leading up to this day, the way Clara described it now was as though she was caught inside Satan's web and soon there would not be any chance of escape—if Kyle didn't come to her rescue soon.

"Distraught, stressed-out, and fucking scared," Kyle said later. "That was how Clara sounded when she called during that first week of December."

"I just had a huge fight with the OG," Clara said. It was now December 2, about "three o'clock in the morning, when she called," Kyle remembered. Clara knew Kyle would still be up because he never slept. Clara was frantic and out of breath: "He said . . . He said . . . Kyle, you are not going to believe this, but he said that when we went to the Virgin Islands for Christmas, he was going to 'make sure' that I didn't come back."

Kyle was stunned by this. He could tell Clara had been crying for a very long time.

The OG had plans to take Clara and her siblings on a Christmas vacation trip to the Virgin Islands. It was going to be a chance for them to get away and spend some time together as a family.

"Don't go," Kyle said.

"I don't know what to do."

"Don't go." It was as simple as that. Tell him you're going and don't show up at the airport.

"You have to protect me," Clara pleaded, ignoring Kyle's request for her not even to go. "Kyle, listen to me. . . . You have to protect me. He's going to *kill* me."

Clara feared that the OG was going to use the trip to execute her while they were in the Virgin Islands. She didn't say how, when, or if she had told anyone else, but the OG had made it damn clear that Clara would not be returning from this trip.

"Look, calm down," Kyle said. "Chill. Everything's going to be fine. I'll protect you. No need to worry. Please don't worry."

It took some time, but Kyle was able to calm Clara down and make her understand that there was not going to be a trip to the Virgin Islands and she did not have to worry. All she had to do for the next few days was watch her back around the house. Keep clear of the OG. Kyle said he was going to fix everything. She had to believe in him.

After they hung up, Kyle popped on his headphones and downloaded some music. He sat and thought about what needed to be done. He didn't want to see Clara suffer the way she was; it was beyond the point of scaring the OG now.

Kyle Hulbert prided himself on being a blood-drinking, sword-carrying vampire.

Kyle was eighteen years old when the state of Virginia emancipated him, freeing him from its psychiatric and foster care system.

Clara Schwartz was a straight-A student in high school with a promising college career at James Madison University ahead of her.
(Yearbook photo)

Clara's father, Robert Schwartz, was a fifty-seven-year-old, well-respected biophysicist/researcher whose work focused on DNA when he was murdered inside his Leesburg, Virginia home on December 8, 2001.

Mike Profl met Kyle Hulbert in October 2001, and the two became best friends. *(Department of Corrections, Virginia)*

Katherine "Katie" Inglis was one of Clara Schwartz's best friends. The two had known each other since junior high school. *(Department of Corrections, Virginia)*

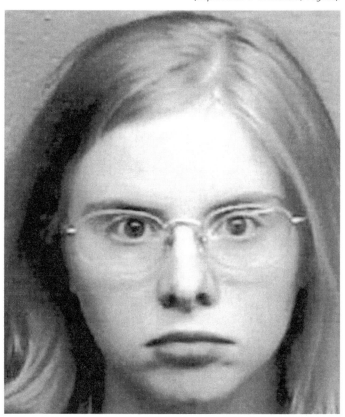

A close-up of the door leading to a side room of the Stone House. Secluded in a wooded area outside Leesburg, it had been in the Schwartz family for several generations.
(Photo courtesy of Shirlina Mann)

The Stone House became a crime scene after it was discovered that Robert Schwartz, widowed father of three and respected scientist, had been viciously murdered.
(Photo courtesy of Shirlina Mann)

Robert Schwartz was attacked in the kitchen of the Stone House.
It appeared that he had his back to his killer when the attack began.
(Photo courtesy of Shirlina Mann)

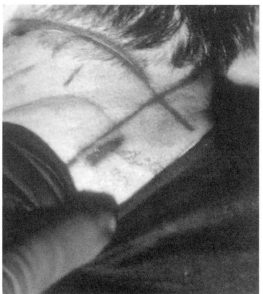

On the back
of Robert
Schwartz's
neck, Kyle
Hulbert carved
an X with the
tip of his
sword, as was
outlined for
him within his
role in the
Underworld as
chief assassin.
*(Courtesy Loudon
County Court)*

In the days following the crime, Kyle Hulbert was arrested for the murder of Robert Schwartz. The story he told police after his arrest was nearly unbelievable.

(Department of Corrections, Virginia)

After police questioned several of Clara's close friends, they believed she had made a detailed plan to have her father executed under the pretense of her Underworld game.
(Department of Corrections, Virginia)

Clara Schwartz was questioned by police.

Kyle Hulbert carried this twenty-seven-inch ninja sword with him wherever he went. It was eventually found inside a closet and forensically tied to the murder of Robert Schwartz.
(Photo courtesy of Shirlina Mann)

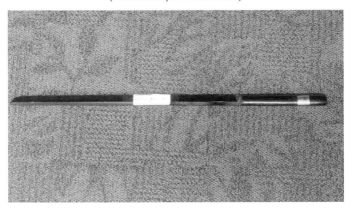

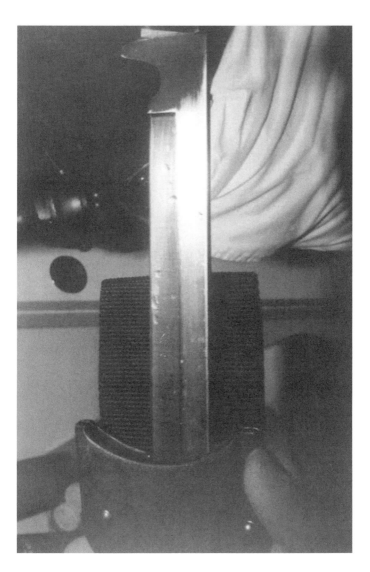

Exam: Mark wounds and medical therapy on body diagram if autopsy not performed at OCME.
A=Abrasion, B=Burn, C=Contusion, F=Fracture, G=Gunshot, I=Incised, L=Laceration,
M=Mark of therapy specify, S=Stab, SC=Scar, T=Tattoo

Decedent: Schwartz, Robert

586

This diagram shows the extensive injuries Robert Schwartz received at the hand of Kyle Hulbert. Of the nearly thirty stab wounds, many entered through Schwartz's back and exited through his front, inflicted by Kyle as he heard voices telling him what to do.

(Photo courtesy of Shirlina Mann)

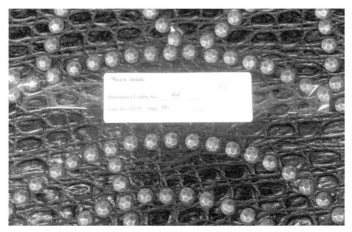

As investigators compiled evidence against Kyle Hulbert, this "shield" was uncovered. Kyle used it to ward off "vampires" and protect himself from evil-doers inside the Underworld.
(Photo courtesy of Shirlina Mann)

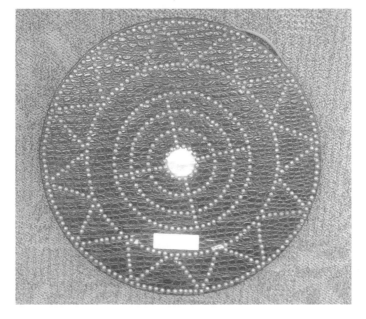

A sampling of the diaries and journals Clara kept,
detailing her hatred for the "O.G." (Old Guy—her father),
Christianity, and her life.
(Photo courtesy of Shirlina Mann)

Police uncovered this photo of Kyle Hulbert, along with Katie Inglis and an unidentified male, at a bank the day before Robert Schwartz's murder. Kyle was depositing a check Clara Schwartz had sent to him that day.
(Photo courtesy of Shirlina Mann)

This surveillance footage clip clearly shows that Clara Schwartz had paid Kyle Hulbert to kill her father.
(Photo courtesy of Shirlina Mann)

Downtown Leesburg, Virginia, where Clara Schwartz
was tried for the murder of her father.
(Photo courtesy of Shirlina Mann)

The Loudon County Courthouse in downtown Leesburg
was the site of Clara's trial.
(Photo courtesy of Shirlina Mann)

Kyle Hulbert in 2014.
(Department of Corrections, Virginia)

What the fuck! Kyle said to himself, with that music banging in his head. Then the conversation Kyle had with his Vietnam buddy came back to him. That advice he had been given: *"Go to the cops."* But also, playing more prominently in Kyle's confused and delusional mind, was the remembrance of his friend explaining because Robert Schwartz was a biochemist, he had access to chemicals that not many people did. Therefore, he could likely kill Clara, and no one would ever know. Thus, it was time, Kyle decided, to confront this clown and explain to him that he would not be hurting his daughter—Clara Schwartz—any longer.

CHAPTER 43

WERE THERE REAL problems between Clara and her father? This was the question many would later ask. Was this all some narrative Clara had constructed to get people to feel sorry for her? Was it your general father-child disagreements taken completely out of context by Clara? Was the OG treating Clara with serious disdain?

Richard Gillespie had been one of Clara's teachers from Loudoun Valley High School. He taught Advanced Placement U.S. history. Gillespie later talked about witnessing firsthand several issues Clara had with her father, although none seemed to be the gloom-and-doom scenario Clara had built them up to be later on.

"The gist of [it] . . . was that there seemed to be significant difficulties between Clara and her father," Gillespie said later (in court). He observed this mostly while being an activity sponsor and working with Clara on certain events and after-school activities. Gillespie "expected," he said, "cooperation from parents" of the children involved in the extracurricular activities he oversaw. He'd seen a commitment from Mr. Schwartz with Clara's siblings, whom he had also taught, but not when it came to Clara. It was mainly transportation problems that spoke of a bigger, more serious gulf between Mr. Schwartz and Clara, Gillespie observed. On a consistent basis, Clara did not have a ride home from her after-school activities. Clara would often cancel plans to go on field trips "at the last moment," Gillespie said. So he'd pull her aside next time he ran into her and ask why.

"I had a run-in with my dad and he won't let me do it," she'd say.

Clara wasn't allowed to drive the family car while in high school because she had crashed it once, so the OG stopped her access to the vehicle. When she did go on field trips, it seemed that she never had anyone waiting there at the school to pick her up when the bus returned. It got so bad that Gillespie asked one of the other teachers what was going on with Clara.

"Well," that teacher told him, "this is the way it's been. We have been taking her home for some time now."

By then, Gillespie had taught for twenty-seven years. One day, shortly after a blizzard in 2000, on his way home from dropping Clara off at the Stone House, Gillespie thought about how it had been only "a handful of times" throughout his entire career "when a parent, even a single parent . . . seemed to abandon a child" in the way he viewed Robert Schwartz had.

One incident with Clara that disturbed Gillespie and made him take notice occurred not long after the Columbine incident. Clara wore a trench coat to school. It was well known then that both of the kids who murdered scores of their peers at Columbine—in one of the most high-profile and horrific school shootings in history—wore black trench coats while roaming the halls in search of victims. It seemed odd to Gillespie that Clara would choose to wear the same type of coat to school, as if either mocking the murders, paying homage to the two murderers, or maybe just looking for attention.

"She . . . also associated with a handful of goths," Gillespie said. They had a lengthy conversation about Clara's choice of

wearing the trench coat and the kids she chose to hang around
with. Gillespie was obviously worried about her.

"If you wonder why kids do this (Columbine)," Clara told
Gillespie, "it's for protection. It's for protection against other
kids who pick on them. You can't get protection against teachers who pick on you. [But] you *can* get protection against
other kids."

Gillespie was concerned. It was a strange and alarming
statement to make. Clara was effectively saying shooting up
a school and killing innocent kids was an okay reaction to
being picked on. He wanted to help. He asked Clara what else
was ailing her.

"Do you know that I am often referred to—and have come
to think of myself, actually!—as 'the troll'? That's why I need
protection."

"She referenced back to the notion of 'needed' protection,"
Gillespie added. "Protection in a sense of, I guess, social
protection. That seemed quite relevant."

From as much as he could observe in talking with her and
witnessing her habits at school, Gillespie's final point about
Clara's life at home was that he believed Clara was "de-
meaned by [Mr. Schwartz]," which "put her in a very difficult
situation . . . that showed in many ways."

As a teacher, it was Gillespie's responsibility to report
child abuse of any kind to the proper authorities, he explained. If he believed Clara was being abused at home, it
would be his duty to report it. He'd seen Clara abuse herself
over the years, such as through cutting, but he had never
witnessed any bruises or any other indicators leading him to
believe she was being beaten.

They talked about the "Clara situation," Gillespie said,
meaning him and other teachers. She had so much potential
as a student. She was wasting it with her behavior and attitude. In the end, he said, "The difficulty with that is . . . we
were all aware of that situation. We are obligated to report
abuse, physical abuse. I saw none they could support. Yet,

there's a reasonably complete record of problems, as the school saw them, with Clara. . . . And yet I think we were more concerned with Clara's emotional well-being and did not have evidence of anything to report. . . ."

Later, when Gillespie went to the police with his concerns about the relationship between Clara and her father, an investigation was launched. One of those investigators looked into it, asking Clara's siblings a series of questions about Clara and Dr. Schwartz. If anyone would have known about the possibility of her father abusing Clara, it would be those closest to both her and Dr. Schwartz. But the investigator found no evidence of any verbal abuse or any other type of abuse against Clara by her father. They had problems, as any family might. But Dr. Schwartz's issues were academic-related concerns. He didn't like the way Clara was valuing her schoolwork. He thought she could do better. And so once again, it was Clara's word—backed up by no evidence whatsoever that Dr. Schwartz was anything other than an overbearing parent who expected big things from his child.

"The only thing I can recall of any note," one of the investigators reported later, "was that the father did not provide transportation after a history club meeting on several occasions." When asked how he would describe the relationship between Clara and her father, as the investigation bore it out, the detective added, "It was pretty typical."

CHAPTER 44

AN ENVELOPE ARRIVED at Mike's house on Friday, December 7, 2001. Katie saw that it was not addressed to Mike, herself, or anyone else in Mike's home, but she knew the name on the overnight package: *Kyle.* Looking at the handwriting—apparently, there was no return address or name—Katie could tell that it was from Clara. So she put the envelope on Mike's dresser and forgot about it. Must be one of Clara and Kyle's little games they're playing with each other. Katie was kind of tired of the Clara/Kyle thing, anyway. She had been ignoring it for the most part over the past few weeks.

"You got a letter here," Mike told Kyle over the phone after calling him at Brandy's later that day.

"Come and get me," Kyle said. It seemed to Mike that Kyle was expecting the letter. Or, rather, he was not at all surprised by it.

Mike and Katie picked Kyle up at Brandy's.

Kyle opened the letter and took out a check for $60.

"Nice!"

There was also a piece of paper inside the envelope. Kyle unfolded it and silently read it: *WHATS NEEDED AND EXPECTED,* Clara had written, misspelling "what's." She signed the note *Lord Chaos.*

"I needed the money to open up a bank account," Kyle said later, hoping to explain what turned out to be a complete inconsistency regarding this letter, why it was sent, and what the money was for. Kyle wanted to clear this up, he told me, adding, "Clara knew I needed some money." Kyle claimed there was no "deal" between them, as in a murder-for-hire plot. The amount alone might back up his statement. Sixty dollars seemed more than ridiculous if you were in the market to hire someone to kill your father. Kyle said Clara was just being Clara and helping him with some cash so he could open up a bank account, buy a phone card, and, most important, show credit card companies that he had a bank account so he could apply for some credit.

"Every time I went over to Mike's, I stayed up all night online," Kyle said. "I didn't have a computer where I lived. I was addicted to porn. I am a sex fiend. All of the porn sites I was surfing required a credit card number, even if you wanted access to the free stuff. So I needed a credit card."

Okay . . .

As for the note, Kyle insisted again, it was Clara's way of reaching out to him and, one more time, letting him know that there was this language developing between them that only they understood. He didn't even recall, years later, what the note said. He believed it was unimportant.

"What's needed and expected" sounds an awful lot like a request.

As for the timing of the money and the note, well, Kyle couldn't explain it.

"I know what it seems like," he said.

And the fact that the letter was sent overnight, express mail.

"Again, I know how it looks . . . but I cannot explain it." Kyle said he and Clara never discussed her sending him money to carry out "a job."

"In the days leading up to December eighth . . . Kyle told Clara he needed money . . . for various things," one law enforcement official later said. "He needed to open a bank account. He needed to charge his phone card. But he also . . . needed money to buy some gloves and something called a 'do-rag,' a head covering."

According to this same law enforcement official, "He told her he needed to make sure he had that do-rag so he didn't leave any hair at the scene when he killed her father."

Kyle doesn't understand where this came from, he said.

"First of all, I do not like wearing stuff on my head—hats and shit on my head. I get terrible cases of hat hair! I don't even like using the term 'do-rag.' It sounds so fucking ghetto—it's not even funny. Gloves? I never wear them."

Kyle disputed it all. He never bought a do-rag or gloves. He believed—and still believes—Clara inserted all of this into the record later on to make it seem as though Kyle took it upon himself to gear up for a fight with the OG.

No receipts were ever recovered proving he bought these items.

"When I read what Clara later told police, I thought I was reading a cheesy script to a B-rated crime movie or something," Kyle said. "Her motives are *so* transparent. It looks that way on paper. She comes across as . . . *'Oh, my God . . . he took what I said as this [and went after] my father. He's crazy. He overreacted to what I had been telling him.'*"

Clara had sent the letter overnight. She needed it to be there before December 8, which was the planned day for Kyle to confront the OG and finally put all of Clara's cards on the table. This, Kyle said, had been an agreement between them—for him to "confront" the OG. Furthermore, it was always believed that the night Kyle had spent on the grounds of the Stone House estate, sleeping in his tent, was for the sole purpose of Kyle getting the lay of the land and scoping out the OG, meeting him and sizing up the man.

"I went to the house to confront him about the allegations Clara had made," Kyle said. "That was it."

CHAPTER 45

KYLE, MIKE, AND Katie were on their way to the bank so Kyle could open that account and deposit the check Clara had sent him. Bank records and video surveillance prove that all three were there on December 7, 2001.

They spent an hour inside the bank. After Kyle opened his account, Mike drove to a friend's house, where they all had pizza and decorated a Christmas tree. It was fun and festive—though Kyle seemed amped more than usual, on edge and wired. He had something on his mind, for sure.

"You guys want to hang out tomorrow?" Katie and Mike's friend asked as the end of the night approached.

"Sure," Katie said.

Mike and Kyle agreed.

Then Mike, Katie, and Kyle went back to Mike's parents' house. Katie and Mike slept, while Kyle spent most of the night online surfing porn sites, before falling asleep at some point just before the sun came up.

The next morning, while they were all still asleep, that same friend called.

"I thought we were going to hook up and go to Springfield Mall?"

"Yeah," Katie said. She sounded groggy and out of it. "What time is it?"

"Noon!" her friend responded.

"We'll meet you there."

Kyle got up. He packed his trusty backpack and flung it over his shoulder. "Come on," he said. "Let's get going." He tucked his sword into its sheath on his side, like a warrior ready for battle. Kyle had another smaller knife with him, which he kept in a holster attached to his hip.

"You bringing *that* thing?" Mike asked, referring to the ninja sword.

"Yeah, I want to get it sharpened at Chesapeake Knife and Tool. It's in the mall."

When they pulled up to the mall, Kyle told Mike he was going to speak with security and ask them if it was okay to bring the sword into the mall to get it sharpened. "I'll meet you guys in the food court after I'm done."

Katie said that was fine. Her friend was supposed to meet them there, anyway.

Kyle found the security guard kiosk and asked about the sword.

The security guard on duty told him no problem. They appreciated the fact that he let them know.

Kyle took the sword to Chesapeake Knife & Tool.

As Katie, Mike, and their friend sat in the food court some time later, Katie explained, "[Kyle] . . . came storming past us . . . looking very angry, and still carrying his sword."

"What's up?" Mike asked.

"They wouldn't sharpen it. Assholes!"

"Why not?"

"They said it was too big."

"Shit, sorry, Kyle." Katie and the others wondered why Kyle was so upset. He could get the sword sharpened some other time. What was the big deal?

They walked around the mall for a while; and by late that afternoon, Saturday, December 8, Kyle said he wanted to leave.

"Where you wanna go?" Mike and Katie wondered.

"Mount Gilead," Kyle said.

This was an area near the Schwartz house positioned on a mountaintop of about six hundred feet above sea level. It's a section of land on the western slope of Catoctin Mountain, between Leesburg and a place that once housed Coes Mill. Kyle liked it up there. It was quiet. He'd camped there a few times since getting to know Clara and felt a kinship with the land. Clara's house was about a five-minute drive from the Mount Gilead area where Kyle had camped. He could walk to the Stone House in about fifteen or twenty minutes.

"Why there?" Mike asked.

"I met someone that night over Thanksgiving, when I camped in the woods."

"You met someone?" Mike asked, confused why Kyle had not mentioned this before.

"Yeah. Let's go. Let's get the fuck out of this mall."

Their friend had left already. Mike, Katie, and Kyle got into Mike's Honda Civic and drove out of the parking lot.

"What are you going to do out there?" Katie asked.

"A job," Kyle said.

As Mike drove, he thought about what Kyle meant by a "job." He knew Clara and Kyle had been heavily into the Underworld game; they had been talking about it daily now for weeks. To Mike, "job" meant assassination. Though he also mentioned that it was part of the Underworld fantasy— a game.

"Who is this person you're going to meet?" Katie asked Kyle.

"Her name's Sara." Kyle didn't share a last name.

CHAPTER 46

THE ENTRY IS undated, but it was recovered from a pile of journals Clara kept during her latter years of high school. It was during Clara's "dark" period, when the Underworld was beginning to consume her thoughts. What's significant about this particular entry is how Clara viewed herself. As she was preparing to leave high school and enter JMU (one might argue: from adolescence to responsibility and the beginning of adulthood), Clara felt "no one" understood her, which was not so much a watershed moment in the life and times of Clara Schwartz. Yet, after making that rather pedestrian entry, Clara mentioned how no one grasped her "mind-set." She saw friends as "black, gray, and white."

Why?

B/C I am a sociopath in mind and nature, she wrote.

"A sociopath"—an interesting explanation of herself.

From there, Clara then talked about how she would not "stop hurting" a person because "they" wanted her to, if it ever came down to it. She gave no context for this comment; it was a simple—however telling—thought, a fleeting glimpse into a feeling she'd had for some time. In contrast, the only way she would stop hurting someone, Clara further clarified, was *[if my] friendship with them has progressed beyond that or I don't give a fuck.*

Clara was firm about her conviction that none of her friends or family could change the way she was. Clara was comfortable in her own skin—though, she would later tell police, her father despised her.

"I was afraid that he would hurt me, kill me, because I'm not . . . I'm not a very liked . . . My dad didn't like me very much," Clara said during one interview with police. "I got the impression that he really hated me, because, you know, he wanted me to be like [my sister], or he wanted me to be popular, be normal, and I just . . . I don't want to be normal. Normal is rather boring." In total contrast with what she wrote in her diary, Clara added: "I . . . liked my friends at school." Then: "I liked dressing in dark colors, listening to dark [music], and he didn't want that."

In Clara's view, people needed to step up and understand that she would never change because someone wanted it—especially the OG. She dissed just about all of her friends, calling each by a name: "bitch," "witch," "slut," "whore," or "asshole." These were all names she used for friends at one point or another. She would hang out with them, she said, but she would never feel any type of intimate connection to them personally. She could not have cared less about their well-being, in other words, beyond what she could use them for.

A true sociopath, indeed.

Clara felt many of her peers believed they were "better than" her and perhaps even smarter. This bothered Clara, no doubt about it. But still, she didn't feel the need to do anything to gain their companionship, get to know them, or even try to get closer. Everything that Clara felt, she kept inside. Betrayal was one thing Clara worried about among her friends. She was concerned that one of her friends would one day betray her trust. She never said how, though.

Ending this entry, Clara made a profound statement. She warned her so-called "friends" that they had better watch out. She was devious and sneaky; and "no matter how strong" they thought they might be, she was stronger. Not physically, of course, but mentally and emotionally.

I am deadly and dangerous . . . , Clara wrote. *I am very capable and know how to murder and get away with it. . . .*

CHAPTER 47

KYLE WAS POSITIONED in between the seats. He was sticking his head up into the front of the car, staring out the front windshield, as Mike drove. Katie was sitting in the passenger seat by Mike's side. It was extremely muddy as they made their way down the dirt road leading toward the Schwartz home and Mount Gilead. It was raining mildly. December 8, 2001, had been a fairly insignificant Saturday by winter's standards. The temp had hovered around forty-six degrees Fahrenheit most of the day, which caused a lot of melting coming down off Mount Gilead, thus saturating the roads. Mike passed the trees on the right and left, the tires of his car splashing through pools of roadside water. It was a bumpy, wet ride.

"Right there," Kyle said, pointing. "Stop the car!"

Why Sara? Why would Kyle lie to Mike and Katie about whom he was going to see and what he was going to do? Why not just tell Mike and Katie that he was going to confront the OG about the allegations Clara had been making?

"I think, looking back, I did that because I didn't want Mike and Katie involved in anything I was going to do in any way," Kyle told me later. "Mike was my friend. He was like a brother to me. I make bonds with people and they mean something. This is why I told Mike to stop the car up the driveway away from the house. I didn't know what was going to happen inside that house. I was going up there to *confront* this guy—and that's all I knew."

It was just after dark now, somewhere between 6:10 and 6:30 P.M., depending on which document and which person you asked.

Mike put on the brakes and slowed down.

"Yeah, this is good," Kyle said. "Right here . . . stop the car. Let me out."

EARLIER THAT AFTERNOON, Kyle's girlfriend, Brandy, and her sister were at home, where Kyle sometimes lived. Brandy's sister was walking by the phone when it rang.

"Is Brandy home?" a voice said.

"Sure, who's calling?" Brandy's sister asked.

A moment of silence. Then: "A friend."

Brandy's sister recognized this voice. It was the same person who had been calling the house all week long and in the weeks prior. In fact, since December 3, Clara had called Brandy's residence looking for Kyle seven times, according to phone records. Brandy and her sister had answered the phone on several of those occasions. She never once said, *"Hello, how are you? I'm Kyle's friend, Clara."* It was always: "Is Kyle home?" No emotion. Nothing personal.

Still, why was Clara Schwartz, Brandy's sister wondered, trying to hide who she was now? And why was she asking for Brandy? Clara knew Kyle wasn't home—he had told her he was out with Mike and Katie.

On the other end of that line, Clara sat in her dingy, messy, unkempt dorm room at JMU. It was 4:49 P.M., about an hour before Kyle and Mike and Katie had made it to the Mount Gilead area. Clara had the phone cradled up to her ear, calling Brandy's house, now demanding to speak to Brandy for what was the first time.

Brandy's sister gave the phone to Brandy and said, "It's . . . Clara Schwartz. She wants to talk to you."

This was strange, Brandy thought. Not only did Clara *never* ask for her, but when Brandy had answered the phone when Clara called for Kyle, Clara never even said "hello." She was always direct. Very terse. Very stoic.

"Hello . . . ," Brandy said reservedly after taking the phone from her sister. The call was so random and unexpected. Kyle wasn't home. What did Clara want?

"Hi," Clara said as if they were old friends.

"Uh, hello . . . what can I do for you?"

Clara started off talking about "college courses, her mother dying, and her father," Brandy later explained. Then, out of the blue, Clara blurted out: "At six-thirty, I have to get off the phone." Brandy looked at the clock. It was just after five. Clara rambled on and on as Brandy listened. Brandy soon realized Clara was purging. She had called to vent all of her secrets. Among them: "I hate my father," Clara said at one point. "He's abused me sexually—and he's trying to kill me."

"That's horrible," Brandy responded. She didn't know what else to say to the girl.

As Clara talked about the OG, she mentioned to Brandy that if he died, she was going to receive a rather large inheritance.

Brandy wondered why she was sharing this. All of it was so random. What was Clara up to?

"Really?" Brandy said.

"Yeah, about four hundred thousand!" Clara explained.

Clara talked and Brandy listened for the next hour and fifteen minutes. When it got to be six-thirty, Clara abruptly said, "I have to go! It's six-thirty. Bye."

Brandy said bye and they hung up.

During the time that Brandy and Clara were on the telephone, Clara talked about things that Brandy had no idea how to respond to. She uncomfortably listened to this girl, whom she did not know, divulge family secrets that were probably better off said inside the confines of a psychiatrist's office or a police station. All the while, during this phone call, Robert Schwartz was about to meet up with a very high-strung, very anxious Kyle Hulbert, who was fighting with the voices inside his head that were trying to dictate his behavior.

CHAPTER 48

KYLE PUSHED HIS way out of Mike's car. He was in a hurry. There was that little thing of the "job" he had to get on with, he told Mike and Katie. Kyle had his twenty-seven-inch sword strapped to his side inside his scarab, and a second weapon, a knife, also in his possession. As he stepped out of Mike's car, his black boots splashed into the mud and rainwater. Kyle wore a black trench coat (which Mike had given him weeks ago as an early Christmas present), jeans, and a blue T-shirt.

"I have a bad feeling about what's going to happen," Kyle heard echo inside his head. It was Nicodemus, Kyle recognized right away, one of his six voices—those so-called "gods" of his. They comforted Kyle at times of absolute duress and stress.

"I remember that Nicodemus, especially, was extremely uncomfortable about everything that was about to go down. I mean, think about it. I am about to go into a guy's house, who, I believe, has been molesting his daughter and is trying to kill her. This is what I believe. And I am about to go in there and tell him that I know what the hell he is up to and what he has been doing."

"Not now," Kyle said to Nicodemus in a near whisper. To himself, Kyle said: *There's a chance I am not walking out of this alive. . . .*

"Don't go up there," Nicodemus urged.

The Schwartz home was about a five-minute walk from where Kyle stood near a fork in the dirt road, one way going to a neighbor's home, the other to the Stone House.

By his recollection, it was unequivocally dark out, so much so that he couldn't really see in front him. "But I have excellent night vision," Kyle said.

"I *have* to do this. I have to protect Clara," Kyle said to the voice. "I have to let him (the OG) know that *I* know what he is up to and what he is planning."

I need to tell him that if anything happens to Clara, I will let people know about what I know, Kyle said to himself as he began to walk.

Mike said, "You saying something, Kyle?"

Kyle stifled Nicodemus. To Mike, he said: "You guys wait here for me. It won't take long." Mike and Katie were sitting inside Mike's car. Kyle was now prepared to walk up the driveway and approach the Stone House door. He could see the faint glimmer of the light on the Schwartz family's front door as he began his trek.

"I'll be back!" Kyle said, looking directly at Mike. "Don't fucking leave. You got it?"

As Kyle walked out of sight, Mike decided to turn the car around. Katie stared out the window at Kyle as he went up the driveway.

"As he was disappearing around the corner," Katie later said in court, "[his sword] was just barely light enough for me to see a glint off of it when he pulled it out."

The way Katie made it sound was as if Kyle brandished his sword as he walked up the driveway, holding it out in front of himself like a *Game of Thrones* character, and made his way toward his enemy.

That statement Katie later gave to police, in which she described Kyle walking away with his sword being pulled from its scabbard, Kyle said, "is totally untrue. That's Katie making things up later on to get herself out of things."

It also, however, says (if true) that Katie realized at that moment what Kyle was going to do. And if this was so, why wouldn't she try to stop him or call someone?

Yet, in reality, it made no sense for Kyle Hulbert to garnish his sword to make a five-minute walk toward the house he was trying to get into in order to confront Clara's father. Would Dr. Schwartz allow a sword-wielding goth friend of his daughter's into his home?

CHAPTER 49

ROBERT SCHWARTZ WAS nationally known in the field of biometrics and DNA. He'd been at the Center for Innovative Technology (CIT) since the company had started, beginning there in 1986. Schwartz was a good-looking man in a Leslie Nielsen sort of way, in somewhat good physical condition, with a bit of middle-aged weight around his belly. He had a Colgate smile and a demeanor that very rarely changed—the guy was serious about life and work.

"We called—our family called Bob Schwartz [by a nickname and he] was my oldest brother," Mary Schwartz said of him. "And he was the oldest of seven of us, in ranges of age from one to twenty—and in that role he was quite a remarkable older brother."

Robert Schwartz had taught his sister Mary how to ride a bicycle and how to punch a bag to protect herself. They played tennis together. What's more, Schwartz was an "involved member" of his family, and was "conscious of our needs . . . and helped my parents," Mary added. He was the type of child who studied especially hard in school so he could get a scholarship in order to relieve some of the financial burden his parents faced with so many children. He was "a kind person." One thing about Robert Schwartz that struck Mary was how he would "bring" her some of the ". . . lab rats and lab bunnies" that were being treated poorly "by their co-bunnies and rats" in the lab. He was concerned about the welfare of the animals. "He always had a gentle touch." Mary could not recall a time that her brother "was ever mean" to her.

This was in total contrast to how Clara had described her father to just about everyone she knew and inside the pages of her diaries and journals. Schwartz had been hard on Clara—there is no denying this—but he had pointed out to his other children that the parental iron fist he made in that regard was for Clara's own damn good. He did not like where her life was headed as he witnessed it from a concerned father's point of view. Those years after her mother died, when the other kids stepped up, Clara bowed down. He did not appreciate that she hadn't yet grown out of her "goth" period to become an adult, like his other two children, who were, by and large, thriving in school and life. On top of that, what perhaps bothered Robert Schwartz more than anything else was that Clara wasn't applying herself. He *knew* she could do better. He *expected* her to do better. Fifty-seven-year-old Robert Schwartz was one of CIT's trusted, highly intellectual, gifted, and motivated employees. The *Washington Post* called Schwartz "one of the leading researchers on DNA sequencing analysis." Beyond his work at CIT, Schwartz was a founding member of the Virginia Biotechnology Association, whose catchy motto of "Discovery is in our DNA" meant something to a guy like Schwartz. He expected his children to follow in his footsteps and learn by the example he set: *Hard work pays off!*

Clara, however, showed her father nothing but hatred and disdain; it seemed to Robert Schwartz that she had given up on life. She had taken the intelligence God had given her and had tossed it all away. This upset the man greatly.

CHAPTER 50

DR. SCHWARTZ WAS in his kitchen on the evening of December 8, 2001, cooking dinner ("I think it might have been fajitas or pork," Kyle said), when he heard a knock at his front door. After drying his hands, Schwartz walked to the front of the house and opened the door to see a kid dressed in a black trench coat, with an angry look on his face. Schwartz had surely recognized Kyle Hulbert as not only one of Clara's friends, but someone he had seen before.

If what Katie later said was true, Kyle had placed his sword back in its proper place on his hip by then and hid it underneath his coat. According to Kyle, he had never taken it out. Regardless, that sword was right on Kyle's hip—there for him to grab anytime he needed it.

"Yes?" Dr. Schwartz asked.

"Is Clara home?"

"No. She's at JMU." Kyle explained that Dr. Schwartz said this in a way that made him feel as if he should have known. ("He had an attitude like, *'What the hell are* you *doing here—again?'*")

Kyle had thought about what to say in order to get inside the Schwartz home. He knew no one else was there at the time.

"Do you have her phone number so I can call her?" Kyle asked.

Dr. Schwartz thought about this comment. "Sure," he said after a pause. "Come in and I'll get it for you."

When you walk into the Schwartz house, there is a bathroom to your right. Walking forward from the doorway, you find the stove, where Schwartz had been standing, cooking his dinner, on the left side; while a "U-shaped counter" began from there and crawled around the backside of the wall. To the left is a rather large open area leading into the living room under an archway.

Kyle followed Dr. Schwartz. As they walked toward a computer area inside the dining area near the kitchen, Kyle noticed as he took a look around that there was a desk attached to the wall.

It felt right—Kyle being in here. This was what Clara wanted—there was never any doubt in Kyle's mind that Clara wanted him to confront the OG about the abuse, about his attitude, about everything he had done to Clara, especially the fact that he was trying to kill her and had plans to take Clara and her siblings to the Virgin Islands and murder Clara while there. Kyle was certain Clara was behind whatever went down inside this house from this point on.

"This is bad," Nicodemus said. *"You should not be here."*

"Can I use your bathroom?" Kyle asked.

Dr. Schwartz, who had sat down at his computer desk with his back to Kyle, turned around and pointed in the direction of the toilet and told Kyle to go ahead.

When Kyle came back from the restroom, Clara's father was writing something on a piece of paper. Kyle guessed the phone number he'd asked for.

Kyle stood in back of Robert Schwartz. Quite casually he said: "So, how have you and Clara been getting along?"

Dr. Schwartz stopped writing, looked up in the air, took a deep breath, and turned his head slightly, not looking Kyle in the eyes. Then his demeanor and tone changed as he stated: "What *business* is that of yours?"

"Because I'm her friend and I care about her!" Kyle said immediately, angrily. His manner had abruptly changed.

Game on.

Robert Schwartz stood. He turned and was now face-to-face with Kyle. According to Kyle's recollection (the only source we have for this entire incident), the older man had a "slight grin" on his face at this point. With that, Dr. Schwartz took a moment and then said, rather sarcastically, *"And?"*

"I know your plans," Kyle snapped back. He was getting antsy. His leg bounced. Kyle could feel a flood of adrenaline flowing throughout his body. He began to sweat. "I know you've been hurting her and you are *not* going to get away with shit like that."

"Leave now . . . ," Nicodemus urged.

Dr. Schwartz didn't acknowledge Kyle's statement with an answer. Instead, he turned his back to him.

"You will *not* get away with it!" Kyle said over the voices in his head.

Robert Schwartz's response angered Kyle even more than Schwartz maybe telling him to piss off. So Kyle took a step closer to Schwartz on Schwartz's left side. He was behind him now. They were standing near the kitchen.

"I won't let you hurt her," Kyle said loudly.

There has never been an indication in all of Robert Schwartz's life that he was ever a violent man. Angry and intense, maybe. Short-tempered, perhaps. But violent? Not by any means. Yet, if we believe the only source available for this moment, Kyle Hulbert said later that it was when he stepped into Schwartz's personal space that Robert Schwartz "backhanded me and made contact just above my left eye." Kyle thought Schwartz must have been wearing "a ring of some sort," because something with a hard steel edge caught Kyle and cut him. "I still have a scar to this day in my eyebrow from where the ring cut me."

Robert Schwartz was now grinning, according to Kyle. Laughing at him.

"He had spun around and backhanded me fast, without me being able to even react. He was a big guy. It rocked me."

Even sent Kyle back a few steps.

When Kyle got his senses back, all he could see was a man laughing in his face, demeaning him, making him feel less than a fool, less than a child. He was made to feel like some *boy* who thought he was going to protect his girlfriend, but he had now realized he had met up with a *man*.

"The level of clarity I have in recollecting the rest of this is frightening," Kyle told me. "I can see every moment of this whole thing . . . I mean *every* movement."

For Kyle, the backhand, the shit-ass grin, the contemptuous attitude—it all amounted to a "confession." He could see guilt in Schwartz's eyes, as in, *"Yeah, I did those things. . . . Maybe I am going to kill her . . . but if so, what the* hell *is some* kid *going to do about it?"* Kyle's mind was fluttering now, shattering into a frenzy of fragmented echoes. Nicodemus (or any of his other voices) was far out of reach. Kyle believed he was staring at the guilt of a man who had been abusing his daughter, all of which was flowing out of him. Kyle couldn't handle it. Those demons he'd always talked about started to stir once again. The vampire in him became electric.

It happened in one fell swoop without Kyle feeling it arise, he claimed. "My mind didn't even think about it." Kyle had his sword in his hand, brandishing it.

Dr. Schwartz went after him.

They struggled, wrestling back and forth. The Schwartz family's dining room/kitchen did not have a lot of room. It was close quarters. On the floor were two of those oval-shaped, braided throw rugs, which made it slippery.

The entire fight, Kyle later surmised, could have been avoided.

"I will say this before I go any further. Had he not struck me, had he not grinned in such a way that haunts me to this day . . . I would have left and let him live," Kyle later said in a statement of this incident he made to law enforcement.

Kyle wielded his sword in front of himself like Conan the Barbarian; then, rather calmly, with determination and confidence, he struck Dr. Schwartz on the back of his neck with a quick slash.

"I remember watching the blade of my sword go up into the air and come down," Kyle explained. The blow Kyle planned on was a carefully focused laceration, meant to "incapacitate Mr. Schwartz." Kyle had studied fighting styles and knew where to inflict a blow on the body without killing someone, but at the same rate would take him down instantly. "There are nerves and such in the back of the neck. You hit someone there with a strike of a blade and it will drop them, maybe even paralyze them."

As the strike went up into the air in motion, Kyle thought: *Damn, this is not going to turn out right. I'm not holding the sword the way I should be.* The handle was loose. Kyle had a bad grip on it.

This particular strike produced no blood. Kyle "believed" he had not "broken the skin" deep enough to inflict the injury he had wanted.

Dr. Schwartz put a hand on the back of his neck, swiped it across, and then looked at it—before shaking his head. He then stared at Kyle. In Kyle's skewed mind-set, he again heard Mr. Schwartz say something to the effect of: *"That did not do anything, kid!"*

They fought—with Schwartz trying to grab hold of Kyle and wrestle him to the ground. But at some point, Schwartz wound up in the back of Kyle, one hand around Kyle's neck; the other, unfortunately, was around the blade of Kyle's dull sword.

Kyle stepped away from Schwartz; and as he did that, he pulled the sword through Schwartz's hand, which made a deep, bloody gash across his palms.

"Somewhere in the back of my mind," Kyle told police, "someone laughed at a fool who would grab an attacker's blade."

It meant a certain disadvantage to Robert Schwartz that he had cut himself badly and was in sharp, penetrating pain now; his palms were undoubtedly throbbing. Schwartz must have known now that this *kid* meant business. He was now in a fight for his life.

Kyle stood a few feet in front of Dr. Schwartz, with his back facing the man. For a moment, Kyle thought to turn around and face him like a warrior, the sword in a position to produce the most violent and deadly injuries imaginable. Instead, Kyle gripped the sword with two hands by its handle, the blade point still facing Schwartz (whose only defense was his hands, both of which were cut and bleeding profusely). Kyle pulled it out, as if preparing to stab himself in the stomach.

It was time, Kyle knew, to deliver a blow that would stop this man.

CHAPTER 51

ROBERT SCHWARTZ WAS standing in back of Kyle, facing Kyle's backside, his hands out in front of himself like a high-school wrestler sizing up an opponent. He was trying to get away from the madman with the sword standing in his kitchen.

With his back to Schwartz, Kyle had the handle of his sword in both hands, the blade "going down the back of my arm." In one motion, Kyle—not thinking about what he was doing more than (he claimed) reacting to the situation— then drove the sword, its point toward himself, backward, just above and to the side of his right hip bone.

The blow struck Schwartz, but Kyle could not tell where.

Kyle turned around and "I then slashed at him" before the two of them "started circling each other."

"I was, at this point even, willing to let him live," Kyle later told police.

To Schwartz, he said, "Back off, motherfucker, let me pass, and I'll be gone!"

Dr. Schwartz did not back away. Or respond.

They continued to circle each other.

Kyle slashed again, this time breezing the back of Schwartz's neck for a second time in the same spot as he had previously, when he tried to place that paralyzing blow but had missed. Unwittingly, without any sort of nefarious plan, Kyle had unknowingly carved an X in the back of Schwartz's neck, which would be the cause of much speculation in the coming days. Many would presume this was some sort of ritualistic wound made by a vampire looking to leave his mark.

"No!" Kyle vehemently denounced that suggestion. "Not at all."

Kyle was more interested in inflicting as much pain as he could. As he began to slash at Clara's father, realizing the older man was not going to back off, he needed to stop him.

"I know anatomy," Kyle said later. "I knew that stabbing him through the abdomen where I did at one point, I would pierce his liver and that would hurt. I'm not trying to kill him—you have to understand. My thought then was *'This guy knows that I know that he is trying to kill Clara and he's going to try and kill me.'* As strange as that sounds, that is the only thought in my head at the time."

According to Kyle, Schwartz laughed at him as they stared each other down and walked in a circle. Kyle was the only one with a weapon, slashing Schwartz when he could. They had broken away from each other after Schwartz gave Kyle a manly shove.

"Step aside. I'm out of here. I don't want to kill you," Kyle told Schwartz. "I will leave."

Kyle said Schwartz smiled at him, but did not say anything. And the fact that Robert Schwartz was so resilient and resolved and not cowering—well, this made Kyle turn even more aggressive.

"I slashed him twice, once in the belly, his hands are bleeding—and the guy smiles at me," Kyle recalled.

Dr. Schwartz "advanced" on Kyle, grabbing him. They wrestled. Kyle lost his sword. So he improvised and drove an elbow into Schwartz's face, causing him to bleed. As they struggled for control, there was a moment when Kyle got some of Schwartz's blood in his mouth.

In the background, whatever Schwartz had been cooking had all but burned up by that point. The stove burner was still on, the pan sizzling.

"And this drove me into a frenzy and I became incoherent," Kyle would later tell police. "I see blood and I go berserk."

Kyle began now to "thrust" and "stab." He recalled, "I am not even caring. . . . I am just stabbing and stabbing and stabbing. . . ."

That metallic taste of blood on his tongue sent a man who was already crazy into an entirely different realm of insanity. Kyle claimed he lost control of his senses—if he, indeed, had any at the time—and blacked out in a violent rage.

When he "came to" several moments later, the first thing Kyle later recalled was "withdrawing my sword from his back."

Robert Schwartz was on the floor, facedown. Kyle had, he told police, "apparently stabbed him several times after [Schwartz fell] facedown on the ground." There was that moment when he came out of his blackout when Kyle said he "could feel the blade tip nick the wooden floor below him—I remember feeling the impact of the blade hitting the floor"—this, mind you, as it pierced through the doctor's body.

Standing over Schwartz, who was now totally incapacitated and not moving, Kyle pulled his sword out of the wooden floor and stood.

He heard something.

Sizzling.

"I can smell blood."

For good reason.

"A droplet had made it to the front burner and it was cooking."

All six of his voices, Kyle later said, were "now yelling at me."

CHAPTER 52

KYLE HULBERT CLAIMING he stabbed Robert Schwartz "several times," as he did in his statement to police, was a gross underestimation. It did not give a complete picture of what happened during that time Kyle said he went somewhere else in his mind and lost memory of those violent, bloodiest moments. In total, the medical examiner reported thirty-one stab wounds inflicted to Schwartz's torso—several of which went entirely through Robert Schwartz's body. Some of these wounds seemed to be meticulous in their delivery—meaning, there was a pattern. A pattern that Kyle later said "was of no conscious design by me." Several wounds were in a sequence of lines, as if Kyle had carefully placed each wound where he believed it belonged. In fact, on the back of Schwartz's neck, clearly visible, there was that large X carved rashly into his skin with the tip of Kyle's sword. But Kyle claimed that this clear X, which marked a spot, was not something he did out of any type of intention to leave his mark.

Quite gruesomely, there were three particular wounds on the front of Schwartz's midsection, all of which made the shape of a triangle: one just below his belly button, one just near his right armpit, and the other near his left armpit. This created a triangular symbol.

"I never intended to do that," Kyle said.

Kyle had passed his sword entirely through Schwartz's body several times. On the front of Schwartz's left hand were several defensive wounds, along with the slice Kyle had said started things off when Schwartz carelessly grabbed hold of the blade.

On Schwartz's right hand was the same: several defense-type wounds.

On Schwartz's face, Kyle left several abrasions and lacerations, including two "superficial incised wounds" on Schwartz's left earlobe.

To consider all of these wounds and study the crime scene photos, there is only one conclusion to make: Kyle Hulbert went mad and repeatedly stabbed this man to death in a frenzy of slashes (much like one of his fantastical delusions or fantasies). But then, strangely enough, he took his time to place several stab wounds in specific places on Schwartz's body, as well as carving an X the size of a cell phone in the back of his neck.

Robert Schwartz was lying on his stomach in the kitchen of his home, pools of blood all over the wooden floor around him. The scientist's clothes were blood-soaked, and sword holes were distinctly visible through his shirt wherever Kyle had stabbed him. The bottom of Robert Schwartz's white sweat socks were entirely saturated with blood, which meant there was a struggle of some sort after copious amounts of blood were present. Schwartz had stepped in his own blood while trying to fight off his killer.

If it was Clara Schwartz's desire—as she had written about, time and again, in her journals and stated to certain friends—for her father to feel excessive amounts of pain, to suffer greatly, then there could be no doubt that her wish had been accomplished. The autopsy report, combined with Kyle's mad tale of a vicious and violent murder, proved that this man had indeed endured suffering for an extended period of time before falling to the ground and breathing his last breath. Robert Schwartz had experienced a lifetime's worth of physical agony in just a few brutal moments.

CHAPTER 53

KYLE HULBERT, AN eighteen-year-old man who claimed to have murdered other men before Robert Schwartz, stood over his victim on the evening of December 8, 2001. The first thing he later recalled was the smell of Schwartz's blood sizzling on the stove.

Kyle took a look at all the blood, the tossed-over furniture, the evil mess he had left behind in the wake of this incredibly ferocious murder. It didn't seem real in that moment. The Stone House was now lonely and vacant, devoid of life, like a beach vacation home during the cold and stormy winter months when everyone is gone. The steely aroma of all the blood, metallic and salty, permeated the stuffy air inside this strange place that had seen so much darkness—even before this terrible moment—throughout its history. But this savage murder of a man who had been trying to make a better life for his youngest daughter by disciplining her and merely wanting what was best—a man who had been on the verge of making groundbreaking discoveries that would have bettered the world (discoveries he'd made already in DNA that would come into play during the investigation of his own murder)—had to be the darkest day the old homestead had ever been through. This murder would define the house from this point on. Kids for generations to come would meander through the forest with their buddies, perhaps playing cops and robbers, and stumble upon this dreary monument, stopping in their tracks. *"That's where that guy was murdered! I hear there are ghosts inside."* Stories would be made up about the place. Tales told. And yet the agonizing truth was that they would all be true: Evil had taken place inside the Schwartz home, and it could never be overshadowed.

Kyle stepped over Schwartz's bloodied corpse and walked up to the sink. He turned the water on and washed the blood off his sword. Like a warrior finished with battle, he could only now think about getting out of the house.

Confident his sword was clean, Kyle shut off all the lights in the house (a detail in his police statement he later said he could not recall), except for those in the living room.

Out of the six voices begging Kyle to run, Nicodemus spoke loudest: *"Make haste! Leave now."*

"I'm going," Kyle whispered.

"The OG's soul has departed," Nicodemus said. *"He's not here anymore—he's gone now."*

Kyle stopped at the door. He took one last look. He sheathed his sword in its scabbard.

Then he left.

CHAPTER 54

KATIE AND MIKE were facing a troublesome predicament—that is, if "haste" was in the cards when Kyle Hulbert returned from murdering Robert Schwartz. Mike had turned the car around while Kyle was gone and had backed into a ditch. Due to the rain and mud, well, Mike's car was stuck like a pair of legs in quicksand. The car was not budging from the suction of the slick and cold mud now encompassing the back portion of the car's wheel wells.

Both Mike and Katie tried "everything possible," Katie later explained to police, but nothing worked. The car would not move. The tires kept spinning and spinning.

The time was between 7:10 and 7:30 P.M. Kyle had been gone a little over an hour.

As Katie and Mike thought about what to do next, Katie heard the subtle sound of footsteps off in the distance: brush crunching, twigs cracking, boots splashing in water.

"All I can remember about going back to the car is branches slapping me in the face," Kyle said. "It was dark. I heard the car as I got closer to it—Mike was accelerating. The engine was really loud. The tires were spinning."

Kyle was back.

Mike got out of the car; Katie followed. Mike sounded panicked and alarmed. "Kyle . . . go back up to Mr. Schwartz's and ask him to come and help us." Mike explained that he and Katie had tried like the dickens to get the car out of the mud, but the tires had submerged themselves deeper and deeper. They were going to need a tow truck or a pickup to pull them out. Maybe Mr. Schwartz could help them.

Are you kidding me? Kyle said to himself. He looked at Katie and Mike with a pompous gaze; both of them waited for a response.

It took some time, but Kyle finally said: "Nobody is home."

"What?" Mike asked.

"Nobody. Is. Home."

"He told us very seriously, twice," Katie said later. "I knew [then] he had done things to Mr. Schwartz."

Kyle tossed his sword into the backseat of Mike's car. He realized if he was going to do what Nicodemus had suggested and get the hell out of there fast, he had better roll up his sleeves and get to work moving the car out of the mud. Thinking the cops were going to be barreling down the driveway any minute was not at all on Kyle's mind. The murder had been rather quiet, as these things go. The closest neighbor would have trouble hearing a gunshot, let alone an argument and a stabbing. Still, Kyle wanted to distance himself from the scene. It was beginning to affect him. He was thinking about what he had done. Not that he was yet remorseful, but he had literally just taken a man's life. A great responsibility came along with having done that, Kyle felt.

"Get in," Kyle told Mike.

Kyle stepped in back of the car and pushed as Mike revved the engine and pressed the gas pedal to the floor.

"He looked like he was shaken up," Katie later explained. She stood nearby, watching. "[It was] like he had just ridden a really scary roller coaster or something, and aggravated at the same time, like something bad had happened."

As Mike hit the gas and Kyle pushed, the car's tires burrowed themselves even deeper into the mud. The mud was now all the way up into the wheel wells.

Kyle then noticed the trench coat he wore kept getting in the way, so he took it off and tossed it on the backseat before resuming pushing.

Katie sat inside the car. She stared at the coat on the seat. She saw a "reddish tint smear" all over the front of it, Katie later explained to police. This "confirmed" for Katie that there had been "blood drawn" back at the house. In her confusing way of explaining her thinking back then, she added how she wasn't "sure Mr. Schwartz was dead. . . . I hoped he wasn't, but in the back of my mind, I knew he was."

Kyle later disputed Katie's recollection. "First of all, I had a black oilcloth [coat] on—a full-length trench coat, the kind you might see in cowboy movies. It was dark out. Rainy. There is no way in *hell* that she saw blood on it."

Mike and Kyle worked at getting the car out of the mud for about ninety minutes. Katie stalled the car several times while Mike and Kyle pushed and the vehicle sank deeper into the mud. There was no use, really, even trying anymore. The car, without some sort of mechanical muscle, was not leaving that ditch.

"Fuck this," Kyle said. He walked up the road in the opposite direction, away from the Schwartz home, toward a neighbor of Mr. Schwartz's.

"Where are you going?" Mike asked.

"I have to call a tow truck or we'll never get this thing out."

By now, Kyle was covered from the waist down in mud. There was dirt and debris all over his face and upper body, too.

When he got to the neighbor's house, he knocked, looking around to see if anyone followed him or there was anyone outside.

The entire incident, Kyle later said, felt as though he was "watching this" and was not part of it. Not necessarily an out-of-body experience, but more like a film. "I could hear myself talking. I could hear myself being very nice and pleasant . . . but I am not feeling it."

"Come in," the neighbor said after Kyle asked to use their phone.

He sat down and explained how they had gotten the car stuck.

"You must be cold," the neighbor's wife said. They were an old couple. Very kind. "Would you like some tea?"

Kyle said he would.

The woman made him sage tea.

"I sat there like nothing had happened. Like nothing at all had happened. I deserved an Oscar, only I wasn't acting. But I really looked like a guy who had just got stuck in the mud."

Not nervous, or wired, or paranoid—like someone who had just butchered another human being. But, rather, cool, calm, and tired.

Kyle said it was not born out of any type of diabolical design or sociopathic behavior. It was, he explained, "me on autopilot. I had just simply detached from the situation. I just did this. The murder. I am now in full-blown psychosis. This is where it goes from me being borderlined to me being royally fucked up. No medication. I've just gone berserk. This is me . . . broken."

CHAPTER 55

KYLE RETURNED ABOUT twenty minutes later.

"A tow truck is on the way. It's going to cost you about one hundred dollars," he told Mike. "But that depends on how long it takes him to get us out." There was now a cockiness to Kyle's walk and talk. He spoke with a different, more confident tone. "That's at least what they told me."

Mike didn't know how to respond.

Sure enough, the tow truck arrived and Kyle jumped out and kept him at bay. Meanwhile, Katie explained, "we put the sword in the trunk." She said they didn't want to "scare" the guy.

Katie waited inside the tow truck as Mike, Kyle, and the tow truck driver worked to get the car out of the ditch.

After the car was pulled from the mud, Kyle and Mike followed the tow truck in Mike's car, while Katie rode along with the tow driver in his truck. They drove to the closest bank so Mike could use the ATM to pay the guy.

"What brings you guys out here tonight?" the driver asked Katie as they bounced along the back roads toward that Leesburg bank.

"Oh, well, um, we were visiting friends. See if one of our friends, Clara, was at home. And we, um, we sent Kyle to the door because we didn't want to upset her dad."

The tow truck driver didn't respond.

"And when Kyle came back and said no one was home, we . . . we turned around and got stuck."

"Oh, come on . . . I know why you went out there," the driver said.

Katie's chest tightened. Her stomach twisted.

"Why?"

"You and Mike wanted to make out!"

Katie laughed.

After they arrived at the bank, Mike went over to the ATM and paid the guy. Katie and Kyle sat in Mike's car and talked.

"He try anything on you?" Kyle asked. He seemed angry, looking for a fight.

"No. No," Katie said.

They were quiet for a time. While Mike stood outside talking to the tow driver, Katie asked: "What happened?"

They both knew what she meant.

Kyle was reserved. After thinking about it, he said, "The OG was down on his knees when he asked me, 'What did I ever do to you?' Then I ran him through!"

"I don't remember him ever asking me anything like that at all," Kyle said, adding that it's quite possible he could have said that to Katie. Some of that night is completely scratched from Kyle's memory. "Personally, with Katie, I think she later said whatever she needed to say to get out of it."

Katie was thinking back on several conversations she'd had with Clara over the past few months, even during a time before Kyle had entered the picture. She remembered how Clara had been banging the same drum, over and over: The OG was the bad guy who was holding her down. When Kyle arrived on the scene, however, the rhetoric changed slightly. Katie recalled one time at JMU that now held some significance in the context of what Kyle had just admitted to her on December 8, 2001. On that day at JMU, Mike was loading the car so they could leave. Katie and Clara had a moment alone together.

"Maybe Kyle can help me with my father," Clara told Katie.

Katie never told police how she responded, or if Clara had elaborated on what she *exactly meant* or what *kind of help* she believed Kyle could offer. But Katie certainly later implied that she believed Clara was talking about Kyle making her problems with the OG disappear for good by doing something to him.

AFTER HE SETTLED up with the tow truck driver, Mike got into the car and drove the three of them back to that same friend's house where he, Kyle, and Katie had gone the previous night to hang Christmas decorations and eat pizza. The friend had been calling, saying she was worried about them because it was so late and they hadn't shown up. Apparently, Katie had said they'd stop by much earlier.

When they returned to Mike's parents' house early the next morning (or the middle of the night), Sunday, December 9, Kyle spent some time on the phone. Clara had been looking for him. She was desperate to get details of what had happened. Kyle knew this, so he called her.

"Your father's dead," Kyle told her. "I'm sorry. I killed him."

"Okay," Clara responded.

Kyle wondered: *Why aren't you crying? Why aren't you saying something? I just told you your father is dead! Why aren't you reacting to this?*

Indeed, according to Kyle, Clara said nothing more than "okay." It was as if her reaction meant: *"Thank you for the information. Now move on to something else."*

Katie said that after Kyle hung up with Clara, they discussed what they were going to tell the police if they came knocking. By this time, about three in the morning, Clara, Mike, Katie, and Kyle knew that Kyle had killed the OG.

Maybe not all the details of the murder, but they all knew the outcome of what had happened inside Clara's house.

"We decided to tell police that we went up to Clara's house to get some notebooks for her and we got stuck in the mud," Katie explained later. She talked about how they'd say they never even made it to the house. They got stuck before they could even go knock on the door. Realizing they were stuck in mud, they'd tell police that they decided Kyle would walk up to the house to ask Schwartz for help, but he knocked and knocked and no one answered.

It was after Kyle had called Clara and told her the news, Katie said, that she and Clara talked about planning a Christmas party and chose a date so the two of them could exchange gifts.

CHAPTER 56

"HI, ROGER, BOB hasn't shown up for work today—and that's very unusual," a coworker of Dr. Schwartz's said after calling one of Schwartz's neighbors, a guy they both knew.

"Huh," the perplexed neighbor said.

"Yeah, and he didn't call in. We had a one o'clock meeting, which was very important, that he didn't make. This is very much out of character for Bob. Can you maybe go over and check in on him to see if he's okay?"

It was about one-fifteen on Monday afternoon, December 10, 2001. As promised, Schwartz's neighbor drove over to the Schwartz house, which was about a mile away from his, to look in on him. What he noticed first was that the Schwartz driveway was "under construction or being bulldozed, or whatever." There were men out there working. The neighbor recognized one of the men as another neighbor.

"Hey, how's it going? . . . Listen, you seen any signs of activity at the Schwartz house today?"

"I've been here since seven-thirty this morning and haven't seen anything," the construction worker neighbor said.

"Would you mind riding up to the house with me—I need to make a welfare check on Bob?"

"Sure," he said, hopping in.

When they arrived, both men got out and the neighbor

walked around to the back of the house to approach the kitchen door; the construction worker went to the front. The neighbor knocked "real hard" on the door.

The door vibrated, which told the neighbor it was not locked.

"I didn't open the door at that point."

He walked around to the front to see if the other guy had gotten any response.

They conferred and decided the best thing to do was to open the back door and go in and check things out.

The neighbor walked in slowly, undoubtedly sensing something was askew. No sooner had he opened the door and taken a few steps, when he found the father of three, a widower, lying in a pool of his own blood. He had been gruesomely butchered to death by what seemed to be a series of stab wounds. What became immediately obvious—even to the neighbor in this frenzied, terrifying moment—was how there had not been any type of forced entry into the Schwartz residence. Whoever had murdered Robert Schwartz, even to the neighbor's eye, had walked into the home without a problem, as if he or she lived there.

He called out to the construction worker, "He's dead!"

They ran back to the car and dialed 911. Turned out, the neighbor knew the dispatcher who answered the phone.

"Did you check for a pulse?" the guy asked.

"No . . . he's dead."

"But you didn't check for a pulse?"

"No. Do you want me to go back and check?"

"Yeah!"

All the neighbor had to do was place his hand on Schwartz's back; there was no need to check for a pulse.

"He was cold and stiff."

A posse of law enforcement soon arrived to begin assessing the situation. Murder like this in these parts of Virginia was about as uncommon as a bear attack.

* * *

CLARA JANE SCHWARTZ had known for no fewer than twenty-four hours that her father was lying dead on the floor in their home, his corpse decomposing in the cold December air. Yet, she did not call anyone or do anything about it—same as when her mother had died.

"We're all stunned," Schwartz's boss, Anne Armstrong, the president of the Center for Innovative Technology, told the Associated Press when the story hit the wires and reporters tracked down where Schwartz had worked. "We don't know anything. What we're assuming is maybe he walked in on something."

It had been Armstrong who sounded the alarm when Schwartz didn't show up that Monday for his usual meeting.

CHAPTER 57

IN HER DIARY, Clara once listed several "carnal sins"—but probably meant "cardinal." In any event, on the top of that list was "witnessing false accusations, either to others or myself." Another was someone "hitting" her on the "right side" of her head. One of the most important, apparently, was someone "trying to assert dominance" over Clara. Yet, the most significant of the bunch was "betrayal of any info," unless you were an "authorized" person within Clara's world.

For her, she surmised that to "experience" death, which Clara claimed she was close to at that time, might be like falling into "ice water."

The first time the bite of it drowns you and bids you under, she wrote.

She said when that occurred (the drowning), you should "just give up."

She wrote this particular undated entry after meeting Kyle, because he was mentioned later on in the same paragraph. Before talking about the regular gang—Patrick, Mike, and Katie—Clara waxed poetic about the ramifications of dying a slow death.

It feels like you're drowning + then you regain control for so long. She claimed to be there now: *Everything is personal. I just want my cat. . . .*

Next, in what seemed to be a portent of things to come, Clara wrote: *Everyone wants me to take a semester off*. . . . However, she saw this type of break from school to be "too much trouble"—interestingly, she had contrarily written before that this was something she desperately needed, but the OG would freak out if she even mentioned it. She wondered whether, after leaving school or taking a sabbatical, she would "move off campus" with Patrick and Mike and Kate.

Many of these entries were written as questions. It was as if Clara was trying to figure out her life and where she wanted to take it next. Decisions about school business and where to live were complex issues, she seemed to suggest in this entry. She didn't want to be a burden on Mike, Katie, or especially Patrick. Yet, the final sentence on the page was where Clara allowed herself some solace in coming up with a solution: *Kyle will spare all.*

What did that mean?

Kyle will spare all.

Sounded like Kyle was the answer to everyone's problems. Kyle would lift the burden because he would be getting rid of the problem.

Kyle later told police with regard to taking Robert Schwartz's life: "I do pity Robert, for he was a living creature. But only so much. He deserved to die. Maybe not in the way I delivered it, but somehow, nonetheless. I still hear his voice and see his smile when I told him that I knew. . . ."

It was that "and?" Schwartz had supposedly muttered to Kyle as they talked about Clara that riled Kyle the most.

"I will never forget that. Clara is now safe. Robert will never harm her again. Whatever happens to us, we will survive."

CHAPTER 58

LOUDOUN COUNTY SHERIFF'S OFFICE investigator Greg Locke had just joined the LCSO in August 2001, after a career that had started out as Locke wanting to dedicate his civil-service life to fighting fires. That career path began back in 1974, when Locke was inspired to join the local Fairfax, Virginia, fire department as a junior member. From there, Locke followed along a path that took him to the police academy so he could qualify as a firefighter. It was a requirement. As many dedicated cops later say, one thing led to another, and Locke found himself chasing felons instead of flames.

Locke was actually in school that day, taking a weeklong class, when he took a call on his pager about the crime scene developing over at the Schwartz residence.

"Look, you guys got that place pretty much secured and under control," Locke told his supervisor, who was at the crime scene. "Why don't I begin by canvassing the neighborhood and talking to neighbors?"

His supervisor told him to go for it.

Since Locke had transferred from the crime lab to the homicide division that August, this was his second homicide case. The first had been the tragic shooting of an elderly woman in Frederick County.

One of Locke's primary concerns with any homicide scene, he explained, "is evidence preservation. Making sure that there haven't been a lot of people tracking through the scene. And yet, right off the bat, the first thing I hope for is a search warrant."

With his supervisor at the Schwartz crime scene, Locke knew it was under complete control. As he drove to the property, he refocused on his current role: talking to people, getting a lay of the land, and seeing if anyone in the Schwartz immediate neighborhood had seen or heard anything.

When Locke arrived, he stopped at a neighbor's house, about a quarter of a mile away from the Schwartz home. There weren't many neighbors nearby.

"It is an area with fourteen-hundred-acre farms spread out all over the place," Locke said.

He parked, got out, and knocked on the door.

Locke didn't say exactly what had happened, but he told the couple who had invited him inside that "there was an incident up the road and I was wondering if you saw or heard anything unusual over the past few days."

Simple question.

The woman and man thought about it.

Locke waited, expecting to ask that same question to scores of neighbors for the remainder of the day.

But sometimes, all it takes is that one crumb.

"You know, last Saturday," the man said, "there was this young person who came to our door and wanted to use our phone to call a tow truck because they had gotten stuck."

This piqued Locke's interest immediately.

We've got our first big break, the investigator thought.

"I drove that road in and where they got stuck, this is a

dead end," Locke explained to me. "Once you go in, you're not coming back out until you leave."

This was significant to him. It meant, in other words, that people didn't pass by. You drove down that road for a reason: to visit someone, to go home, or, in this case, to commit a murder.

"Tell me about that," Locke said.

"Well, they wanted us to call a tow truck for them. We could see other people down at the car. Only one of them came to the door. I offered my phone to him to call a tow truck. He told me, 'I don't really know who to call.' So I said I know of a tow company that I use, do you want me to call them?"

Greg Locke cracked a slight smile.

We've got our second big break!

"Can you give me that tow company name and number and address?"

"Sure."

Locke left, went to the scene, spoke to his supervisor, and explained that he was heading off to the tow company to see if he could get any additional information.

"Okay," the supervisor told him.

When he arrived at the tow company, Locke spoke to the owner.

Hell yeah, he remembered that call, the owner said.

"They stiffed my driver."

Locke spoke to the driver. Within a few moments, Locke was able to get it out of him that the driver had lied to his boss so he could, in turn, pocket the money that Mike had given him that night in the parking lot of the bank.

"You recall the bank and where it was?"

"Yeah," he said. "I have his license plate number, too. His name. Address."

There are two qualities all great detectives share: determination and persistence. They are obsessed over their jobs and do not give up easily when things get difficult. For Locke, at this moment, it appeared he would not have to rely on those characteristics. Things seemed to be taking shape for him without much effort.

This is too easy, Locke thought. *What's the catch?*

Within hours, Locke had Mike on camera at that bank withdrawing money from the ATM on the night of the murder.

"From there," Locke explained, "other detectives went and did surveillance on [Mike's] house."

CHAPTER 59

GREG LOCKE WAS confident that the three young adults who got stuck in the mud in Schwartz's driveway on the night of December 8, 2001, were going to have a lot of explaining to do. Other investigators were working on bringing in Mike, Katie, and that third, unnamed person, whom the LCSO had heard about and had gotten a description of, but did not know how involved he was. As that end of the investigation was rocking and rolling along, Locke took on the grave task of driving to JMU in search of both Clara and her sister to inform them of the terrible news that their father had been murdered. It was early evening, December 10, when Locke pulled up to Rockingham Hall. Obviously, this was not his favorite part of the job.

After knocking on Clara's dorm room, Locke introduced himself. Clara appeared in sweatpants, her eyes red, "as if she had been crying or had some sort of eye irritation," Locke later noted.

"If we might speak with you, Miss Schwartz," Locke said after identifying who they were.

Clara said something, but Locke could not understand her. She then closed the door and disappeared for "one minute," Locke said. When she returned, she handed Locke her driver's license, as though he'd asked for it. He noticed that "her hands were shaking and she held her wallet with both hands."

"We don't need to see your license, ma'am. But we'd like to come in and speak with you, if we could."

Clara opened the door.

Locke was astounded by what he saw. The room "was in disarray, with clothes and food wrappers lying on most all areas of the floor." Clara was a slob. She'd not cleaned up after herself in what seemed like weeks.

"Would you like to sit down, Miss Schwartz?" Locke asked.

Clara sat on the edge of her bed. She never asked why they were there or what the problem was.

"I'm afraid I have some terrible news. I'm sorry to have to tell you, but your father has died."

"How?" Clara asked immediately.

Locke had to be careful. He could not divulge details about the crime scene or how Schwartz had been murdered. He was involved in an investigation. "He was found inside the home earlier today."

Clara did not respond. *[She] did not cry, and seemed to exhibit little or no emotion upon hearing the news . . . ,* Locke wrote.

"Her expressions and body language at that time, when I told her that her father was dead, told me one thing," Locke told me later. "Clara knew about her father's death before we delivered that news to her."

Good detectives develop intuition they use to guide them—that is, until evidence sends them another way. As an investigator, you have to rely on your gut. Sometimes it's the only way to gauge people, work a case, or develop new threads that become actual leads. Clara's lack of emotion and immediate questions told Locke straightaway that someone who was there at the house had told Clara about her father. It was the only way she could have known. The news had not been released. Clara had not spoken to her neighbor, a man she didn't even really know. Nobody else could have given her the news. It was either that, the inquisitive detective determined, or "she was involved in that death somehow."

"Your father's death is under investigation," Locke explained to Clara as she stood emotionless and taciturn in front of him. "Which is the case with any unattended death."

Clara didn't ask any questions or say anything more.

Another red flag.

Locke asked, "Would you know where we might locate your sister?"

Clara got up and went over to her computer to check a message board. After reading it, she turned and said, "[She's] in the library studying for exams."

"Would you mind coming with us to her dorm room?"

"No problem."

Locke had brought a counselor from JMU, a police officer from campus, and a second investigator from the Loudoun County Sheriff's Office.

Clara rode with the counselor and arrived moments before Locke had with the other two cops. As they approached Clara's sister's dorm room, they assumed Clara had broken the news to her sister, because they heard a scream, followed by "No . . . no . . . no!"

Clara's sister was devastated—a normal, common response to such news.

It struck Locke that Clara and her sister had reacted so differently to the same news.

After calming Clara's sister down, Locke pulled Clara aside and asked if he could run a few questions by her. They found a space in the dorm where they could speak alone.

"When did you last speak with your father?" Locke asked.

"Friday night. We talked about me coming home for the holidays. There was discussion and concerns because I didn't have a vehicle at school. We, in fact, argued about me wanting to bring my car to school and he wouldn't let me."

"You haven't spoken to him since?"

"No. He was actually supposed to come here today so we could chat more and have some dinner."

As they talked, Locke paid careful attention to Clara's emotional state. It was flat. She didn't come across one way or the other. She talked about her "boyfriend," as she referred to Patrick, and how he had recently moved to South Carolina. She never asked about her father and how he was killed, or what happened, or if they had any suspects. Nothing. Locke had gotten more emotion (and questions) from a smash-and-grab victim.

"Do you have any other friends you can tell us about?" Locke knew something, for sure. The fact that he was inquiring about Clara's friends told her that.

Clara brought up a boy named Bradley Dander (pseudonym), who lived in Leesburg, she said. "We have a common interest in knives and swords. We share a storage unit together, where I store a sword and utility knife." She gave Locke the town and unit number, where they could find it. She said she'd be happy to allow them to see the weapons.

Locke thought this was odd: Clara having brought up these facts. Offering up weapons. They had not told her that her father had been stabbed to death. What was she implying with this information?

Is she telling us she didn't do it? "Here, check out my weapons."

"Brad works at [a local supermarket], and he was discharged from the army . . . and determined to be 'mentally unstable.' I've known him about three years."

"Can you tell us about anyone else?"

She mentioned Mike, telling them how old he was and where he lived. "His girlfriend, Kate Inglis, also lives there with Mike at his parents' house." Then she lied, for some reason: "I've known Kate about three years." They'd known each other since middle school. "She was also in the navy, but discharged—she's, like, nineteen, I think."

Then she brought up Kyle.

"He lives with his girlfriend in Maryland," Clara offered. She talked about how she had met him at the Renaissance Festival that fall. She said Kyle, Katie, and Mike had come to visit her at JMU recently. "Kyle was at my house during the Thanksgiving weekend. While we were 'sparring' with staffs [once], I fractured my thumb. I was prescribed pain medication after going to the clinic here and it made me fall asleep during class."

"What else can you tell me about"—Locke referred to his notes—"Kyle Hulbert?"

"He was recently arrested at the mall for carrying daggers under his cloak." It was odd language, but Locke was getting used to the way Clara spoke. "He stays with Mike once in a while. Mike had taken Kyle to court for that, because Kyle doesn't have a car."

"How'd that turn out for him in court?"

"I'm not sure. I've heard two different stories. One that he received community service, and another that he was fined. . . ."

"When have you last spoken to him?"

"Earlier today," Clara said. "I called him at his girlfriend's house."

That was enough for now, Locke surmised. He could always call on Clara if he needed to speak with her again. Locke made plans with Clara to meet anyone Clara could get over to the Schwartz Stone House on December 12. Locke said he'd like to interview everyone in the Schwartz family formally, if they did not mind. It would help the investigation immensely.

Clara said no problem.

After saying their good-byes and offering condolences, as they walked out toward their car, Locke turned to the detective with him. "Clara Schwartz knew that her dad was dead before we told her."

"I'm with you on that."

Before getting into the car to head back to the LCSO, Locke took a look at the building where Clara's dorm was located. He shook his head.

She knows a heck of a lot more.

CHAPTER 60

WHILE SCORES OF law enforcement personnel pored through Robert Schwartz's house at the crime scene, Dr. Schwartz lying stiff and bloodied on the floor of his kitchen, Mike, Katie, and Mike's mom were shopping at the mall.

After spending the day eating at the Chinese buffet, going to a computer store, and buying gifts, Katie later explained, she, Mike, and Mike's mom drove to Walmart to buy some Pedialyte. Then they went home. Katie was wrapping presents in Mike's mother's room when the phone rang. Mike's mom, of course, had no idea what was going on. She was, in a way, another innocent victim being dragged into what was careless behavior on Mike and Katie's part.

"It's Clara," someone in the house said.

Katie took the call.

"What's going on? Hey, I got you some Christmas presents today," Katie told Clara, as if it was any other day.

"Be careful," Clara warned. She sounded not so much scared, but in her protect-the-secret mode. "The police have your names. The OG was found this morning. They came here to my dorm room."

Katie listened and it seemed to her that Clara had been crying.

"How are you feeling about this, Clara?" Katie asked.

"I'm sort of sad," Clara told Katie. "Not sure what I am going to do."

"Sort of sad" was her comment.

"Where will you go?"

"I'm gonna stay with my grandparents for a while in Maryland."

Katie asked about the cops having her and Mike's names. What was that supposed to mean?

"They might be contacting you," Clara said.

After they hung up, Katie hopped into bed with Mike downstairs. She could tell Mike was worried.

"What's wrong?" Katie asked.

"We could be charged with accessory to murder for driving Kyle up there," Mike whispered. He had a nervous look to him. He was pale and tense. He knew they were in big trouble—even if they didn't know what Kyle was going up there to do.

"The future isn't set yet, Mike," Katie said as reassuringly as she could. "Who knows what's going to happen?"

"I don't know," Mike responded. "All that abuse she talked about. We don't even know if it's true!"

What a time to pose that question! Such a strange comment, and Katie never elaborated on what was said after it. But what did Mike mean by it? That if Schwartz had abused Clara that Kyle butchering him to death was justified and he deserved it?

Later, Katie recounted what, exactly, Clara had said over the past few weeks regarding the so-called abuse, encapsulating it into a sound bite.

"She had told us that her father had hit her on several occasions and tried to kill her more than once. She told me that he had tried to poison her at least eleven times, not just kill her. [Clara] had been considered to have serious mental illnesses, such as schizophrenia and . . . depression, by more than one psychiatrist."

CHAPTER 61

AS CAPERS GO, this one was not going to require the tenaciousness or acumen of Lieutenant Columbo to solve—at least not in the sense of who murdered Schwartz and who had driven him to the scene. Maybe arresting the mastermind behind it all, if there was one, was going to take some time and effort. However, finding the murderer wasn't that hard for Investigator Greg Locke and the LCSO. The fact that Kyle had gone to the neighboring couple's house and called a tow truck driver, and no sooner had Mike used that ATM and the tow truck driver took down his license plate number, than the LCSO had a bead on Mike and Katie.

Mike was on his way to a local body shop to get an estimate on his car on Tuesday, December 11, late afternoon, when he realized there were many police cruisers following him.

"Shit," he said to Katie, who went along for the ride, "look."

There were several plainclothes officers already in place around the shop. It took only a few moments for police to barge into the reception waiting area of the body shop (according to one report), put Katie and Mike in handcuffs, and read them their rights.

As Katie was brought down to the ground by cops, this

same report of the arrest claimed, she allegedly yelled, *"We didn't do anything. . . . What's going on?"*

A second testimonial had Mike and Katie being pulled over for a routine traffic check near the body shop and taken into custody there.

Mike and Katie were, of course, separated. Eventually the local police department that had arrested them called in Greg Locke and his LCSO boys and girls to question Katie and Mike to find out where this thing stood. For investigators, the murder posed a lot of questions, the first of which was fairly obvious: What was the motive? It certainly wasn't robbery. Nothing had been taken. So, why else would several young people get together and kill the father of a so-called friend—that is, if Katie, Mike, and Kyle actually had done it?

Mike had been with Deputy Michael Eiland, of the LCSO, who booked him into custody, as they waited for Investigator Locke to arrive. Basically, Locke had taken over the lead in the investigation. As they waited, Eiland just sitting, not saying much, Mike said, "It's too quiet in here."

"So talk," Eiland suggested.

Mike mentioned *The Lord of the Rings* and how he liked the movie. Then: "I'm scared what's going to happen to my girlfriend." Katie was being booked somewhere else.

"Why?"

Mike thought about it. "I was there," he stated. "I saw blood."

This piqued Eiland's interest: "Continue. . . ."

"Kyle went up to Schwartz's house. . . . I stayed outside the house and prayed for Mr. Schwartz's soul to go to Heaven."

Interesting comment from someone at the scene. Neither Kyle nor Katie ever claimed that Mike went up to the house with Kyle. But here was Mike, with his own tongue, claiming he waited for Kyle outside the house, which told Eiland that Mike knew about the murder before it had occurred.

Mike was then transferred to another part of the jail as he waited for Locke. He spent some time with a deputy.

"You have anything sharp on you, Mr. Pfohl?" the deputy wanted to know.

"Nope—but I wish I did. I don't like myself very much right now."

Locke arrived and took Mike into a small room to talk. It wasn't an interview suite, but was more modest and comfortable, nonthreatening.

Mike told Locke he would ask for an attorney, but he didn't have any money. He asked the investigator to fire away with questions and he'd answer best he could.

It didn't take much for Mike to spill himself. He talked about Katie, Kyle, and Clara. "I spoke to her on Monday, Clara. She didn't cry. But she didn't talk about his death, either. . . . I drove Katie and Kyle to the Schwartz residence on December eighth to see Clara. I hadn't seen Clara for a long time. None of us realized she might be in school. But as I drove up the dirt road driveway, I thought about that."

"What happened next, Mike?"

"While driving up to the house, I believed we were going the wrong way, so I turned around. Kyle said he needed to do a 'job,' but I knew that meant 'assassination.'" It was implicit in Mike's confession here that he recognized that Kyle was there to kill Robert Schwartz.

"So you stopped. . . . What happened?"

"I got stuck in the mud and did not drive all the way to the house. So Kyle went up to the house to see if Mr. Schwartz could pull us out. He was gone about thirty-five minutes and said the house was locked and no one was home. Kyle came back and looked like he had a bad day, like he saw something up there he didn't want to see." He then explained how Kyle went to a neighbor's house to call a tow truck.

The conversation turned to Clara and her father, their relationship.

"No one who knows Clara," Mike explained, "likes what

she said about her father—the way her father treated her! She was not close to her family and did not get along with her father. He didn't like her friends."

"What about Kyle Hulbert?"

"Kyle always carried a sword," Mike said, adding that Kyle "had one with him on Saturday, December eighth. There was a circle of us friends and Kyle was the protector. Kyle believed it was his responsibility to look after me. And Kyle took everything with Clara and her problems with her father very seriously. He believed he needed to watch over and protect Clara from her father. Clara told us that her father was trying to poison her. Kyle even tasted poison when Clara brought him a pork chop one day. Clara thought the poison was sulfuric acid."

Locke wanted to know why Mike drove Kyle out there. Important question, from a legal perspective.

"Betrayal is the worst possible thing and I did not want to betray my friend Kyle," Mike said. "He is my brother."

Had Mike just set his future in motion? Had he just admitted that he knew his friend was going to commit a murder, but he drove him to the scene, anyway?

Throughout this conversation, Mike clearly admitted that he *and* Katie knew Kyle was going to kill someone that day when Kyle mentioned he had a "job" to do. But he claimed he didn't know the target was Schwartz until they got close to the Schwartz home—and even then, he contradicted himself by stating that he didn't know Kyle had killed Schwartz until Kyle returned to the car after going up to the house. Mike explained to Locke: "Kyle said, 'No. One. Is. Home.' I still didn't understand until Kyle repeated himself." And Kyle said back to Mike: "'I said, nobody is home!'"

Locke wanted to know if Mike knew where the murder weapon was now.

"Wrapped in a towel in a downstairs closet in my bedroom under some other towels. Kyle gave it to me and told me to clean it with alcohol. The blade looked dark and burned. He told us about the incident and said this 'was the first' that really bothered him," implying that Kyle had killed before and it hadn't bothered him.

"Did he talk about the murder?"

"Yeah, he said that Schwartz asked him, 'What did I ever do to you?' Schwartz was on his knees. It was then that Kyle said he drove the sword through his abdomen." Mike said further that Kyle had told him and Katie about the entire thing that night.

Locke asked about getting stuck.

He explained how they decided to call a tow truck. "Kyle said he's done other 'jobs,' which we knew to be homicides. He said he buried one victim behind the victim's house."

"What do you think should happen to Kyle?"

"He should probably go to jail for the rest of his life."

Locke explained to Mike that he was not under arrest, but he wondered if Mike was willing to write out an "apology" for what happened out there at the Schwartz home. If he was truly sorry for what happened, Locke explained, why not write it out on paper? For Locke, it was a way to get Mike to say what he knew about the crime.

"I don't think that [he or Katie] knew the depth of their involvement or the culpability that they were involved in this," Locke later explained. "I believe that they both knew what Kyle planned to do once he got out there. . . ."

"Sure," Mike said. Writing an apology sounded easy enough. It also gave Mike the impression that if he apologized, well, perhaps he was going to be given the option of getting out of this mess. As far as Mike's role in all of this, according to Kyle, Mike did not know anything about what was going to happen inside the Schwartz home until it was over, later on that night. Further, if you asked Kyle, he would tell you that Mike didn't know he was driving Kyle to the house to kill someone.

One of the many off comments Mike made in encapsulating the entire evening of December 8, 2001, and his role in the events: the murder, getting stuck in the mud, keeping the secret about Schwartz's death—all of it. To Mike, when asked, he called it one "big oopsy."

CHAPTER 62

FOR KATIE'S PART, as she began her conversation with Investigator Greg Locke, she started out by telling a series of lies. Katie said how she, Kyle, and Mike got stuck in the mud by her mother's house and needed to be towed.

Her mother's house?

Locke knew this was a total fabrication, but he allowed Katie to continue.

"Kyle went to a neighbor's house of my parents' to call a tow truck," Katie said. "No one was home at my mom's and I didn't have keys to get in."

Locke smiled to himself.

From there, Katie broke into an elaborate explanation, actually rambling, describing the events that night Schwartz was murdered and the following days. Locke and other LCSO investigators could tell she was mixing lies with the truth because of the information they had already gathered. But they listened, anyway, allowing Katie to bury herself deeper and deeper. Each lie, effectively, became more ammo for the LCSO.

"Clara called me near midnight Monday, she was pretty upset . . . and told me her father was dead."

"Look," Locke finally said when Katie seemed to be finished with her little soliloquy. "We know that you did not go to your parents' house, Miss Inglis."

Katie looked at them. She tried to look puzzled. Then, after a long pause, she said: "Okay. We went to the Schwartz residence." Then she told Locke what she knew. Her story was basically the same as Mike's; however, Katie offered more detail and insight into the relationship between Clara and her father. "Her dad was violent . . . ," Katie told Locke.

She next told investigators that Kyle had washed the sword at her mother's house; they could probably find what she believed to be blood in the drain. Yet, Katie played down her knowledge of anything other than knowing about the murder after the fact.

As Katie talked, Locke went back and spoke to Mike, who was in a room not far away. Locke wanted to verify some of the things Katie was saying.

"We know you're speaking in half-truths," Locke told Katie at one point when he returned. "Stop it. It's time to be one hundred percent honest with us."

"I admit," Katie said, "I knew Kyle was doing a 'job,' and that Kyle is an assassin. I knew Kyle was going to kill somebody when we went up there, but didn't know who. Not then. . . . I saw blood on Kyle's coat. I also know that he cut his coat." She repeated what was a familiar story by now: Schwartz on his knees, pleading with Kyle. . . . Kyle stabbing him in the stomach. She said Kyle had told them the same story on the night of the murder. "Kyle has injuries on his hand and scalp. He called Clara on Sunday—and Clara knew her father was dead then, because I remember Kyle telling her, 'I did it.'"

"Katie, would you be willing to write out an apology letter detailing your part in the events on Saturday night?"

"I can do that."

They left Katie alone. When they returned, one investigator asked Katie if she knew where they could find Kyle.

"Yes . . . he stays at his girlfriend's house."

Katie provided the address in Maryland.

CHAPTER 63

PATRICK HOUSE SURFACED after it was reported by the media that Dr. Schwartz had been murdered. He wanted to reach out to Clara and talk to her. After doing some checking, Patrick heard Clara was at her grandparents' house in Maryland. With his parents by his side, he took a ride out to see her. They went to a restaurant to have lunch.

Patrick knew Clara was somehow involved. How could she not be? She had tried to get him to kill her father before she took Kyle under her wing. What Patrick wanted to know was "Why did you involve someone as innocent as Katie?" Patrick was invested in Katie more than any of the others; he had known Katie the longest.

This was not the same Patrick whom Clara had described in her journal during this same time period. The guy she described—you might think by reading her entries—was someone she had never and would never stop seeing. You would assume that they could never sever their ties.

"Why?" Patrick asked again, when Clara didn't respond.

"I didn't mean to" was all Clara said.

For Patrick, this lunch and their relationship had reached the complete end. *Finished.* He did not want to see or hear from Clara ever again.

Patrick's next stop would be the LCSO.

CHAPTER 64

DR. CAROLYN REVERCOMB, with over seven hundred autopsies under her belt, took over the task on December 12, 2001, of taking a look at Robert Schwartz's body to see what she could find out about his murder. Ultimately, every human being dies of the same cause: cardiac arrest. Whether cancer, a blow to the head, liver disease, strangulation, stabbed, or shot, the heart eventually stops and we expire. Revercomb, like everyone else, knew that Schwartz had been stabbed repeatedly and those wounds led to his death; that wasn't a difficult conclusion to deduce. But what could she determine during the autopsy that could help law enforcement further its investigation? Were there clues present to who had murdered Robert Schwartz? Was there evidence left behind?

Revercomb noticed almost immediately after she began with a cursory inspection of Schwartz's body that he had suffered two stab wounds to his neck that went entirely through one side of his body and—quite alarmingly—out the other. She counted twenty-seven stab wounds to his torso, along with several additional stab wounds, some superficial, some penetrating the skin an inch or more, some going all the way through his body.

There was serious rage in this killer's heart. That could never be denied.

What became clear from her postmortem was that there had been numerous stab wounds to Schwartz's back that seemed to be administered after he was dead. How did she draw this conclusion?

"Many of the wounds to the back were associated with defects in his clothing that do not have blood on them."

Effectively, the doctor was saying, many of those back stab wounds going all the way through Robert Schwartz's body "were inflicted when he was not moving and did not have blood pressure."

This was significant. Schwartz's killer repeatedly stabbed him after he had breathed his last. So Schwartz was on the floor, facedown, not moving, and his killer was standing over him, jabbing that sword over and over into his back.

The doctor noticed a pattern to several of the wounds, which she pointed out to investigators. There were three particular wounds in a group on Schwartz's upper left back "very close in space" that appeared to be in the shape of "a three-leaf clover."

The suggestion might be that these three wounds were somehow ritualistic or placed there for a purpose other than to inflict pain and death.

Revercomb finished her autopsy and did not find anything out of the ordinary other than this pattern, along with those stab wounds administered after death. It was clear to this doctor that whoever murdered Robert Schwartz had gone into that house with a plan to kill. This person carried that plan out with emphatic precision—this opinion based solely on the number of wounds the killer had left behind. Moreover, there was good reason to believe Schwartz's killer was male. The strength involved, the fact that Schwartz had defensive wounds, made this clear. Beyond that, there was clear evidence that Schwartz's killer *meant* to kill him. There was no question about that. With the amount of blood and stab wounds present, there was no way, investigators knew, that Schwartz's killer could claim self-defense or some other harebrained reason to get out of what was a ferocious, mutilating, and horribly violent murder. The new task at hand, however, became to find out why. In reviewing the autopsy report, investigators were certain that once they knew the *why,* the *who* would fit into that scenario like a gun slipping back into its holster.

CHAPTER 65

CLARA DID NOT make a habit of dating her journal entries. She had, of course, but not with any repetition or consistency. One date of particular interest that was later found in a journal by the LCSO was *December 12, 2001, C.E.* This was just days after her father had been murdered—and certainly after the LCSO had visited Clara at JMU, delivering that horrible news.

It's a peculiar entry. Clara began by talking about feeling "so isolated" and being "shoved away" by family. She called herself "useless." She focused predominantly on Patrick and "wanting him" near her at this time. She said "everyone" in her life wanted her to "forget" about Patrick and move on. But it was now, at this juncture, that she claimed to need him the most. (Patrick, however, was already finished with Clara—something he made clear to her.)

Clara wrote about being upset that they were not including her in family discussions of what was going on. Then, almost as if planting a thought because she knew it would sooner or later be read by law enforcement, she penned this gem: *I know the sentiment and all. . . . Robbery, but whom. He died violently.* Then the entry seemed to skip ahead, as Clara talked about not wanting to see "their name smeared," although it's hard to tell whom she was referring to. *They aren't evil,* she added. Did she mean Kyle, Katie, and Mike? Or did she mean her family?

As she continued, it seemed that "they," her family, were "lumping" Patrick in with her friends, meaning Kyle, Mike, Katie, and a few others. Clara viewed this as unfair and unwarranted. She then went on to say how she would marry Patrick "in secret" on that night, at that moment, if he wanted her.

On the same day she made this bizarre entry in her journal, Clara accompanied her brother and sister to the LCSO so they could be interviewed more formally. Locke and the LCSO agreed that it would be better for them to be spoken to at the precinct rather than at the Schwartz home. By now, the LCSO had a clear indication that Clara Schwartz was going to have some explaining to do at some point. She knew about the murder days before her father had been found. That alone was enough to cause great concern among investigators.

Clara, Jesse, and Michelle Schwartz arrived at the LCSO near three o'clock in the afternoon. Michelle and Jesse were interviewed first, while Clara waited. Both interviews were rather uneventful: two grieving kids, confused, sad, upset, mad, and not really sure how or why anyone would want to hurt their father. Both were baffled by the murder.

Investigator Rob Spitler, along with Greg Locke, sat Clara down in an empty room inside the LCSO as soon as Jesse and Michelle had finished. They began to talk with Clara on a more candid, official basis.

"You're not under arrest or anything like that, Miss Schwartz, but we do have some questions," Locke began. "You're free to leave at any time."

Clara said she understood the protocol—however arrogant and snooty she came across.

"Okay . . . ," Locke said right before Clara, without warning, launched into a narrative as she "initiated" a conversation almost as quickly as she sat down—Locke later wrote this observation in his report of the interview. This made it clear to Locke that Clara had something to say; she had an agenda and needed to get some things across to them.

At first, it was centered on her "home life" and her relationship with her father. Clara seemed to want to talk about this to get it out in the open, for some reason.

Locke and Spitler were all ears. If Clara wanted to ramble, this was the place to do it—and they had all night long to listen.

"He never approved of my friends and always made me feel like I wasn't good enough," Clara said of her father, right off the top. "He said my friends were 'spooky,' and he never liked the way I dressed. He even tried to throw out my Doc Martens."

These were rather odd details: a daughter apparently dissing a dead man, like Clara was, banging on and on about how her father (who had just been murdered) never liked anything about her. Why would she do such a thing? Especially now, and especially on this particular day?

There was one friend, a girl (not Katie), whom Clara said her father truly and inherently despised. He once told Clara, "I don't *ever* want her here."

"He once threatened me about my grades," Clara explained. "He told me that if I ever got bad grades, he would withdraw my funding for school and take away my stocks."

"How did you get along at home?"

"I stayed in my bedroom, for the most part. He didn't like that. He would make me come downstairs to watch TV. He hated it, though, when I taped shows like *X-Files* and *X-Men*. I once attempted suicide while in high school. It was because of him! I cut myself. I did it to relieve the pain."

They couldn't stop Clara from going on and on, even if they had wanted. Clara was on a roll. She had a narrative she needed to get out—to vomit from her mind. She couldn't contain herself.

She talked about how her father had "verbally abused" her

often, and the abuse occurred "quite frequently," and that he also "taunted" her for her "entire life." She "couldn't stand it!"

Clara revealed that "he even punched me in the arm once and sometimes slapped me."

"When was this?" Locke wondered.

"Right after my mom died."

She mentioned her storage unit she'd rented with a friend, again giving them the address and unit numbers, reiterating how they could find a sword and knife inside. It was almost as if because she knew that the murder weapon was Kyle's sword, she wanted them to find her weapons and test them for blood.

Clara next talked about how she had mainly just hung out with Mike, Katie, and Kyle now, abandoning most of her other friends.

"My father never told me that Kyle was not welcome at the house, although my father didn't want *anyone* around."

They asked about those friends (Mike, Katie, and Kyle), since she'd brought them up.

"I was always lending them money. I'm upper-middle class," Clara added.

"How much money are we talking about?"

"My friends? Oh, in total, they owe me about four hundred to six hundred dollars. I'd also give them gas money when they drove me places."

They wanted to know how she was feeling over the past few months, how her life had gone with her father. It was one thing not to get along with your parents as a college student; some parents and their children fought all the time. Yet, it was quite another thing, however, when you sat and admitted fighting with your father at a time when he was sitting on a slab in the morgue, waiting to be buried after being viciously murdered. It didn't make sense. Most kids, Locke thought, would be kicking themselves and sorry for all the fighting, looking back at the what-ifs and what-could-have-beens.

Instead, Clara was bringing up things she didn't need to mention.

"I would write down my thoughts in journals," Clara offered. Clearly, she wanted this information known. She needed them to have it. "I listed incidents of abuse toward me in my journals. Even those incidents when he tried to poison me! He once told me," Clara added angrily, "that the only way I would ever get any money from his will was if I 'fed him strychnine.'"

"You tell anyone about your father allegedly trying to kill you?"

"I know I told Kyle and [another boy], Kate and [someone else]."

Here came the bus. Clara was preparing to toss one or more of her friends into its path.

As the conversation continued, Clara mentioned how these days she mainly just "kept" to herself. The longer the interview went, the more relaxed, composed, and not at all restless or nervous, she seemed. It was as though she had prepared for this, rehearsed it, and knew that she had a recorded history of what had gone down over the past year, especially the last few months. Out of nowhere, she added how she "doesn't trust people" around her anymore. Her relationship with her father, she then said for no reason, bouncing from topic to topic, deteriorated after her mother passed away. The abuse she suffered from her dad got much worse after her mother was gone. "But I've learned to keep my emotions to myself. I don't cry in front of people."

She had an answer for every question that was never asked.

They were curious about a motive her father might have had to kill her. Indeed! If Dr. Schwartz was planning and scheming to kill his daughter, he had to have a reason.

Clara's answer would become classic: "Well, look, the cost of a funeral is a lot cheaper than forty thousand dollars for college tuition."

"You think it's possible that any of your friends could have hurt your father?" Locke asked casually.

The bus was closer now. This was Clara's chance.

In his report of the interview, Locke wrote that when they asked Clara this question: *She never really answered. . . .*

Instead, Clara spoke of what she knew about "the incident," adding, "I spoke with Kyle after my father's death, by telephone." (The investigators did not ask her how she knew it was *after* Schwartz had been murdered.) "He had mentioned to me about 'going up there,' meaning my house. He said to me, 'I made Mike park somewhere, and Mike and Kate drove me . . . up to the house. . . . He's not going to hurt you anymore.' Patrick and Kyle, I should tell you, were both afraid that my dad might kill me."

Locke asked how close Clara was to Kyle.

"Kyle would do anything for me," Clara said.

That bus had just passed—Kyle, Mike, and Katie being dragged underneath it.

CHAPTER 66

BRANDY AND KYLE were lying on Brandy's bed, cuddling, watching a movie. Kyle later said he'd just taken Brandy out to a barn nearby and had sex with her on a couch inside the creaking, cold wooden structure. He recalled this only because Brandy had asked him why he had been so rough during intercourse. Kyle said he had never been that way with Brandy.

It was December 12. Clara was still at the LCSO in Virginia, where she was answering questions. Kyle and Brandy were in Brandy's room. Kyle had not really heard from anyone since the murder and that following day when he spoke with Clara. He was still, he later claimed, running on autopilot, going through the motions. In the back of his mixed-up mind, he was waiting for the ball to drop and the doors to come crashing in.

"I was just there. My body [was] experiencing what was happening around me. There was no thought to anything I was doing."

This was how Kyle described the days before his arrest. He had been just hanging around, not doing much of anything. He'd had a job. He was paid $50 a week to clean up after some horses and feed and let them out. He did that on

December 12, but he could not recall much of anything else he had done since the murder.

As they watched television, Brandy and Kyle did not hear the commotion going on in another part of the house. At that moment, cops were piling into Brandy's home, in full regalia, weapons drawn, searching for Kyle.

The next thing Kyle knew (or could recall), he was literally staring down the barrel of a rather large gun that was pointed directly at his head, between the eyes.

"Don't fucking move," the cop said.

Brandy froze.

The barrel was so close to Kyle's face that he remembered saying to himself, *Wow, those are some pretty large rounds in the chambers!*

Kyle had a fleeting thought about darting, trying to get out the window in back of where he and Brandy were lying, and then taking off down the street, running as fast as he could.

"Brandy's eyes were as big as saucers," Kyle said. "She . . . was pressing into me."

Kyle was trying not to move, but somehow also shield Brandy by shoving her under and in back of him at the same time. This was not her fight. She and her mother had nothing to do with this. It was a thought that kept Kyle from doing anything stupid.

After this event, the next thing Kyle Hulbert recalled was being in lockup, waiting for the LCSO to come and extradite him to Virginia to face charges for the murder of Robert Schwartz.

"I could only think [how] Robert Schwartz would not be able to hurt his daughter any longer," Kyle later said, analyzing that moment after his arrest. "And that was a good feeling for me then."

CHAPTER 67

INVESTIGATOR GREG LOCKE sat with Clara Schwartz and another investigator and talked. Clara had come into the LCSO for an informal conversation about her life and her father's death. By now, Clara knew that her friends had been arrested—Katie and Mike. She was in no position *not to help* when the LCSO asked her and Jesse and Michelle to come in. Although, the best thing Clara should have done for herself right away was go to a lawyer—whether she was guilty of anything or not—and allow that lawyer to speak on her behalf. Yet, in all of her hubris and narcissism, Clara believed—as she had always believed—she was going to be able to talk her way out of this. She would calculatedly feed the LCSO the information they needed to bust Mike, Katie, and Kyle as she, of course, walked away into the sunset, dusting off her hands.

On the other hand, as Locke thought about Clara over the past few days, he focused on one thing with regard to her: "You always want to leave the door open for a way out. That's what I was doing with Clara. I've found it's much easier to give someone a way out than to push them." Locke was conducting what he called "a soft interview" this first time with Clara. He wanted to get a feel for her personality; he really didn't know her.

Clara talked openly with the LCSO as she dissed her dead father repeatedly. But there came a time during that conversation when Locke asked probably the most important question thus far: How did it make Clara feel when she heard from her friend Kyle that her father was dead? By this point, the LCSO knew that Kyle had told Clara right after he had killed her father.

"I didn't think he would ever do anything," Clara said rather defiantly. In one breath, her argument was revealed: *"I didn't know. I didn't think he'd go through with it. I thought he was just talking."* But in another, she added, "Yet, he did give me the impression that he *might* do something."

Two answers. Could Clara Schwartz have it both ways?

Locke would allow it today. He was still gathering information, getting a sense of who she was.

"How have you been feeling about your father's death?" Locke smartly followed up.

"It didn't really sink in until we were doing the casket stuff. . . . I've lost a lot of friends over the years. It doesn't always sink in. But my mom's death . . . made it a reality for me. . . . Now it takes a while for it to sink in. It may not hit me until the funeral."

"Casket stuff"! What an odd choice of words.

Locke brought up Mike next.

"He had a vision," Clara explained. "He spoke to a dragon. He told me that if I went to the Virgin Islands at Christmas with my father, I wouldn't come back. I was afraid to go at first, but then I thought it would be okay as long as we ate out at restaurants while we were there."

The interview went on and on, for most of the afternoon and into early evening. Clara talked about her life as a pagan. How she considered herself to be the "priestess of high chaos." She talked repeatedly about "discounting" anything

Kyle had said about her father, but she failed to answer a direct question posed by Locke regarding if she had ever heard Kyle say pointedly or to the effect of "I'll take care of this." Instead of answering the detective, Clara stated how she was used to receiving "ten to fifteen death threats" per year, adding, "Kyle told me once that he was thinking about going up to the house to 'have a talk with him,' and then he said, 'Maybe I should make sure he never bothers you again.'"

Locke wondered if Clara had ever given Kyle the impression that she wanted her father dead.

Clara shrugged, shifting a bit in her chair, and looked away. "Um, I might have said some off-side comments like, 'I wonder what it would be like if he was dead. . . . Life would be better without Dad in the picture.'"

"Had you made these comments to Kyle on the same day he talked about your father never bothering you again?"

"I don't think so, but maybe he pieced a bunch of things together."

Locke stared at Clara. *She's trying to convince me that she didn't have anything to do with this.* Here she was offering information he had not asked for; she was trying her best to put out every fire she could before it started.

Clara then told Locke a few familiar stories about her father yelling at her, following that up with the fact that Mike and Katie did not like the way Mr. Schwartz treated Clara and they had made it clear to her that they worried about her.

Backpedaling, Locke thought. He could almost hear Clara thinking: *He knows something—I need to try to find a way out of this.*

"How are you feeling now?" Locke asked.

"I am still confused," she said. Then, as if the detective insulted her: "What the heck!"

"Do you think Kyle would do this?"

"I thought he was just joking. He did tell me once, 'I will

kill your father,' but I thought he was just venting and that I didn't take it at face value."

"So you just blew it off then?"

"Well, yeah, but I probably didn't use those words. I think Kyle, if you want to know, would have worked on his own. Mike told me that he didn't know what Kyle was doing. I definitely think Kyle acted on his own."

Funny, she didn't add: *"If he did this."* Locke found that lack of questioning to be quite revealing. Clara believed Kyle killed her father, Locke knew right then.

"How do you get along with your family?"

Keep her talking. That was the strategy. The more she talked, the deeper Clara Schwartz buried herself. It was clear as glass that she was trying her best to downplay her role in this thing. Otherwise, why divulge so much information without being prompted?

"My sister doesn't like my friends. But she doesn't matter! I sort of dissociate myself from my family. . . ." She stopped and thought for a moment. Then, as if she'd had an epiphany, Clara asked, "Did I do something wrong?"

"Did you?" Locke asked.

"No! Aside from not taking Kyle seriously, I guess. . . . No!"

"Why didn't you tell me about your father's death when I visited you at James Madison just a few days ago to notify you of his death?"

Clara grew quiet. She'd forgotten that one little problem. She thought about what to say. "It all seems like a dream since September eleventh—it all seems like a dream."

Locke came out with it candidly: "Did you *know* what Kyle did?"

"Yeah," she answered immediately, "but I never said he was an assassin."

She never used the word "assassin"? Locke considered. What was *that* about?

Catching herself, Clara followed this by saying, "He didn't use *that* word. . . . He mentioned it other times."

"You mean Kyle used the word 'assassin'?"

"He may have. I might have blocked it out."

"Perhaps Kyle used the word 'assassin,' but you just didn't like it?"

Backpedaling even more, Clara reiterated: "I blocked it out!"

CHAPTER 68

AS CLARA SCHWARTZ tried talking her way out of a terrible jam, Investigator Greg Locke kept up the pressure. This was where his skills as an interrogator—and Locke had the chops, no question about it—came into play.

As an investigator, you have to know what to ask your interviewee, what not to ask, and what to push back on hard. For Locke, all he needed to do at this point—certainly because Clara had been so open about her relationship with her father—was keep the focus on Kyle (whom he now knew to be the murderer) and her father. Just keep Clara talking about both. She'd do the rest.

"I have gaps in my memory," Clara claimed. She was more subdued at this point. She kept hopping all over the place, though sticking to one main narrative: Her daddy was the bad guy. "Like, for instance, my entire eleventh-grade year is missing." By "missing," she meant she could not recall anything about it. Then she became quiet—almost like she was beginning to sink into herself after realizing she'd probably said too much. "There were other things," she added, "beyond the physical and verbal abuse."

Locke wondered what she meant by that.

"When I was in ninth grade . . . a freshman in high school, my father touched my butt. My mom was there. She said,

'Stop molesting her!' This happened while I was walking past my father. He smacked me on the butt."

"Was there any *other* type of sexual abuse?" Locke didn't know how important a question this would become, because Clara had bullhorned this allegation to Kyle over the past several months, taking it far beyond a slap on the butt. Kyle recalled Clara telling him several times that the OG had fingered her. He was certain of this.

"No," she said. "That was it. Just lots of yelling, I remember, and slaps and punches."

"You think you blocked things out?" Locke asked.

"Possibly."

"Is there anything, looking back on all of it, that you would now do differently?"

"Taken Kyle seriously." Then she changed the subject entirely, adding, "You know this will be the sixth funeral I've been to since September. I cannot take more of this. I am the priestess. I *preside* over funerals. I've done two since October. . . ."

"Why would Kyle do something like this—kill your father?"

She shrugged. "Maybe he did it because he figured if he did it, I wouldn't have to worry about my grades. I was really worried about getting bad grades and how Dad would react."

"When was the last time you saw Kyle?"

"Thanksgiving. He has not been back to the house since then."

They discussed how much school Clara had missed recently. She said only a few days. Locke then asked if someone might have brought her up to the house between December 3 and 7.

Clara said no.

"What if someone says you were there in town on December sixth?"

She became riled. "They're lying!"

"Do you know when your father died?"

"No."

"Did Kyle mention it?" Locke was pinning Clara down now to specifics. He was asking for dates and times and what she knew, and when she knew it. This would help later, especially when they interviewed Kyle. "I'm under the impression," Locke continued, "that he might have shared that information with you."

"Maybe," she offered. "I've been out of it, like I said. You know, he didn't give a date—just that, 'I did it.'"

"What do you think should happen to Kyle?"

"He should go to prison."

"For how long?"

"Life, probably."

"You think he'd kill again?"

"He might for a just cause," Clara said.

That was an extremely telling answer for Investigator Locke, who took this as a clear indication that Clara believed there could be "just cause" to murder.

From that point forward, Clara explained one of her theories. She said Kyle might have gone through one of her journals and had taken what was written and had blown it all out of proportion to suit his own twisted needs. She called Kyle the "warrior type." Then she described how she had been in and out of the hospital for terrible migraines recently. She said she wasn't at all angry with Kyle because "I don't get angry anymore." Since her mother passed, Clara said, she'd had a tough time with relationships in general. She would sometimes take friends out to her mother's grave and introduce them to her. She called Kyle a "loner," adding that she could relate to aspects of herself in him. She said Katie was her "twin sister," whom she "truly loved." She then talked about the fact that Mike liked weapons, although he was a nonviolent, "philosophical" person.

"We're social within the antisocial," she said, referring to the four of them.

After being asked, Clara said Mike and Katie should get "suspended" sentences or even "parole" for their roles in her father's murder.

"You know, I thought Kyle could do it, but really didn't think he would."

Typical for Clara, she then changed the subject abruptly, saying, "I carry runes." Runes are stones, letters, or even symbols, generally used in Viking or Nordic and Celtic tradition.

After Clara said this, she reached into her pocket and "rattled" something, Locke heard, but he couldn't see what it was.

"This whole semester," Clara continued, "I felt like something would go wrong. . . . I had an epiphany in early to mid October, near the twenty-third of the month. I also had a vision of my mom dying before she did. I have also been having terrible nightmares."

Locke asked about her supposed visions.

"Well, my vision recently stated, 'Your dad is going to die within two months. . . .'"

Locke stared at Clara. There sat this young woman in her frumpy clothing, rumpled, unkempt hair, no (or very little) makeup, working her smarmy attitude, as if she could somehow sit down and explain everything away and her life was just going to go on as it had. Clara was narcissistic to the core—her hubris so overwhelming that she didn't even notice how stupid her answers sounded coming from her lips. This conversation was all about Clara and what the people in her life had done to her: *Poor Clara Schwartz. No one understood her. No one treated her right. No one understood what she was feeling. No one cared. She lived in darkness.*

Thus far, Clara had never once said she was sad or upset that her father had been brutally stabbed to death, that he was dead, and his life cut short. She never once said she hated her supposed friend Kyle Hulbert for killing her father. She never once stated that she wished it had never happened. Instead,

Clara sat there in front of these cops and believed she was talking circles around them.

"I think Kyle snapped," Clara explained. "He even told me he was a danger to everyone."

"Has Kyle, do you think, ever killed anyone before your father?"

"He said he has. He mentioned it before."

"What did he tell you about your father's death?"

"He said my dad asked, 'Why?' And he told my father, 'Because you hurt my sister.'"

"Your father asked, 'Why?'"

Clara said: "He just smiled at Kyle."

The conversation turned into a rapid-fire back-and-forth exchange. Locke was keeping up the pressure as Clara began to fall on her words and simultaneously added details to the items that Locke found most interesting.

"I wish Kate never met Kyle. . . . All of this could have been avoided. Kate and Mike are good people, but Kyle can be very persuasive. I bet he either persuaded them to drive him to my house or he paid them. I even gave Kyle a check to start a bank account."

"When was that?" Locke wondered. This was significant. Clara had known Kyle for several months. In all of that time, when was it that she "gave" him the money?

"On December sixth," she said. "I sent it next-day delivery so Kyle would have it for that Friday."

"Why?"

"So he could start an account! He said he would pay me back soon."

"Does Mike or Kate owe you any money?"

"Mike owes me, like, fifty-five, and Kate owes me, like, thirty."

Locke took a moment. He thought this thing through a bit. Then he asked, "Now, explain to me why, again, you would overnight a check to Kyle?"

"I don't understand how Western Union works, but I do know how to send a check."

"Why did Kyle want this money again?"

Clara changed her story—again, adding more to it.

"To buy a do-rag and some gloves." She then laughed and said, "I told Kyle, 'I don't know any black people. . . .'" More seriously, she then said, "Maybe Kyle *was* planning something?" She said this as though figuring it out just then as she explained it to Locke. Like the entire scenario Kyle had instigated and it had just now made sense to her. "He said something about getting gloves and something for his head. He told me that he needed something for his head so he wouldn't leave anything at the scene. I blew him off. I was tired. I really wasn't paying much attention. All I remember was that he was going to use the money to charge up his phone card. It sounded like he was rambling."

In his report of this interview, Greg Locke underlined and made bold this entire section where Clara admitted that Kyle Hulbert explained to her that he needed the tools to cover up the murder of her father and that he needed Clara to send him the money to buy those tools. Her explanation for this, as she told Locke and his colleague, was that she didn't quite hear him or take it all in because she was tired.

"What were you doing on December eighth?" Locke asked next.

"I slept from about eleven in the morning to four that afternoon." She claimed to be at JMU.

"Which night was it that you spoke to Kyle about this check and the gloves?"

"Either Tuesday (December 4) or Wednesday. I called him. The reason I recall not paying attention is because I remember the tiredness."

They talked about the check and an e-mail Clara received that same week from one of her professors regarding one of her grades being extremely low and how worried she was to tell the OG about it.

Locke was piecing this thing together. It felt like a conspiracy. It had all the makings of a murder-for-hire plot. There was motive and means and muscle.

It all fit.

"If you didn't think that Kyle was serious about killing your father," Locke asked, "why did you send him a check?"

Clara didn't hesitate to answer: "I zoned in when he started talking about the check. . . ." She then must have realized how rash that sounded as it came out. She added: "I think that you are trying to get information about this while I am tired. . . . Some of that money was for Mike to buy gas to go and pick Kyle up in [Maryland] and bring him back."

Sounded to Locke like Clara Schwartz funded the entire plan.

"You need to take a break?" Locke asked.

"Yes," Clara said.

CHAPTER 69

CLARA TALKED ABOUT feeling "abandoned" in her journal entry dated December 12, 2001. She felt "segregated" and "locked in a cell" with a "sentence" of "solitary confinement." There was that common word she used repeatedly to describe her life: "isolated." The pessimism and sadness she experienced, however, was not because her father was gone and now she was totally parentless. According to Clara's own words, it was because she had "witnessed the demise" of three horses "years ago." Those memories came flooding back, "plaguing" her, Clara explained. She now blamed herself for the death of one horse in particular, Kee, who had been acting strange all that day, especially when Clara went to feed it. But then Clara said she "forgot to check" on the horse on the night it died. She thought she might have been "able to save" the horse, but it died, anyway.

CHAPTER 70

THEY TOOK A ten-minute break, Locke knowing that his time with Clara was now limited. She was fading. He didn't want an abrasive interview to follow. He needed Clara fresh. He had her on the ropes, however, and now was a good time to poke her with serious questions that seemed directed at her potential guilt.

Locke brought up Kyle as soon as they sat back down. He wanted to understand the conversation Clara said she'd had with Kyle about the gloves, the do-rag, and the money.

"He told me," Clara blurted out. "We talked about it. I didn't think that . . . Look, maybe he would just scare him a bit . . . just talk. Kyle said he was going armed. Kyle said he went there armed."

"What was it that you thought your father and Kyle would talk about?"

"The poisoning!"

"Well, did you *think* that Kyle was trying to scare or intimidate your father?"

""Whatever!" Clara snapped angrily.

"Okay, let me get this straight. Why would Kyle need gloves just to, as you said, 'go and talk' to your father?"

Fair question.

"He's weird like that."

"Why do you think Kyle told you to give him money to buy gloves and a head covering and he would get your father out of your life?"

Clara was agitated with this line of questioning. She was shifting in her seat more than ever, feeling the pressure Locke was putting on her. However, she didn't back down.

"I honestly thought he was going to use the money for the bank card." Then, as an afterthought, "He did say something about borrowing gloves. About that check . . . Kyle told me he was leaving [Mike's] on Saturday and I didn't want Mike to get the check."

There was a lull—a moment of quite repose. Clara was thinking . . . deeply. She knew she needed to come up with something that was going to get this cop off her back. Locke was in a perfect position to keep pressuring Clara for answers. She had contradicted herself so many times, he could ratchet up the weight of the circumstances by threatening arrest.

But then Clara spoke again. "I want to go straight," she said. "In my heart of hearts, I *knew* he was going to do that"—*referring to Kyle killing her father,* Locke wrote in his report—"though it would be more like . . ." She stopped. "It wasn't like I was *paying* him to kill him. . . . [He] was using the money to pay back a friend. Kyle was supposed to give some of the money to Mike for gas. . . ."

"So the money wasn't necessarily to kill your dad, but you knew that Kyle was going to?" Locke wanted Clara to be clear on this very important point.

"Yes. But he didn't use the word 'kill.'" She paused. She stared Locke in the eyes. "Does this make me a bad person? Sometimes I thought it would be better if he killed him."

"Did you think it was a matter of time before it was you or him?"

"You are putting words in my mouth. I feel like you are pushing me into a corner. What would you have done if I didn't come down today?"

Locke didn't answer.

"I'm tired," Clara said.

They took another break.

Clara dropped her head onto the table and slept. Fifteen minutes later, she popped back up. Locke noted that she appeared "refreshed" and "alert."

"I'm ready," Clara declared.

Locke looked at Investigator Spitler.

Strange girl . . .

Clara explained that as she took her little catnap, she thought about how she could be of more help to Locke and Spitler. She said she'd gone through a lot of "what-ifs" since her father's death. She again mentioned that vision she'd had, saying how "maybe deep down" she now believed that "maybe" Kyle had "done it. You have to understand Kyle. He's controlling. He insisted that I call him every day."

"Okay, which day did you last speak to Kyle?"

"I think it might have been Tuesday [after the murder]. I questioned everything . . . but thought he was bullshitting me. . . ."

"When do you think Mike knew what Kyle was going to do?"

Clara didn't hesitate once again to offer up her friend Mike: "Maybe when he picked Kyle up on Thursday."

They talked about the prospect of Clara getting some counseling or if she had ever gone to see a therapist. She said she had tried it after her mother's death, but it didn't work.

Locke asked, "Listen, Clara, how did it make you feel, you know, after Kyle told you what he had done to your father?"

"I wasn't listening. It's like a horse I had when I was young. . . . If I had paid more attention to it, she would still be alive today. Same as if I had paid more attention to Kyle, my father would be alive."

Clara seemed to drift off. Locke noted in his report that she stared at him and Spitler oddly, as if looking through them. Then she randomly said, "The road has been fixed? Can I assume the road is better?"

There was a "WTF" moment there as they tried to figure out if she was speaking in metaphor or had really meant what she said. Then it dawned on Locke.

"The road out to your house . . . oh, yeah, it appeared to be better than it was."

"Clara, I have to ask you, are you under the influence of drugs or alcohol right now?"

"No."

She was finished for the day.

Locke escorted Clara into the break room inside the LCSO, where her sister and brother were waiting. As they walked into the room, Clara turned to Locke and said, "I need to ask you a question."

"Go ahead. . . ."

"No, in private." Then to Michelle: "Do you mind if I talk to him alone for one moment?"

"No, go ahead," Michelle said.

Locke took Clara out to the main lobby. Nobody was there.

"Is this okay?" Locke asked.

"Yeah . . . ," Clara said. Then: "Can she cut me out?"

"I'm not really sure what you're referring to?" Locke asked. It was an odd statement.

"If my sister is pissed at me, can she cut me out of the will?"

"Again, Miss Schwartz, I am not really certain what you mean."

"My sister is the executor of the estate, and some of my family is really upset with me. If Michelle is upset with me, too, can she cut me out of the will?"

Before Locke could even respond, Clara broke into a rant about her father's estate and its worth, saying how the house was recently appraised at a "half million and Dad said we could probably sell it for six hundred thousand. His stocks are worth about seven hundred thousand. That's about one-point-two million! That would be almost four hundred thousand each. Could she cut me out of that? I mean, the money would go into a trust until I was twenty-five, but I would probably leave it there longer. I'll probably buy a house or something."

"I'm not familiar with the details of wills and estates—you'd be better off asking an attorney about that."

Clara hugged Locke and then walked back to the break room.

As Clara reunited with her family, Locke could only think that Clara was picking up on doubts that her sister must have had about her potential role in the murder. Locke had a feeling even since first talking to Michelle that she had questions surrounding her sister, Clara.

"Am I going to be able to get any money if my sister thinks that I am involved in this?" Locke believed Clara was asking herself.

"And that told me one thing—she'd had something to do with it."

CHAPTER 71

KYLE HULBERT WAS in custody and talking. On the same night Clara gave him up, Kyle told investigators that on the previous Saturday night, his plan consisted of nothing more than to "go see Mike, Katie, and Clara."

Murder was not on the agenda.

Kyle told them when and where he met Clara. During his "oral statement" to LCSO investigators John W. Russ and Mike Grau, Kyle said all his friend Mike did was drop him off at the fork in the road near the OG's house. Kyle said he went to Mount Gilead that evening to see Clara. He had no idea she wasn't going to be home. He explained how he had knocked on the front door, but there was no answer. So, instead, he went around to the back of the house, where he saw the OG's truck. After knocking on the glass door and getting no answer there, "I walked back to Mike's car and found that they were stuck."

While they were trying to free the car from the mud, a rock flew up and cut his eyebrow, Kyle explained, giving a reason why he had a gash there.

"That's how I got this injury," he added, pointing to it.

Not a bad lie.

Kyle next said he went to the OG's neighbors. Called a tow

truck. They got the car out and hit the ATM. Then he, Mike, and Katie went to Katie's friend's house to hang out. Beyond that, not much else happened.

Kyle talked about being in foster care and how he was protective of people he viewed as "family," meaning Mike and Katie and Clara. He claimed to have been taking his medication regularly. Because he took the drug Neurontin, an anti-hallucinogen, he was in good spirits, generally speaking. If he ever felt as though a violent episode was in his future, Kyle stated, he would simply seclude himself somewhere until it passed. He had control of his emotions, he seemed to say.

Investigators asked about Clara and his relationship with her.

"I spoke to her last Tuesday. . . . She sounded like she had been crying. She said her sister was hysterical because they had just found out that their father was dead. The school was watching Clara, afraid that she would hurt herself because she had done it in the past."

Kyle said he'd do anything for Clara. "She loves her father, but he doesn't love her. He's abused her. He's made death threats against her and given her lemons with sulfuric acid."

Both investigators kind of looked at Kyle as the interview progressed, as if to say, *"Right, kid."* They didn't even need to tell Kyle that Clara had already given him up. After a period of staring and not much being said, Kyle, instead, offered, "Okay, you guys want to know the whole story, right?"

Of course, they did. It would make things much easier.

Kyle took a moment. He was caught.

"I knew that they had me," Kyle said later. "So I told it like it happened."

He focused on the six voices plaguing him, the constant belief that Clara was going to die if she went to the Virgin Islands, and that pork chop story. He said Clara vomited once after eating something her father had prepared. He told the story of how he knocked at the door and how he walked in. He recounted how Schwartz got nasty with him and how

Schwartz smiled at him. He detailed how Schwartz laughed in his face and backhanded him.

The scuffle.

The sword.

The blood.

"I'm a vampire. . . . When I got a taste of his blood in my mouth, I went into a rampage."

Washing his sword.

"Katie knew what was going to happen. With Mike, I told him the less he knew, the better. Katie cleaned [the blood off] my face in the car. . . . It had to be done." He then told them where they could locate the evidence to back up what he was saying.

When he was finished writing out a full confession (in which he signed his name followed by the word "Demon"), Kyle was told he would be indicted on first-degree murder charges—they could sort out the details and decide if he was crazy at a later date.

As Kyle sat in his cell by himself, he thought about the events. Why hadn't Clara come to visit him? Where was she in all of this?

I'll do three years in a mental hospital and be out! Kyle told himself. *I feel deserted.* He'd found out after the murder about the inheritance Clara was set to get. *Clara is going to get that life insurance money and count me out of it.*

That quilt made up of the four of them was already coming apart.

"I never knew about Clara's [so-called] inheritance until *after* I was locked up," Kyle claimed. Although Clara had told Mike and Katie and Patrick that she stood to receive almost a half-million dollars when the OG died, she never once mentioned it to Kyle (according to him). "Then I find out there is, like, millions in liquid assets and all sorts of money and it hits me. I finally knew why I was locked up!"

The sucker.

Clara was very careful whom she told about the inheritance. She revealed it to those people she knew might bite at the chance to get their hands on some of it by participating. But with Kyle, she had to make an emotional plea. She knew that if she ever told him about the inheritance, he might figure out he was being used.

CHAPTER 72

CLARA WAS STEWING. As those days after she was grilled by investigators passed, there was an always-looking-over-her-shoulder feeling surrounding everything she did, everywhere she went. In her journal, dated December 13, Clara wrote about Patrick and his family being her "new family" and "I love him." Strange she wrote this about a guy who—with his parents in tow—told her to her face that he wanted nothing to do with her anymore.

It had been the "first time in days," Clara wrote, that she didn't have to "lock" her door for fear of her own safety. She claimed that her family was treating her like a killer: *I might as well have done it. . . .*

She raged about not ever changing the way she was—for anybody. She would never become somebody else to make another person happy.

On December 14, the *Washington Post* named Clara as being connected to Mike, Kyle, and Katie, just stopping short of calling her a "suspect." *Post* writers Josh White and Maria Glod reported, *Law enforcement sources said detectives are investigating whether [Dr. Schwartz had been murdered because] he would not allow Clara to associate with [Kyle, Mike, and Katie]. Clara Schwartz has not been accused of any wrongdoing.*

What pissed Kyle off when he saw the newspaper was that the *Post* had reported that he "was known to some as 'Demon.'" This was a name that Kyle wanted to keep private at the time. Kyle's biological father was interviewed for the article and told reporters Kyle had "serious, serious mental issues" and had been off his meds for quite some time.

The LCSO was working diligently behind the scenes, subpoenaing phone records, writing warrants, and getting ready to dig deep into Clara's life to see how much she was involved in her father's murder—if at all. Did she sanction the murder? Did she convince Kyle to do it? Was she an unsuspecting victim in it? Did her fantasy world clash with a man who could not interpret reality from fantasy? Had Kyle taken it upon himself to kill Dr. Schwartz without her knowledge? These were all questions the LCSO had to answer before bringing an arrest warrant to prosecutors with Clara's name on it.

Locke and Spitler believed she was as guilty as Kyle. The circumstantial evidence alone was overwhelming. Spitler wrote up one of the warrants to search Clara's dorm room and get that computer of hers into the forensics lab so they could get inside and see what she had been up to online. Everything, whether you delete it or not, can be extracted from a computer's hard drive—the only safe way to destroy data is to drill holes through the drive itself. Save for Clara taking a Black & Decker to hers, they were going to find a cache of evidence.

The main probable cause for the warrant, Spitler pointed out, consisted of the communication between the players: Mike, Katie, Kyle, and Clara, and how Clara hadn't told anyone she knew her father was dead and who might have done it. Clara knew her father had been murdered, the warrant spelled out, as early as December 9. The LCSO believed that the information they could get from Clara's dorm room and her computer would further prove that she was involved.

Kyle had told them that he spoke to Clara about the murder online, in chat rooms and via e-mails.

Meanwhile, Clara detailed in her journal what was going on around her. She claimed they had "raided" her dorm and "stole" her computer.

I will not be so stupid in the future, she wrote.

She went on to note how "they" had "likely raided" her storage unit, too, adding how she was going to "demand" her "religious staff" back. Oddly, she then mentioned: *They have discovered 'the other.' I will die for my religion.* She believed law enforcement was tapping her phone. Yet, beyond this, it was her own family, she complained, that the police would have to protect her from the most: *[Because one of them] threatened to kill me + make my life miserable. He also choked me + placed his finger on my windpipe.* She said because of that and the treatment they had shown her, none of them would ever be "invited to a wedding, if there is one."

CHAPTER 73

HERE'S THE THING about the unexpected, abrupt end of a life: To those who truly loved the person, his bodily presence might be here one day, gone the next. However, in those days right after the death, the unbearable pain of his memory is permanent, raw, and palpable. Robert Schwartz's favorite shirt was still hanging in the mudroom of his home. His shoes, with horse shit and dirt still stuck into the cracks of the soles, his hat, his keys, his closet filled with his personal belongings, and his wallet—all of the things in life that defined him were still there in the Stone House for those loved ones to touch and feel. The kids could smell him and see him as they walked from one room to the next. They could feel his bold personality resonating throughout every room of the house. His things, indeed, were there, but Robert Schwartz himself was still missing.

Patrick, Robert's younger brother, was down at the Stone House during those days right after Robert's savage murder. The place was being cleaned. Pat did some dishes. Then he got on his hands and knees and scrubbed his brother's blood off the wooden floor.

"I threw out the last can of beans that my brother ate," Pat Schwartz recalled later.

Clara came by.

"You want to go for a walk?" he asked. He wanted to be there for his niece and comfort her during such a terrible time.

"Yeah," she said.

As they walked, Clara opened up. "Do you know that he was trying to poison me?" she said. "On several occasions, he tried."

Pat was taken aback by his niece's statement. In truth, he didn't know what to say. "I saw this as she didn't know what reality is," he commented later.

The main problem with Clara's accusation, her uncle Pat surmised, was that Robert Schwartz was a biophysicist. "He's professionally trained. He's a smart guy. If he wanted to poison her, he would have poisoned her."

She'd be dead.

"Look, Clara," Uncle Pat said as they walked. "This doesn't ring true with me."

"But . . . but . . . this is my life. I had to be careful about everything he was doing, because he was trying to kill me."

Paranoid, Pat considered, listening to his niece. *She's paranoid.*

And delusional.

Over the course of the few days that Patrick Schwartz and his wife spent with Clara after Robert's death, he observed how Clara was going in "ten different directions at the same time." She had "confused thinking patterns. . . ."

And this caused great concern for Robert's brother and sister-in-law. They wondered what Clara was going to do, and they worried that she'd harm herself.

CHAPTER 74

AS ROBERT SCHWARTZ was memorialized and laid to rest on one end of town, Kyle Hulbert appeared in front of a magistrate on the other side of town. During that brief December 18 proceeding, Kyle talked about his condition of suffering from hallucinations for as long as he could recall, and spending the last ten years of his life in and out of mental institutions and foster homes. He claimed that Schwartz's murder was "not premeditated." He explained that he should have had "more control" over his emotions, but he had snapped. He said Mike and Katie "did not know" what he was going to do.

Kyle, Katie, and Mike were charged with murder. Mike and Katie had buried themselves by telling law enforcement they had been involved in the planning, getaway, and cover-up. They were all being held in Leesburg Jail without bond.

During that memorial mass held for Robert Schwartz, his son, Jesse, spoke highly of a man "who wouldn't want to be remembered as a murder victim." There were approximately 150 people in attendance, so it was clear to anyone there that Robert, despite what Clara had said about him, had touched the lives of many.

Monsignor Thomas Cassidy put the pain everyone was feeling into context and words by saying how it was the "way in which he was slain [that] leaves everyone bewildered and horrified." The good priest then likened Schwartz's death with the World Trade Center attacks, saying how it "mattered little whether the assault on human dignity occurred" in New York City, at the Pentagon, or "in the bucolic hills of Mount Gilead. Such heinous realities appall our sense of human decency. . . ."

"I remember him not as a man who won awards," Jesse Schwartz said of his father, holding back the tears, standing in front of the large crowd, "but a man who wore an oil-stained shirt with blue jeans."

Michelle Schwartz was a wreck. Her world had crashed and burned with the death of her mother and now her father. She spoke of a man she adored, loved, and honored. She told the crowd that she was her father's daughter, his little princess.

Clara did not speak. Instead, she documented the day in her journal later that night, mentioning how she had observed a "distinction" during the burial that "bothered" her "a lot." She felt that everyone in her family was "accepted," but her. She felt shunned that their "boyfriends" were "welcome," but hers was not. *I am evil and to blame,* she wrote. In conclusion, Clara reckoned, *I am not to trust anyone I did before. . . .*

Clara had taken her father's last moments on earth during his burial and—once again—made it about her.

CHAPTER 75

A COLLECTION OF evidence was uncovered inside Mike's home. Law enforcement seized what seemed to them to be the makings of a group of dark and twisted kids playing around with the occult. Investigators found various knives, documents, and swords, which they claimed had been used in "killing and human sacrifice in a Wiccan fashion." Although quite erroneous and rather over-reported by the media, the case was turned into a "coven" of witches running around the Leesburg region in search of fresh blood and violent confrontations. A story like this, even in its infancy, could send the media into a frenzy of speculation and wonder—and it certainly did.

The X that Kyle had haphazardly carved in the back of Schwartz's neck became the talking point of the murder having "occult overtones," and seen as part of a much broader, more organized satanic religious cult that involved Kyle, with members Katie, Mike, Clara, and several others standing right behind him. This was, of course, all blown way out of proportion. But the fact remained: All eyes were on the Schwartz home and Clara's possible connection. Had Kyle, acting as her assassin within this group of occultist peons, murdered her father under orders from the high priestess? Though the media stopped just short of describing Clara as a suspect, word was that law enforcement had been gathering evidence of a conspiracy to murder Robert Schwartz—his Wiccan witch daughter leading the pack, barking out orders, running the entire operation.

Perhaps sensing this same finger being pointed at her, Clara called the LCSO on December 19. Investigator Greg Locke wasn't around. He returned the call later that same day when he got back to the office.

Locke recorded the call. He and Spitler had a strong suspicion that the more they spoke to Clara, the more they'd uncover her involvement. It was all there; the LCSO just needed to pull it out of her.

"How are you doing?" Locke asked Clara's sister, Michelle, who answered the phone.

"I'm fine."

He asked for Clara.

"I'll get her for you."

Clara said she'd just remembered some information that might be useful and wanted to share it. The feeling was that Clara had been experiencing the pressure of becoming a suspect. She felt it inside her home, in the community, and certainly within herself. So Clara became proactive on her own behalf, hoping to put out fires before they became downright blazing infernos.

She first explained that she had a "thyroid appointment" the following day and could stop by the office if he wanted, or simply over the phone tell him what she remembered.

Locke told her to spit it out now. After all, tomorrow, he knew, she could be lawyered up.

"In talking to Jesse about this event, my memory is not incredibly good anymore," Clara explained. She went on to add that she had been speaking with Jesse that previous weekend and "asked him what would happen if he was to end up in jail, and he said something about since he's a danger . . . he would end up in solitary confinement."

Locke was confused.

She's talking about Jesse?

"I think this happened Sunday or Monday. . . . I think we were talking about the murder weapon, but I thought they were doing more like hypotheticals, because with . . ." She was stumbling over her words, clearly bouncing around, not making much sense. "I remember saying something like, 'If the sword smells bad, then perfume it,' because I think we were doing stuff like, 'What if the sword smells bad?' and 'What if the blade is damaged from heat of something?'"

Locke piped in, "Now, let me back up just a minute. . . . Was this *Kyle* you were talking about?" (Clara had mentioned "Jesse.")

"I think it was Mike," she said. Then she explained that she believed they were talking about the murder weapon—that was the hard point here.

Locke wanted clarification about the timing. Was this before or after the murder?

Before, she said.

Clara continued, saying how she thought Mike, at one point that weekend, said, "'I think your old man is dead.' And I said, 'I don't believe you. I won't believe you until the cops come knocking at my door.'"

This was great. Clara was setting herself up with an alibi. Locke made sure the phone call was indeed being recorded.

It was.

As Locke tried to ask questions, Clara kept interrupting. The argument she was trying to get across was that Mike and Katie and Kyle had told her that her father was dead, but she did not believe them.

So Locke asked if she had called her father that weekend.

"I had no reason to," she answered.

Strange—they're telling her that her father is dead, yet she's now saying she had no reason to phone him?

Locke made a note.

They talked about Clara's schedule that weekend and when she was expected to call home and when she expected the OG to pick her up at school or come and meet her for dinner. She tried to say that calling home cost a lot of money, so she only did it when absolutely necessary. This had been a contentious issue between Clara and her father. There had been a phone bill for $1,000 once and he had gotten really pissed at her.

This led them into a discussion about money and her father providing her with funds to live on. She had a job that summer at Bob Evans, but it didn't amount to much.

Then they talked about who owed Clara money and how much. She said she had never lent Kyle any money, besides that one time she sent him the check for $60.

Locke maintained a calm, peaceful, content-to-listen demeanor that clearly made Clara feel comfortable. She kept talking.

"Do you remember Kyle talking to you about other victims?" Locke asked when he found an opening.

"No," she responded, "I don't think he mentioned anything else."

Clara knew she needed to get it out there that she had talked with Kyle on IM several times. So she explained to Locke that just recently, in fact, she'd spent six hours or so online with Kyle and had invited him during that talk to come stay in the woods near her house.

All of which, of course, Locke and the LCSO would find out from searching her computer.

For a time, they discussed Kyle and the potential of him killing other people and where he might have done it. Clara brought up the fire at the apartment that day they took off to the store—the morning after Kyle had that vampire experience in the woods. He had buried somebody, she thought he had told her, in the woods somewhere near there. She couldn't recall exactly where, however.

As they got deeper into Clara's relationship with Kyle and "the things that he said," Clara made a point to note that she didn't really believe him whenever he told a story: "Because there's so . . . I don't know . . . lies mixed with truth, I guess. . . ."

As they began to speak about Kyle's foster parents, Clara indicated that her sister had to use the telephone and she had to get off.

"Okay," Locke said. "Well, was there anything else that you needed to tell me?"

"Um . . ."

"Is that pretty much all that you remembered?"

"Yeah, I think."

They decided that if Clara recalled anything else, she would call Locke immediately.

After hanging up, Locke sat back in his chair. He considered the call. He now knew that he needed to get Clara back into the LCSO in a more formal interrogative setting. He had to put a little bit of pressure on her, see where it went. She was obviously trying to backpedal and cover her tracks. How deep was she involved? That was the question. Right now, Clara was her own worst enemy—another few hours of interviews and she might crack.

CHAPTER 76

ON DECEMBER 19, not long after Clara and Locke had spoken, Jesse Schwartz called into the LCSO. He wanted to let Locke know that he, Clara, and Michelle were heading back to school on December 21. So, if the LCSO needed to speak with them again, their best bet would be on December 20.

"Could we set something up for tomorrow?" Locke suggested.

They did.

Michelle got ahold of Locke after hearing about the scheduled interview. She wanted to drop off some paperwork that the LCSO needed, anyway, and wondered if he'd be there to have a chat. So she made plans to go down on the twentieth with her grandfather, Robert's dad. When they arrived, Michelle's paternal grandfather, who seemed to be a bit perturbed, said he wanted Locke to understand something up front.

"I have some concerns about you questioning Clara," he explained, sounding like any concerned grandfather whose grandchildren now had no mother and no father.

"Okay. Tell me."

"I think I want to have an attorney present if she is going to be reinterviewed."

Damn . . .

Locke had been afraid of this. So he thought fast on his feet. "Look, would it be okay with you if Michelle sat in on the interview? Would that be acceptable?"

"If it's okay with her, I feel like that would be fine."

"Michelle, would that work for you?" Locke asked. She was standing nearby, listening to the conversation.

Fingers crossed.

"Sure, that's fine with me," Michelle said.

"At that point, Clara had not requested an attorney," Locke said later. "Once she did, I knew that if an attorney came in, that attorney was going to tell her to shut up, and shut us down completely."

The next day, Locke made sure the administrative office was vacant for the interview. He didn't want to come across as intimidating in any way. The goal here was to keep Clara talking. Make her feel safe. Comfortable. This was not an interrogation.

They arrived near noon on December 20, according to a transcript of the interview. Locke didn't make them aware that the entire interview was being recorded on videotape. He wasn't bound by any law to do so. Locke and Spitler had talked beforehand, and they wanted a record; so, if nothing else, they could go over it afterward and gauge Clara's reactions and explanations. "Body language is everything to me in the beginning," Locke explained.

Indeed, one can tell a lot by the body movements and speech patterns of a subject such as Clara Schwartz.

They all sat down. Locke began by asking Clara to clarify everything she had heard from Kyle—especially what Kyle had told her about the murder itself and how it had transpired. He wanted details, as many as Clara could recall from her conversations with Kyle.

Clara, in turn, stuck to the same script that Kyle had been reading from: the knock on the door, Kyle asking the OG for Clara's phone number, the backhand, the argument, the scuffle, the OG "grab[bing] the sword" and Kyle drawing it "out of his hand," and then, of course, the gruesome murder.

Locke asked where, what time, and what was said.

Clara explained that Kyle had told her it all started "somewhere near the bay window."

They discussed the "smell" of the sword and what Kyle had done with it. Locke knew Kyle had hid it at Mike's because the LCSO had the bloodied weapon bagged and tagged and sitting in the evidence room.

Habitually, when Clara didn't want to answer a specific question, she simply ignored it and moved on to something else.

Then they arrived at a point where Clara said Kyle had called and asked her about the sword and how to clean it. This was significant to Locke, so he wondered if that question by Kyle had "raised" Clara's suspicion at all that something had happened to her father. It seemed almost impossible for her now to deny knowing anything before the fact.

"I wasn't really sure. I mean, well, maybe in some part of my mind, I did, but I was just like, you know, just really confused by that kind of stuff."

The guy had asked her about cleaning DNA from a sword, and the best she could manage was: *"I was . . . confused by that kind of stuff."*

As Clara said it, Michelle looked at her quizzically.

Clara claimed to have "tuned" Kyle out for the most part whenever he discussed those types of dark, evil things. Yet, Locke knew that they had, in fact, talked about the OG's murder online, because Kyle had told the LCSO this fact during his interview.

Locke moved on to Kyle supposedly telling Clara he had killed someone before. Locke was interested in this. He wanted to know more about it.

Clara described that walk she took with Kyle that morning to go get coffee. She mentioned the apartment fire and the body that he said he left in the woods.

They discussed Kyle telling his stories of battling bad guys, the weapons he owned, how Kyle liked to talk a big game that was likely all BS, which led Clara into saying how she never knew what to believe.

Sitting and listening intently now, Michelle piped in a few times to clarify certain basic things—times, days—for Clara as Clara stumbled her way through the interview.

That weekend that Patrick blew Clara off and Kyle replaced him came up next. Locke wanted to know everything about Patrick and his potential role in this crime. He asked Clara when the last time she had spoken to him "before your dad's death" had been.

Clara said they had chatted on that Saturday, near 4:00 P.M., just hours before Kyle knocked on the OG's door.

"Did you call him or he call you?"

These were easy, important questions. The LCSO could later determine if Clara was truthful by checking phone records.

"He called *me.* . . ."

They talked about where Patrick was calling from.

Clara said South Carolina, where he had gone to see a family friend.

Locke asked if Clara had called Patrick after she found out about her father.

She said, "Yeah. I called him, and he was like, 'Oh, my god. You know, I'm so sorry.'"

"He seemed surprised?"

"Yeah. . . ."

Locke wanted to know if Clara called anyone else with the news of her father's death.

She said, "Mike and Katie."

"Why would you call *them*?"

She stammered and stumbled again: "To tell them that, you know, the police told me and, you know—"

"But, I mean," Locke said, "you *knew* they were the ones that did it!"

"But that was—when you showed up at my door, I was like, 'Oh, man . . . Okay . . . so now it's real.'"

"But—" Locke tried to say as Clara interrupted.

"I told you that that was just to call them and tell them—"

"But they already *knew*!" Locke said again.

"Yeah. I just—I don't know."

Clara was backtracking. She was trying her best to answer each question the way in which she believed the LCSO needed to hear it. Although she never said it, Michelle had to be questioning her own sister at this point, simply because Clara came across so guarded and obviously watching her words so closely.

"Michelle had questions about her sister's involvement as that interview proceeded," Locke explained. "I think she began to see that there was a possibility that Clara might have been involved."

As Clara tried to explain how she just wanted to "let them know," Locke asked a smart question: "But wouldn't you be mad at them? I mean, they just—"

"I don't . . . ," she tried to interrupt.

"They just *killed* your dad?"

CHAPTER 77

LIARS ARE OFTEN caught when they forget the smallest details: what you claimed to have eaten one night, the color of a car or house, a phone call you forgot you made. You have to worry and ask yourself: *Did I say I was sleeping, or did I say I was out?* As the old saying goes, you don't have to remember the truth.

"This was someone," Locke said of Clara Schwartz during that December 20, 2001, interview, "that still doesn't get what has transpired. Her dad was murdered! And there she is, thinking about herself—it's *all* about her."

Clara claimed she didn't get mad at people the way she used to, which was why she wasn't angry with Mike, Katie, and Kyle for their roles in killing her father. She compared it to her mother's death and the same reason why she never got mad at her mother for smoking.

Locke couldn't believe what he was hearing. It didn't make sense—that is, if Clara had had nothing to do with her father's murder. If she did, well, then, it made perfect sense. She was trying to crawl out of a corner she had been backed into.

Even Michelle couldn't believe what her sister had said, comparing the two. "Well," Michelle broke in, speaking harshly, "that was a *little* different situation." She looked skeptically at Clara, who had been referring to the cancer killing their mother.

"Yeah," Clara finally agreed.

"I mean, someone came and took your dad's life away from him," Locke reiterated. It wasn't a slow and agonizing death brought on by cancer, which had been brought on by smoking. What the hell was Clara trying to say?

"Well, now I'm really angry at them," Clara said. "Like— but I was just—I think I was in shock. . . ."

Clara finally said her reason for reacting the way she had was that she didn't believe them. The bottom line? She thought they were lying.

Again, for Locke, if Clara truly believed they were lying, why did she react the way she had? Locke wanted to know why Clara hadn't shared any of this with Michelle, who was probably sitting there asking herself the same question.

"Because I thought they were lying. I didn't believe them. . . ."

(So the cops tell you your dad is dead, your friends tell you they know this, and that one of them did it, but you *still* don't believe any of it?)

Locke restated and asked Clara once again, why hadn't she told Michelle about Mike and Katie and Kyle *after* they had chatted and then police came and made the death notification? That had made it all real enough, didn't it?

Clara said she had "blocked" out that part of it, meaning Mike and Katie and Kyle. She explained how she had lain on her bed for thirty minutes after she spoke to them, before telling herself, *I need to take a shower. . . . I need to take a shower.*

"When Kyle told you that he killed your dad, why didn't you try to call your dad to find out if he was okay?"

Fair question.

Michelle looked at her sister, waiting for an answer.

"I guess I just . . . If I don't . . . I didn't want to sort of bother my dad. I didn't want to wake him up or bother him, have him, you know . . ." Her voice trailed off.

Locke asked if she ever wondered whether Kyle was telling the truth at *that* time.

Clara's response: "Sort of. . . ."

They then got into the technicalities of that $60 check Clara had overnighted Kyle the day before the murder. They also discussed how Clara called Mike and Katie and asked them to have Kyle dropped off, and how she had supposedly heard from Kyle that he wanted gloves and a do-rag to make sure he didn't leave any forensic-type evidence behind. They discussed the sword and all the prior knowledge she had of this murder, and the fact that she now said she didn't believe any of it when Kyle talked about it. There was nothing in what Clara said that made this experienced detective stop and ponder. He never once thought, *Well, maybe she's* not *involved?* Everything Clara said, to the contrary, all of her body movements and speech patterns, made the investigator question her involvement even more. As he sat listening, it seemed Locke was speaking to the mastermind behind her father's murder—the person who had put it all together and planned it long before she had even met the man who carried it out.

"There was little doubt in my mind at that point that she had been actively involved," Locke said later, "even if she wasn't there present at the scene of the murder. When she told us that she had sent Kyle money and he was going to buy a do-rag and gloves . . . she was admitting as much as she was going to admit."

Still, Locke knew time was not on his side. This was going to be the last opportunity he had to crack Clara, so maybe he needed to push her just a little bit more.

Locke wanted to know everything Clara could tell him about Kyle. If he was such a pathological liar, as she had suggested more than once, what else could she share about his background, about the "lies" he had told her?

After Clara talked about the foster families Kyle had mentioned to her, his childhood, his tenure inside dozens of mental hospitals and institutions, but not much else, Locke asked Clara what she had told him about her father.

"I had said that he was abusive, that he—"

"How?"

Clara took a moment. She stared at her sister. "I'm not sure Michelle wants to really hear this, but there were times that he had pushed—pushed me to take a certain steak. I remember this one time he had pushed me to take a certain steak, and I was . . . and I didn't want to take it, so I took the other one, and he got sick."

"What?" Michelle said, clearly shocked by the allegation. It sounded absurd, even if true, the way Clara had explained it.

Clara started to say, "There was—"

Michelle interrupted, "What do you mean—a *steak*?"

In other words, WTF! What in God's name was Clara talking about?

"Like dinner. And stuff like that. Like, I remember one night I got . . . I took a steak. He had fixed up like this huge . . . steak . . . big enough for two people." Her dad had had a TV dinner, instead, Clara explained. "I ate half of that and was sick for a week. I gave the rest to the dog over two nights and the dog was sick."

Locke asked about the pork chop.

Clara recalled the date. The twenty-fourth, she said without hesitating. "They were stuffed pork chops." She said after she ate half of one, she had to go to the toilet and "puke."

Locke asked what happened later on, when she saw Kyle that night.

Clara said she gave Kyle a piece of the chop and he said it tasted like ammonia.

Michelle, Locke noticed, began almost to back away from her sister at that point. Locke could tell, simply by watching

Michelle, that she was now beyond the doubt ceiling of suspecting her sister was somehow involved. Michelle was now questioning everything.

Locke had Clara talk about her steadfast belief that the OG was trying to poison her. She was sure of it. She was also certain it started on "February 13, 2001." But then Clara changed her mind and said, "No, 2000." She said there had been eleven separate incidents she had documented. All involved meat. It was the sole reason why she had stopped eating meat altogether.

Michelle interrupted and talked about how Clara would "go into the fridge and eat all the food" at times. It seemed as though she'd binge—one explanation for why she had often gotten sick. Did Clara have an eating disorder that she tried hiding by claiming her father was poisoning her?

Clara explained how she'd fast as part of her core spiritual belief system (although she never made clear what that actually was) and then go on an eating binge to break the fast.

They moved on to Kyle again. Locke wanted to know anything Clara could recall about what Kyle had said to her regarding going to her house on that Saturday evening he killed her father.

For some reason, this led Clara into a discussion about how she liked to cut herself in tenth grade after her mother died and how she began to feel less than others. She said her father started to yell at her a lot back then, and this was near the time she started to buy knives and collect them.

They talked and talked. Locke kept going back to one question that had bothered him from the moment he and Clara had started a dialogue: After Kyle started to talk about hurting her father, why hadn't she gone to her sister or her father or someone else and told them what was going on? This was where it became very serious, Locke explained. Clara might have *thought* Kyle was some bullshit artist, especially where fighting and being a vampire was concerned.

However, the moment he began to talk about killing or even hurting her father—this after she had specifically told him that her father was trying to poison her and she hated him— well, things had gone from not believing the kid's stories to maybe she should take him seriously, even if it later turned out she was wrong.

Clara seemed to agree. In fact, all the signs, according to what Clara herself had said, were there. Kyle wanted a phone card. He wanted gloves and a do-rag. He had said, for crying out loud, "I'm going to kill your father. . . ." Why in the world *hadn't* Clara said anything to anyone about this—if only to protect herself? And why—another question might have been asked (although it wasn't)—hadn't Clara Schwartz ever written about this in her journals? Why had she never penned an entry about how much of a liar Kyle was and the fact that he was starting to talk about killing her father? If Kyle had been such a storyteller and bizarre creature in her world of faeries and gods and goddesses, staffs and swords, why had Clara *never* written much about him?

Hindsight, Clara said, was clearer for her now that she'd had some time to make the connection between what happened to her father and what had been said. But, at the time, she just didn't believe any of it. She'd blacked it all out because it seemed so enormously transparent and not at all possible.

Clara steered the conversation back to how violent her father had become after her mother died—to the great surprise of Michelle. Clara claimed the OG pulled her hair, hit her, and screamed at her.

"I was worried about my dad. I didn't want to die. . . ."

The low grades she was getting had set him off, Clara claimed. It was that trip to the Virgin Islands that worried her most.

An hour into the interview, Clara asked to take a break.

When they returned, Locke and Clara spent some time

talking about the injury Clara had suffered while "sparring" with Kyle. Kyle had missed and struck Clara on the thumb while they were practicing sword techniques with sticks in the woods near her house one afternoon when Kyle visited (one of the three times Kyle had met the OG). Clara had a scoring system she'd designed to rate the performance of those she said she trained in fighting with sticks/swords. Kyle was a four, she said. Not bad.

This led them into Clara talking about the Underworld. She spelled it all out for Locke, although not clearly. Locke had a hard time following along. Yet, after figuring things out, the investigator was able to ask pertinent questions, a main one being, "Is there any type of ceremony when you become a master?" Locke was thinking: *Is murder the ultimate sacrifice or a rung in the ladder on your way to becoming a master?*

Clara broke into a long explanation that made little sense, so Locke brought it back to Kyle and his role in the Underworld.

Kyle was a good student of the Underworld, Clara said, but not great.

There came a point when Michelle chimed in and talked about how her father would get very upset with Clara when she lied and didn't do her chores around the house, like feeding the horses and cleaning up after them. Michelle said there had been a "lot of arguments" between them that past summer, but they were "arguments."

They were nothing more.

Locke asked Michelle if she was ever aware of her father hitting Clara.

"I had been home before when he snapped at her—he had snapped at her because she had said some rude things. I had been home when he had done things like that because of things that she had said and things that she had done."

If there had ever been a moment when he might have hit

her, Michelle seemed to say, it would have been then, when he snapped. But she had never seen him raise a hand to Clara.

Clara claimed he had "smacked" her across the face several times with an open hand.

Michelle recalled it being Mrs. Schwartz, their mother, who had done the smacking, not Daddy.

Clara wrote off her father hitting her, just like that, crediting the mistake to having "huge gaps of memory from my past."

By the time they got into the specifics regarding her father striking her, Clara was adding provisos to a lot of what she said: "If he did" or "If I remember it right." Yet again, it seemed to Locke that she was constantly and consistently backpedaling from what she had said earlier. Because Michelle was there contradicting what she was trying to get across, Clara was implying, *"Oh yeah . . . I forgot about that. Yup. That's the way I remember it happening now."*

The next half hour consisted of them talking about the relationship Clara had with her father when the other children were home and when they were away. Clara talked about a guy who was, essentially, two different people. Michelle talked about a guy who was calm, talkative, and also a broken man who missed his dead wife very much.

Clara brought up how the OG didn't much care for her friends.

Michelle agreed, adding that neither did she.

They spoke of religion, and how her father didn't favor any one religion and didn't want to raise his children in a religion because he didn't agree with it as a whole. This gave Clara the opportunity to tell Locke that she grew up with Catholic grandparents who often took them to mass, but there came a day when she told them she didn't believe in God.

"I mean, I guess the best way to describe my origin is polytheistic, not monotheistic, sort of, I guess. . . . I think it would be closer to Norse or Celtic than anything else."

"What do you believe about death?" Locke asked.

"Death is natural. Death is a journey, nothing to be feared. I still fear it because, you know, it's . . . We don't know what happens. . . . I'm afraid of dying, but I know it's . . . There's always a possibility of death in life. I just thought *I* had a greater chance."

"Because of the possible poisoning and threats?"

"Yeah."

CHAPTER 78

THEY THEN GOT on the subject of Clara's driving skills as the interview began to wind down. Michelle pointed out that Clara was a terrible driver and their father was worried greatly about her driving. This was an interesting exchange for Locke to hear. It gave him some insight, from Michelle's point of view, into how Robert Schwartz thought about his daughter. Clara had described a man who despised his youngest daughter—and she could do no right in his eyes. She talked about a man who had been planning, plotting, and scheming to kill her.

"He was always worried, because every time that you were late," Michelle said, addressing Clara, "he would always say something like, 'I hope she didn't get . . . in an accident. . . .' Every time you were late."

As Clara talked about showing up home late a lot and the OG not really saying much of anything about it other than pointing out the fact that he was worried, Locke again questioned this versus what Clara had been telling him. He wanted to know if it surprised Clara that her dad never yelled at her for being late. Here was an opportunity and reason for Dr. Schwartz to be genuinely pissed off at his daughter, and yet he wasn't.

She ignored the direct question and instead talked about

how her brother dissed her for being late, and her father, Clara admitted, actually stuck up for her.

"I mean, sometimes my dad and me had a nice relationship, like we were nice to each other and sometimes we were just horrible."

Clara brought the conversation back to her and how she had thought about killing herself while in high school.

Locke allowed her to stay on her high-school days of fighting and lying to her father and getting into trouble and taking drugs. He mostly listened, asking questions that kept her chatting. Clara did most of the talking, mentioning how "weird" her father had gotten after her mother's death. "Like I honestly thought he was insane or going insane."

This mention of the word "insane" brought up a conversation between Michelle and Clara about their mother. Michelle figured that Clara must have thought their mother was insane, but Clara reacted bitterly and said no way.

"Our mother was manic-depressive," Michelle told Locke. Then she relayed a story about their mother once having a "manic episode" in which she stripped naked in the middle of the night and ran throughout the house, yelling and screaming, "Where is my watch? Where is my watch?" She hid under the bed, Michelle added, "because she thought she was a German alien, and she thought there was . . . [She was] telling me things like the reason there were serial numbers on the back of road signs was so people could track where you were at."

Locke took a breath. He listened as Michelle told even more bizarre stories about their mother and the meds she was on, along with how paranoid she had become right before her death. Then Locke turned to Clara. "Let me ask you something, Clara. Do you think that some of the same things that your mom had might be the reason you thought your dad was trying to poison *you*?"

Clara swallowed. "Um . . ."

"Do you think that's possible?" Locke asked again when

he didn't get a response. Locke didn't believe for one moment this was possible, but he wanted to offer Clara, as he later put it, "a way out of this."

"Like, I think, like, honestly, I've read some stuff on bipolar, and I don't think I have it. I just . . . I think I have depression."

Locke kept asking Clara if she was simply paranoid, like her mother had been, and that was why she thought—or she believed, rather—that her dad was trying to kill her.

"What I find hard to reconcile with," Clara said, "is the amount of times that I got diarrhea, that I puked, that I felt dizzy, nausea."

Michelle said, "My father was actually afraid Clara was manic-depressive."

"Did you know that?" Locke asked Clara.

"Not until recently."

Locke wanted to know more about what Clara had "told" her "friends" about her father. Specifically, what "role did Kyle see himself in" within your life as it pertained to your relationship with your father?

"Protector," Clara said immediately, without having to think about it.

"Protector?"

"Well, to an extent . . . ," she said, again backing off.

Locke cranked up the pressure a bit, asking her directly what role Kyle played in her life.

Clara agreed to some degree that he was her "confidant," but that she saw him more as her protector against the dangers of herself rather than anyone else.

"Tell me about Kyle being the protector," Locke pushed. "How did he see himself in that role?"

"What do you mean?"

"Did he feel like he needed to protect everybody?"

"I don't think so. I think he, just, well, um, ah, well, the thing was, he also liked me and—"

"Liked you in what sense?"

"Like, wanted to date me. And I just found it uncomfortable with him. . . ." Clara also claimed here that all of her friends knew she didn't have sex with guys and wouldn't have sex until it was time, she shared, to make children.

"So how 'bout you and Kyle, have you ever fooled around?"

"Once."

"Once?"

"And Patrick knew I didn't want to have a relationship with him."

Locke finally got Clara to talk about December 5 and 6, after asking, "You [and Kyle] had a conversation on the phone about him killing your dad—you said that he had referenced that once prior to that. When did he reference it prior to that?"

"What do you mean?"

After some discrepancy about dates, Clara said, "I think it was Friday or Saturday. . . ."

As they talked it through, Clara maintained that Kyle had never said anything about killing her father until the day before he did it. "And I started going, 'Yeah, right, whatever. He's lying.'"

But Locke focused on what Clara had told Kyle. There was a fine line here that both were walking. In telling Kyle that she believed her father was trying to kill her, and her drilling that point into him, was Clara asking her friend to end her misery? Was she knowingly telling Kyle, in beating that drum of *"He's abusive and trying to poison me,"* that she wanted Kyle to do something about it?

"Do you think that you could have let it slip and said, you know, *'I would be better off with my dad out of the picture. I would be better off if my dad weren't here'*?"

"No, I don't think so," Clara said. "I don't think I would have, not—"

"Even inadvertently, just in conversation," Locke suggested. "Do you think it might have slipped, or something?"

"There's . . . I mean, there's always a slim possibility. I don't think I ever joked around or anything like that. I . . .

I mean I think there may be a very faint possibility, but I don't think . . . I don't think I trusted him enough to talk."

"Because I am trying to find out why he went that extra step—why this would have happened—and I thought that, you know, maybe something was said that he took the wrong way. . . ."

Clara explained how she thought Kyle maybe "didn't want Dad to hurt me. I think he both . . . I guess, I think that he was sick of it happening. I guess he took his own initiative. . . ."

The investigator wanted to know if Kyle had seen "any incidents of . . . violence" toward Clara?

"No," she said.

"Just what you told him?"

"Yeah . . . I don't remember. I don't think Dad yelled at me that one time that . . . that he was there. I'm almost positive that he didn't. . . ."

Michelle said she didn't recall her father yelling at Clara while Kyle was ever at the house. Michelle remembered the times Kyle was there because she thought he was so "creepy." She couldn't forget him.

Clara explained that the first time they met each other, Kyle and the OG were cordial.

"So, what would have driven him from point A to point B—from 'Hi, I'm Kyle' to killing your dad?"

"Well, he didn't like my dad when he met him. Kyle didn't like him. He said that to me. He said he didn't like him."

Locke asked what Kyle specifically didn't like about him.

"I don't know," Michelle said, again piping in. She shook her head, disagreeing with Clara. "I think Dad didn't say *anything* to Kyle."

"I know," Clara responded. "But I'm saying maybe, just maybe, I don't know. The only thing I got from him is like, 'Well, what do you think about my dad?' He said, 'I don't like him.' I said, 'Okay. Well, what about Michelle?' He goes, 'You guys don't look anything alike.'"

Locke finally got Clara to admit that she believed Kyle

might have been protecting her from her dad. Clara said she needed protection; she was scared of her father.

This back-and-forth exchange went on and on. Locke would bring Clara right to the edge of her possibly admitting her role in the murder, and then she'd pull back and break into some story about high school or college.

"Look, in my mind, by this point in that interview," Locke recalled later, "I believed that she had known all along that they were going to kill her father. . . . A financial gain is what I think she was looking at from this. Did she have a perfect relationship with her dad? No. I think her dad was probably strict and probably held her feet to the fire, and did not allow and did not want her to just rip and run with all of her friends, as she would have liked to have done." Because of it, Locke observed, "she resented that."

Locke wanted to get a few things straight. He acted like he was confused, hoping Clara would clarify and, in turn, back herself into a corner and admit to something.

"So Kyle referred to you as his 'sister'?" Locke asked.

"Yes."

"So he told your dad, 'Because you're trying to kill my sister'?"

"Or something—something involving sister. And he said that Dad smiled . . . and he said that Dad showed no remorse. I just remember thinking, 'Okay. . . .'"

"How did that make you feel?"

"That kind of creeped me out. I couldn't believe he—"

"That he *didn't* show any remorse for what he had done?" Locke wanted to clarify.

"Yeah."

"You thought your dad should have said, 'I'm sorry'?"

Michelle stared at her sister, waiting for a response.

"Well," Clara answered, backpedaling yet again. "What was really creepy was Kyle said, 'When all the others did that, they showed remorse.'" (Clara was referring to the other victims that Kyle claimed to have killed.) "And I'm going,

'Oh, God.' It's sort of like, I guess, when someone realizes that they've just talked to Satan or, you know, 'Oh, God! What, you know . . . *Who have I been friends with?*'"

Locke asked if Kyle meant that he had maybe made a mistake in killing Dr. Schwartz.

Clara said she didn't know.

As they discussed what Kyle and Schwartz were talking about right before Kyle killed him, Michelle asked if she could leave. Apparently, she'd heard enough.

Clara asked her to stay.

So she stayed.

Jesse came in at one point and asked how things were going.

Clara indicated that her throat was parched. She needed some water.

Locke brought the interview back to Kyle and what Clara thought a good punishment might be for him, when all was said and done.

She stumbled and said something about how she had thought about this and was unsure, because she wasn't so clear that "he's actually done anything. . . ." However, if he had, "I think it would be better off if he got the death penalty."

"For Kyle?" Locke asked. He was surprised.

"Yeah!" she said. But here came that bus again. "I think Mike definitely played some—I'm not sure how much—but he should definitely, because he, I mean, even following, gets to a point where you have—I'm not sure if it's morality—it's having a conscience. I can't get the right word."

After Locke helped Clara figure out what she was trying to say, Clara restated how she believed Mike "honestly, probably, most definitely [deserved] the same punishment because he's aiding, and what are we going to do if one of his other friends becomes a murderer, too, you know."

"What about Kate?" Locke asked.

"Honestly, I think Kate is more of a—in terms of souls— I think she has probably a more innocent soul than the others do. Like she's just dating the *wrong guy,* happened to be in the *wrong car,* you know." Clara stopped. Then she thought some more about it. "But I still think prison, counseling, you know."

Seeing a clear opening, Locke asked, "What about your dad? What kind of soul does he have?"

"Well, I know Catholics don't believe in it"—actually, Catholics do believe in it—"but I think he should go to Purgatory for a little bit and then go to Heaven. Purgatory is for a Christian to pay a penalty."

"I'm familiar with Purgatory," Locke said.

"I think, overall, he was a good, good man, because I think he—if—I wonder whether this all would have happened if Mom stayed alive, if Mom hadn't smoked, stopped smoking, you know, would have lived, because I think most of it can be attributed to—"

"That time in Purgatory, would that be for what he did to you?" Locke asked.

"Yes . . . and any wrong that he did to the rest of society—anything else that none of us know about, that he kept in his heart, because I don't think to my knowledge that he ever went and confessed or whatever. . . ."

Clara didn't sound like the admitted atheist that she claimed to be—apparently, she believed in some of the tenets of the Church.

Locke wanted to know where Clara saw her soul.

"My soul is on earth." Then she went on to say that she believed her soul would one day end up in Purgatory, too—once again contradicting her disbelief. "But . . . Kyle will go straight to Hell. But that the others will spend a couple of millennia in Purgatory . . . I mean, Mike did help him, so Mike will go to Hell, but I think Kate will spend time in Purgatory and then go up to Heaven."

Just about five hours after they started, Locke indicated he was done.

CHAPTER 79

IT WOULD TAKE some time, but by February 1, 2002, Investigator John Russ obtained a first-degree murder warrant for Clara. Russ, along with Greg Locke and Mike Grau, took a ride to JMU and were told by campus police that Clara was inside her dorm room. Like most of the time, she was probably alone.

As soon as Clara opened the door—she was on the phone at the time—and saw Russ standing there, she tried closing the door in his face.

Russ said, "Come on." He stepped in front of the door so it couldn't close all the way. "Don't you do that. Get off the phone now, please, Miss Schwartz."

Clara played stupid. "I thought you were a reporter," she said, opening the door and letting the investigators in.

"That's nice," Russ said. "You are under arrest, Miss Schwartz. . . . Get your shoes and coat on."

Locke looked on as Russ read Clara her Miranda rights. Inside Clara's dorm, Locke noticed, "were items indicative of Wiccan and gothic ceremonies." For Clara, nothing had changed since her father's death and the pressure the LCSO put on her. She was still practicing her witchcraft, thinking she was the high priestess of the new order.

Russ escorted Clara to a waiting car outside; the others

followed behind. Along the way, Clara asked Russ what she was being arrested for.

"First-degree murder!" Russ said.

On the way to the JMU Campus Police barracks, sitting in the backseat of the cruiser, handcuffed, Clara said, "I want a lawyer."

Too little, too late, but what the hell!

Sitting by her side, Locke explained her rights again. Then she asked why they were headed to the campus police station and not the LCSO?

Locke said she would have to be booked there on campus first.

Protocol. Jurisdiction.

After they settled up with the campus police and Clara used the restroom, they headed out to the LCSO. En route, with Locke sitting again by her side, Clara, without being prompted, said, "I had a dream that I was going to be arrested."

"Yeah . . . ," Locke responded.

Clara stared out the window and watched the trees go by as cars passed. Men and women were out in the world going about their daily routines. Life went on. Clara, though, was going to jail. Was it real to her by this point?

"I also dreamed that my father's grave was desecrated," Clara added when Locke didn't say much in response. "The only difference [in my dream] was that I was arrested at the Stone House."

"We cannot ask you any questions," Russ said from the front seat. "You've asked for an attorney, Miss Schwartz."

Again, keeping the conversation focused on her and her life, Clara ignored the comment and instead babbled on about school and how she had cut back on her classes since going back. She mentioned something about a powwow at the Stone House coming up that weekend with Jesse, Michelle, and other family members, although she had chosen not to go.

"Why?" Locke asked.

"Because of everything going on with the family."

"Was that because of the *Washington Post* article?" Locke wondered. It was clear from that published article that Clara and her siblings were at odds and Clara was somehow being ostracized. Again, the article fell just short of naming Clara as a suspect in her father's murder. Her family knew, however.

They spoke of menial things for a time; then Clara asked, "What will happen if this is all determined to be a misunderstanding?" She was almost smirking, laughing out of the corner of her mouth, as if to say the charges would never stick. It was that Gen X sense of entitlement that she seemed to possess. Clara could not stifle it, no matter how hard she tried.

"Not quite sure what you mean," Locke said. "But there are several steps in this process. You'll go before a magistrate tonight. They will determine if there is a bond." Then Locke explained how there would be a preliminary (like a probable cause) hearing, a grand jury, and then a trial, if it went that far.

"What are my plea-bargaining possibilities?"

Locke shook his head. Here she was, on her way to being processed for first-degree murder, already trying to cut a damn deal.

"You'll have to discuss that with your attorney, Clara."

"What are the different types of offenses as applied to my case?"

"You are being charged with first-degree murder." It was as if she just *didn't* get it. Locke explained the lesser charges associated with homicides: second-degree murder and manslaughter. "But you need to discuss all this with your attorney, not me."

As they pulled into the magistrate's office on East Market Street in downtown Leesburg, Clara said, "Huh, this is where I went to see a shrink." She recognized the building.

"Come on, let's go," Locke said, helping Clara out of the vehicle.

The magistrate saw Clara right away. He explained the process more clearly than Locke had. There would be no bond. Not now. Probably not ever. Clara was going into the local county lockup until her case was given to a prosecutor and her attorney—appointed or hired by her family—and the process of justice was initiated.

"Do you have any dependencies on drugs or alcohol, ma'am?" the magistrate asked as a final question.

Clara didn't speak right away. She stood, silent. Then, after a few moments, she said: "No." It seemed she was finished, but then she added, "Wait . . . although it can be debated as to whether I have a mental illness."

They all looked at each other. What a strange comment to make right after you were processed on first-degree murder charges for having a role in your own father's death.

Clara was released to the county jail, where, it being Friday night, she would spend the weekend before any action in her case went forward.

CHAPTER 80

PUNXSUTAWNEY PHIL WAS busy in Punxsutawney, Pennsylvania, searching for his shadow northwest of where Clara was being held on Saturday, February 2, 2002. She was in the tank with several other inmates, who were waiting to be sent to a state prison or let out on bond. One woman watched as Clara made a phone call to a student friend at JMU. The woman cozied up near Clara so she could hear the call—or at least Clara's side of it.

Clara tried the same number several times, but the boy was not around. When she was finished, she sat down next to the woman.

"I met him after the murder," Clara said, referring to the boy she was trying to get ahold of. "He knows all of the secrets."

"Why are you locked up?" the woman asked.

"I messed up. I was five minutes late to the movies on the day my dad was killed and I didn't have a ticket stub. . . . I told my friend Kyle I was being mentally and physically abused by my father and he took it upon himself. . . . He was going to take the blame because he could be ruled mentally insane. I was going to introduce Kyle to a game. This game is led by this person named Mike, but he's in Russia." Clara paused. Then, as an afterthought, she felt she needed to add what was the only truthful thing she might have told this woman on this day: "After I got what I needed out of them (Mike, Katie, Patrick, and Kyle), I get rid of them."

The woman was staggered by this last comment. Clara's case had been big news in town, so most everyone knew the bare facts. The woman was reeling from what Clara had just told her, but then Clara added, "We talked about the homicide before. . . ."

"Who do you mean 'we'?"

"Kyle and me . . . we had planned . . . to go into the house and kill him, my dad." But Kyle went alone, she elaborated. There was some indication that Clara decided she didn't want to go through with it.

"Did your father fight?" the woman asked.

"Oh yes."

As Clara talked about not wanting to go through with the murder, the woman wanted to know, "Why didn't you call your dad?"

"I didn't really believe him (Kyle). If someone told you they were going to kill your dad, would you believe him?"

"If I had friends like you, I would!" the woman said.

"It was all because I was mad at my father. [Kyle] called me, you know, and he told me that he killed my father with a one-piece ninja sword. You can go online and look at Atlantic Cutlery and you can see the sword there that he used. I don't like that type of sword, actually, the one-piece. I like a staff better."

The woman listened.

"He (my father) was abusing me because he didn't like me. You know why he didn't like me? My intelligence far surpassed his. I'm smarter."

After they were finished, the woman was sent to another jail. Clara stayed in the holding pen. Once the woman had a chance, she asked to speak with LCSO investigators in charge of the Schwartz case. She had one hell of a story to tell.

CHAPTER 81

AFTER SEARCHING CLARA'S dorm room under a warrant, the LCSO uncovered more incriminating evidence of her involvement, including instant-messaging conversations with Kyle and Patrick, Katie and Mike. Clara, with her narcissism so fatefully blatant, had saved them all in a file marked with Kyle's name!

As the noose tightened, group loyalty began to dissolve. Katie was talking the most, tossing Mike aside like garbage in order to save her own ass. By February 13, 2002, defense attorneys got into the public forum by discussing the case with the media. Clara's attorney, Corinne Magee, went after Kyle and his mental-health history, an undoubtedly argumentative issue of this case. Magee wanted Kyle's entire mental-health history so she could evaluate what she and Clara were dealing with. The statements Kyle had given police would be put to the test under a legal dispute that Kyle was probably not stable enough to give such incriminating statements.

A judge denied Magee's request for the prosecution to turn over such records so early in the judicial process. Then the judge placed a gag order on all parties involved. During the hearing, Clara sat wearing leg shackles and did not speak a word. She looked tired and more morose than usual. The few weeks she had been jailed were taking their toll. If she hadn't thought any of this to be serious before her arrest, she most certainly now realized that it was not part of her Underworld fantasy, but she was looking at real time behind bars.

ON MARCH 17, 2002, Kyle, Mike, and Katie were brought before a judge inside the Loudoun County General District Court and formally charged with first-degree murder. Loudoun County was a place that had posted a mere six homicides in all of 2001. This was the country. Leesburg, in fact, is one of those East Coast towns, just out of the Washington, DC, Beltway, that comes to mind when one thinks of the Founding Fathers and how America was once a nation, however young, built by men and women unafraid to fight— often to the death—for what they believed. The Revolutionary War had roots in and around Leesburg. It was a place where people rarely thought about a distinguished doctor of biophysics being brutally murdered inside his own home. It was unfathomable that it could be carried out by a group of Wiccans playing in the dark corner of the universe, apparently thinking there was no penalty for meandering within the blurred lines of fantasy and reality.

Asked to enter a plea on the charges, all three pleaded not guilty and were prepared to take their cases to trial. That meant four separate trials for four defendants.

This was a judicial fiasco—not to mention a major burden on taxpayers.

To no avail, Clara's attorney kept beating the defense drum that "prosecutors did not prove my client had prior knowledge of the crime." Yet, during a probable cause hearing that same week of March 17, 2002, Greg Locke testified that, indeed, Clara Schwartz did have prior knowledge. She had admitted as much to him.

It was up to a grand jury to decipher if there was enough evidence to charge the four and indict; no sooner had they convened, did those indictments come raining down.

After Mike, Katie, Clara, and Kyle were formally indicted, Clara's co-counsel, James Connell, told reporters that Clara was innocent. Prosecutors were "casting a wide net and have no unified theory of what happened."

Commonwealth's Attorney (CA) Owen Basham would not comment when Connell accused the prosecution of throwing poo "against the wall" to "see what sticks."

The indictment claimed that Clara had been "trying since June 2001" to get someone to kill her father—several months before she had even met Kyle.

Finally, after Connell kept talking to the press, Basham spoke to reporters, offering a statement that finally shut the defense up: "I won't comment on specific evidence," Basham said, "but these charges are conservative, and the defense team should wait and listen to my opening statement."

Things went quiet for months. A long winter turned into a warm, sultry spring; by June, as Katie faced possible years and years behind bars for crimes she kept saying she had no knowledge of beforehand, the prosecution went to Katie with an offer.

One that Katie could not refuse.

CHAPTER 82

IN THE LETTER of immunity that Katie Inglis's attorneys brokered with the Commonwealth of Virginia, Katie agreed to testify against everyone. She would tell all she knew about the murder, before and after, and leave no stone unturned so the prosecution could go after those who they believed had plotted, planned, and carried out this horrible crime: Mike, Clara, and Kyle. Once Katie could pass a polygraph and answer the state's questions "truthfully" (that word was printed in bold in the letter), she would be released on a $100,000 bond.

More important than all of that, if she passed the polygraph, Katie would not only be awarded bond at a special hearing, but during that hearing the state would amend her murder charge to "accessory after the fact." Katie would be looking at perhaps a few years behind bars, at most.

On June 4, 2002, with her hand shaking like a skid row alcoholic's, Katie Inglis signed that deal. She would have been an idiot if she hadn't.

Katie dished on it all. She changed up her story just ever so slightly, but the gist of it was there: Clara conspired with Kyle to murder the doctor; she and Mike knew about it all, but did nothing to stop it and actually helped to cover it up afterward. In doing this, Katie was saying Mike was a willing participant with Kyle in the murder.

Katie was obligated under this agreement to testify against Clara and Mike and Kyle for both the prosecution and the defense whenever called. The only crime it appeared Katie had committed, according to the deal, was not doing anything after the fact—not telling anyone what she knew. And in all fairness to Katie Inglis, this was probably true.

CHAPTER 83

THROUGHOUT THE MONTHS of July, August, and September 2002, both sides hammered out details of an imminent trial for Clara, which everyone agreed would begin that fall. At first, it was thought they would be ready by August; but when Investigator Greg Locke had to undergo major back surgery that summer, October looked more likely. Mike and Kyle would be tried after Clara.

In an interesting development, as Clara's attorneys fought for bond in July and early August, Clara's family got together and signed a letter to the court. Not to support her and ask for the judge to sincerely consider bond, but rather it was to say they did not agree it was a good idea to release Clara. In total, nineteen members of Clara's family signed a letter that stated Clara might harm herself or someone in the family if released on bond. Clara's attorneys were trying to get Clara released to her aunt and uncle, Dr. Schwartz's brother and sister-in-law.

Loudoun Circuit Court judge Thomas Horne, who would be presiding over the trial, said no dice. There was not a chance Clara was getting out of jail before her trial.

The family breathed a sigh of absolute relief.

One of Clara's cousins, Dr. Schwartz's nephew, was the

most outspoken of the bunch. He came out and said that if Clara was released: "I feel she would attempt to flee and have no scruples about the method she would use to accomplish this act."

With that comment, it was clear where Clara's family came in on whether they believed her tales of woe and abuse.

CHAPTER 84

JENNIFER WEXTON BEGAN her career with the Commonwealth of Virginia, Loudoun County, and quickly became the go-to prosecutor in cases ranging from simple and major felonies to misdemeanor criminal and traffic charges, all the way up to cases of sexual assault and domestic violence. Wexton had a soft spot for mental-health issues. She felt this was an important part of the justice system that needed constant scrutiny and attention. People needed to keep an open mind about the mental-health crisis affecting the country.

Living in the Washington, DC, area for most of her life, Wexton graduated with honors from the University of Maryland at College Park. In 1995, she earned her law degree from the College of William & Mary in Williamsburg. Tall and blond and unassumingly attractive, Wexton could handle any type of situation she found herself facing while fighting for the state inside a courtroom. In the coming years, she would go on to fill a substitute judge seat and then, after a special election, earn a seat in the state senate with a blowout victory over two veteran Loudoun County career politicians.

In October 2002, not a year since Dr. Robert Schwartz's vicious murder, Jennifer Wexton found herself facing off against Clara Jane Schwartz, who'd had some time now to sit in jail and think about the defense she wanted to mount.

By then, Clara had convinced even herself that she'd had nothing to do with her father's murder. It was October 7, 2002, and Clara was twenty years old. Waiting for the first day of her trial to start, she wore a blue sweater and black skirt. Her long, thick dark hair was braided and coiled around her shoulder as if she had a pet snake with her. Effectively, Clara was on trial for the crime of parricide—or the act of a child murdering one (or both) of his or her parents. It is a crime committed mainly by males. Experts claim, however, when females get involved, they generally contract the murder out and rarely do it by their own hands.

That dark and gloomy Wiccan witch from a year ago, with the despondent and melancholic look of utter despair on her face, was nowhere to be found in Judge Horne's courtroom. Clara's lawyers had clearly schooled her: *"Look upbeat and positive. Don't slouch! You are fighting for your life here."*

Wexton explained out of the gate during her opening argument that Clara initially had tried to convince Patrick House, her boyfriend at the time, with her deceptive, manipulating skills, to kill her father by poisoning the man. But after meeting with resistance from Patrick time and time again, and then meeting Kyle Hulbert at the Renaissance Festival, Clara realized she'd found herself the perfect murder weapon.

The perfect piece of clay to shape and mold.

The perfect assassin.

"Clara Schwartz wanted her father dead!" Wexton reminded jurors. "She'd hated her father for a long time." After a bit of detail regarding Clara's college life at JMU, Wexton reiterated, adding an important point: "Clara Schwartz wanted her father dead—but she wasn't going to do it herself."

Indeed, that was what this trial came down to: the idea that Clara, although she talked about it often and supposedly feared for her life and considered herself an expert sword fighter and high priestess of the Underworld, did not want to commit the ultimate act of evil herself. She wasn't gutsy enough.

"She was going to find someone else to do it for her."

Wexton then quoted from one of Clara's many online conversations with Kyle that the prosecution had transcribed and would enter into evidence: "'All I ask is that it not trace back to me.'"

The Underworld game Clara had created was next. The prosecutor talked about how all of the players Clara had recruited were there for one purpose: to protect her from those other players and bad people from hunting and hurting her. Wexton made jurors understand that Clara had kept track of this elaborate game on her computer and in her journals. Her writings had become nothing more than a "tool" allowing Clara to talk about her father's murder under the guise of a fantasy, weighing who was willing to take it to a reality level and who was unapproachable. In other words, she had created this world in order to hide the true meaning of wanting her father dead and looking for someone to employ for that task.

Wexton told jurors, however, that Clara did not want to discuss the murder online. Clara told Kyle once: "I hate talking about this kind of thing on here. . . ."

Wexton mentioned Patrick by name again. As soon as Patrick figured out that his girlfriend was serious about wanting her father murdered and how "Clara made it clear to him that it *wasn't* a game [and that she] . . . wanted Patrick to kill her father," he ran as far away from her as he could.

Closing out her rather brief opening, Wexton said that Clara hated her father with a fevered passion, and the true motive for the murder was that age-old reason of having "stood to receive a large inheritance when he died." The weekend that Kyle had been invited by Clara to camp on the grounds of their secluded stone farmhouse in the woods after the Thanksgiving holiday was for one purpose only, Wexton added near the conclusion.

"So he would recognize Robert Schwartz" when he later

went back to the house to kill him. Clara wanted to be certain Kyle didn't make a mistake and kill the wrong person.

Over and over, Wexton used that phrase: "Clara wanted her father dead." It was the theme, no doubt, that the prosecution would carry into the trial as witnesses were brought in to prove it.

"Clara Jane Schwartz wanted her father dead, but she didn't want it to trace back to her," Wexton said finally. She then looked over at Clara, who sat, stone-faced, staring straight ahead, not at all interested in what was being said about her. "Well, ladies and gentlemen, the murder of Dr. Robert Schwartz has traced back to his daughter Clara, and that's why we are all here today."

CHAPTER 85

THE DEFENSE LAWYER James Connell stood and asked jurors to understand one thing about his client: Clara Jane hadn't created this Underworld game to hide the murder of her father under the cloak of a fantasy, but rather as an "innocent escape" from what was an extremely solitary social life of being alone and depressed and out of touch with her classmates.

"Clara Jane Schwartz is no cheerleader. She's not the most popular girl in the school," Connell stated. Then, oddly, he added: "She's not the brightest girl in school. She was not everybody's first pick for party invitations. . . ." It was because of that societal desolation and alienation, he said, that Clara "turns to this fantasy world."

And so their message was clear: Poor Clara Schwartz, an outsider not liked by many. She was a girl who felt alone in the world. Not fitting in where others did. Misunderstood. Reserved. Depressed.

Next, in a dramatic turn of phrase, Connell explained that during the "fall of 2001, the silly, dark world of Clara Schwartz collided with the dark and dangerous world of Kyle Hulbert."

Now came the gist of their defense: Kyle Hulbert took it upon himself to commit this murder after listening to a friend describe the horror of being abused by her father. Clara, by gosh, had no idea that she was dealing with a mentally ill psychopath who would take what she said and spin it into a murder plan. She never asked this boy to do it. She never beat around the bush about wanting him to kill her father. She never paid him to do it. That was all speculation and insane innuendo on Kyle's part now that he faced the potential of going away for a very long time.

"Because of his mental illness," Connell said, Kyle "misinterpreted conversations with Clara" in which she had never wanted her father to be killed.

What about Clara soliciting Patrick first, however? How would they explain that little problem?

Connell was saving that for his cross of Patrick, apparently, because he didn't broach it here during his opening. He stuck to Kyle. Like when Kyle talked to her about killing her dad, for instance, which he clearly had online, Clara's argument was that she never took him seriously. She believed that they were dabbling in the Underworld and Kyle understood this.

"Ladies and gentlemen, at the end of this trial, the evidence will show you *two* things," Connell concluded, holding up the peace sign to indicate the number two. "Number one! Clara Jane Schwartz did not kill her father. And number two! Clara Jane Schwartz did not *intend* for her father to be killed."

Done.

Time to get it on.

CHAPTER 86

AS TESTIMONY BEGAN, Jennifer Wexton got to work with witnesses called for a specific purpose: to lay the foundation of the state's case. The day itself was long on legalities and bench conferences. After a few minor witnesses needed to establish place and time, near the end of that first day, October 7, Wexton put up the neighbor who had found Dr. Schwartz. This offered the commonwealth the opportunity to inject a bit of veracity and realism into the situation right from the start. Photos of Dr. Schwartz lying in a pool of his own blood were displayed, and the brutality and violence behind the crime became material.

The neighbor spoke of how he and the construction worker found Schwartz. As he testified, photographs of the house, the X carved on Schwartz's neck, and the massive amount of blood spilled during the murder were shown to jurors.

Buzzing around the room was a whisper that Clara's sister was up next. Someone had seen her enter the building. Many wondered—with Michelle torn between sibling loyalty and the love she had for her father—what she would say. Michelle was smart, far more intelligent than Clara. She had a feeling that Clara was involved. That interview with Locke and Clara that Michelle sat in on turned out to be very telling for a sister who had always considered Clara a bit eccentric and dark.

One couldn't walk out of that conversation without feeling that, at the least, Clara knew beforehand and afterward, and did nothing to prevent it or report it. Still, what would Michelle now say about her sister?

Deputy Commonwealth's Attorney Owen Basham, Jennifer Wexton's co-counsel, began by asking Michelle to describe the sibling family tree for jurors; then he worked his way straight into Kyle Hulbert's presence in Clara's life. He asked Michelle if she recalled meeting Kyle during that Thanksgiving weekend, which was one of the state's key moments in this crime.

Michelle said she had met Kyle that weekend.

"And who else was present that weekend at home?" Basham asked.

"My father was home. My sister was home. And my brother traveled up, but he spent most of the weekend visiting friends in the area."

"And did you have the occasion to see and meet Mr. Kyle Hulbert that weekend?"

Michelle spoke with confidence. You could tell by the way she used her voice that there was no doubt in her mind that what she was saying had happened the way she said it had. Jurors picked up on this.

"Yes, sir, I did."

Basham asked her to explain.

"I remember him dressed in a black trench coat down to his feet. . . . I think his hair might have been wet. . . . He [had] a sword with him."

Michelle went on to talk about how Kyle had pulled the sword out and showed it to her and Dr. Schwartz. She described how Kyle "touched the blade and . . . said it was dull."

A few questions later, Basham asked Michelle to describe an instant message she received from her sister on December 8, 2001, the night of the murder.

Michelle spoke of a quick back-and-forth with Clara that night. Clara made a point to tell her that their father was coming down to JMU and that she was in her dorm at the time of the instant message. These both seemed like odd details to add. The conversation had taken place somewhere near eleven that night. Michelle said she wasn't prone to getting instant messages from her sister: "Only when she *needed* something." With that declaration, jurors understood the reason why Basham had asked about this was because the prosecution wanted to show how Clara was creating an alibi for herself by letting several strategic people know where she was and what she was doing.

As Michelle continued, the day got short on time and the judge recessed until the following morning. After being asked, Connell said his cross-examination of Michelle was going to be lengthy, so why start and stop? Maybe just tabling it till morning was best.

WHEN MICHELLE RETURNED on October 8, James Connell began his cross-examination by asking where Clara lived on campus, as opposed to where Michelle lived: close by. He established how Clara and Michelle had never really seen much of each other because they, essentially, lived separate lives, with different friends and different interests and hobbies. Then Connell brought Michelle back to that Thanksgiving weekend and a conversation she'd had with Kyle. Michelle said Kyle had told her he was "born holding a Guns and Roses album" and had been "abandoned at birth by his parents." She claimed Kyle wouldn't stop talking, so she kind of zoned out and stood and listened. She felt right away that she was talking to a liar—a kid who was making things up to make himself appear cooler, more important, and the center of attention.

Michelle called all of her sister's friends "a little strange," but said she never made blanket "judgments about people." She quickly realized and sympathized with a generalization she'd made that Kyle, especially, had been "affected" by his life of living in foster care.

Connell tried to trip Michelle up about times she had testified to during her direct testimony as being different to what she remembered now, but it meant nothing in the scope of Clara's case. It only proved that Michelle might have said two o'clock when she actually meant one.

Big deal.

Regarding that interview with Locke that Michelle sat in on, Connell laid out how the family had discussed going into the LCSO and that Clara, particularly, had "agreed that it was a good idea to go to the interview."

"She never said [that]," Michelle testified, "but she didn't show any hesitation. I believe that she was pretty open to it."

So much for Connell trying to make it appear as though it was Clara's idea to go in and give the LCSO any info that investigators needed, as if fully cooperating.

Connell then brought in how, back in July during a preliminary hearing, Michelle testified to the fact that Clara actually said it was a "good idea" to go down for the interview. So, why was she now saying she didn't recall Clara saying those exact words?

"Yes, the *family* agreed it was a good idea," Michelle made clear.

"Including Clara, ma'am?"

"Yes."

Establishing that fact, Connell spent very little time discussing the content of the actual interview with Locke that day, likely because most of it would destroy Clara.

A few more inconsequential questions, and that was it. Basham checked his notes one last time, whispered something to Clara, and told the judge he was finished with Michelle.

CHAPTER 87

THE KILLER HIMSELF walked into the courtroom next. There was no disputing this fact: Kyle Hulbert killed Robert Schwartz in a premeditated act of utter violence. It was a murder so bloody and savage that he had blocked the worst moments from his unstable memory. Kyle was not denying that he committed the murder. The Commonwealth of Virginia wanted him to destroy Clara—rip her story to shreds. Refute, piece by piece, the tale of the poor little confused and depressed girl, who misunderstood the mentally insane psychopathic vampire, and bury Clara for good. Many inside the courtroom believed Kyle would do that exact thing; while others were on the fence, not really knowing how far Clara had her hooks in this guy. Was she still able to control Kyle's thoughts and behaviors?

So the question remained as Kyle, dressed in his prison johnnies, that gaunt and chiseled look of a man who didn't eat much, made his way to the witness stand. Would he take down the high priestess of the Underworld, Lord Chaos herself, and tell jurors she had pressured him and manipulated him, asking repeatedly that he murder her father? As a result, Kyle only did what was asked of him by a smarter, more calculating witch.

Basham approached the admitted murderer. He asked him to state his name, date of birth, and Social Security number.

Kyle did what he was told.

"Mr. Hulbert, do you know the defendant in this case, Clara Jane Schwartz?"

Here was Kyle's chance to swat Clara in the face. He cleared his throat. He sat up and moved in close to the microphone so everyone could hear what he was going to say. Then, without much flourish or drama, Kyle uttered: "At this time, I respectfully choose to invoke my right afforded me under the Fifth Amendment of the Constitution and respectfully decline to answer this question or any other questions you may have."

According to Kyle, "I wanted to testify. My lawyer told me to plead the Fifth." The main message Kyle wanted to get across in testifying—had he not listened to his lawyer— was that Mike, his "brother" and best friend, "did not have anything to do with this. He wasn't aware. He didn't do any of this. But my lawyer wouldn't let me."

It seemed really odd. Kyle claimed that his lawyer told him that answering one question meant that he would be subject to answering any question they had for him.

"And that was a road he didn't want to take," Kyle said later.

Yet, Kyle was screwed, no matter what he said. He'd admitted killing Schwartz. What would it matter what he now said? He couldn't be punished any more than life in prison.

Kyle sat back in his chair inside the witness-box. He had pled the Fifth! He didn't want to incriminate himself by telling on poor Clara. In doing so, Kyle would have to say he was the murderer. Apparently, he was preparing a defense for himself and didn't want to muddle that. The idea of trying Clara first might have just backfired on the prosecution— although, to their credit, they never tried to cut a deal with the Devil and ask Kyle to testify on their behalf. Hell, they had Katie for that.

Basham asked if this was going to be Kyle's response to every question.

Clara stared at her former friend and minion. If one looked close, there was even a slight crack of a smile on her face, Kyle later said, as if she had gotten her way once again.

In lieu of Kyle clamming up under his God-given right, Wexton argued to have his lengthy, detailed confession read into the record in open court for jurors. It would be just as good as Kyle sitting there and telling jurors what had taken place inside the Schwartz home. Maybe even more powerful because it was written days after the murder.

It took a few minutes, but the judge was able to find a clerk of the court to read Kyle's confession.

And there it was for everyone to hear: Kyle's detailed account of killing Robert Schwartz, tasting his blood and going into a feverish "frenzy," stabbing him repeatedly, all because Clara Schwartz had asked him to do so, and had convinced him that she was being abused and Mr. Schwartz was going to kill her.

Wexton and Basham looked at each other and said nothing after the clerk was finished with the read.

What would Clara do now?

CHAPTER 88

INVESTIGATOR JAMIE KOONTZ was next up for Basham and Wexton. Koontz had uncovered the sword inside Mike's house that Kyle had used in the murder. Wexton and Basham offered up photographs of the sword and where it had been found. If you looked close enough, Koontz noted as the photographs were displayed, you could make out "droplets of moisture" on the blade. That would be "moisture," indicating that "someone may have washed or cleaned it," Koontz testified.

After Koontz, John Russ sat and answered questions. Wexton asked him several inconsequential questions about evidence collection to establish how the chain of evidence had been followed to a tee. Then he cut him loose.

Both investigators had set a tone for the state's next witness.

Patrick House.

Clara's ex-boyfriend, the first appointee to the ambassadorship of the Underworld's top assassin, was of average height and had red hair. His goatee and mustache were still part of his look. In the scope of it all, Patrick was a good kid. He'd gone through that stage of Dungeons & Dragons and fantasy worlds and come out of it okay, maybe even still dabbling just a tiny bit in it all. Patrick had had his share of issues and problems, certainly; yet he was smart enough to know serious trouble when he ran into it. And just last year, Patrick would say, in not so many words, that trouble came knocking in the form of a cerebral-looking, goth, gloomy girl he thought maybe he could see himself with for the long term—that is, before she started talking about him murdering her father.

Patrick spoke of meeting Clara and the beginning of their friendship and the Underworld she was so fascinated with and had created on her own. He called Clara the "dungeon master" of that world, and he had soon been given the roles of "assassin" and "bard."

"How about Clara's father? Did he have a role in the game?" Wexton asked.

Patrick shifted in his seat. It was an uncomfortable question.

"No, ma'am," he said.

Wexton rephrased it: "Was there a *character* that was made to represent Lord Chaos's father?"

"Yes, ma'am."

Patrick was a detail-oriented witness. That was a good sign. He further explained that Clara had created his role in the game. He said his job was to protect her from those who wanted to kill her, one of whom was the OG, adding how the term "'tay' was an acronym that she used for the word 'kill.'"

"Did she often speak in acronyms?"

"Yes, ma'am."

Important fact in this case.

Wexton asked if this language Clara used was central only to the Underworld game.

A second important fact.

"Not particularly," Patrick said, exemplifying Wexton's

point. "It was more something that she used on a general basis."

"Did she tell you . . . why it was that OG needed to be killed?"

"She would . . . She used references to poisoning, among other things."

Wexton wanted to know if Clara had made several requests of Patrick to kill the OG, or was it just one time.

"Yes, ma'am," he said, meaning several.

They next discussed how Patrick's character Path had the sole job of taying the OG, and how he and Clara had an agreement about this.

"And can you explain what the particulars of that agreement were?" Wexton wanted to know.

"The agreement was when the assassin had met her character's father an equivalent number of times to the times her father attempted to kill her."

They talked about Clara's journals and how Patrick would sit and sometimes read them: how Clara had written that her dad had tried to kill her. Not the OG character in the game, but *her real father.* Patrick explained further how her journals might have started off as a map and narrative of the Underworld game, but as time went on, "toward the end of August and September, I was seeing more of the journals that had less to do with the game."

Patrick hit every note the prosecution needed from him. He spoke of talking to Clara about killing the OG. How the lines between reality and fantasy blurred into all reality, and he eventually realized she actually wanted him to kill her father. And how "she made reference to money she would get from her inheritance."

Question after question, Patrick spoke of a young adult who was obsessed with the notion of seeing her real father die. He told jurors about that time inside her dorm when Clara handed him that herbal medications book and had it opened to a chapter on poisoning. It was about then that he realized, "She no longer appeared to be inside the game. It appeared to be all reality to her then."

After Patrick talked about those times that they went out to eat and Clara freaked out, thinking the OG had somehow gotten into the kitchen of the restaurant and had poisoned her meal, Wexton moved on to postmurder questions. Patrick said that one day he did talk to Clara at a time after the murder had been in the news; he asked her why she had involved Katie in it at all.

"What, if anything, did Clara respond?"

"Her response was that she didn't mean to."

There was a bench conference regarding several online conversations investigators had uncovered from Clara's computer that she'd stupidly saved. They were between Patrick and Clara. The argument was that asking Patrick about a lot of that material would be leading. If they were both "in character" during the conversations—not even using their real names—how could jurors expect to take what was said as reality?

They hashed it out and Wexton, after Connell objected several times, handed Patrick over to Clara's team. Patrick had done his job for the prosecution, anyway. He told jurors that Clara had asked him to kill her father. He believed it was a genuine request. Once he realized she was serious, he ran. Everything else he added to that had been gravy.

CONNELL BEGAN BY asking Patrick if he had been involved with other "role-playing" games at the time, besides the one with Clara.

He said he had.

Then Patrick was asked to explain what a role-playing game actually was, just in case jurors didn't know.

And he did.

"Now, in real life," Connell asked, "you are not an assassin—is that right, sir?"

"No, sir."

"You never killed anyone?"

"No, sir."

"Your character might go and kill monsters or people as part of the adventure, correct?"

"Yes."

As the discussion carried on, the point was that the life Patrick had with Clara, either online or in person, always had elements of fantasy, so there was no way Patrick could have deciphered whether Clara was talking real world or Underworld. And then, regarding those online conversations, Connell made a point: "On any particular occasion, you could not be one hundred percent [sure] that the person using [Clara's onscreen name] was Clara sitting at the other end of the computer as opposed to some . . . hacker, correct?"

"Generally, the conversations I had with her, yes, I could be sure."

If the goal for Connell was to confuse jurors, or show them by example how close the line was between the game and reality, he did a fair job of it by bantering on and on, asking Patrick all sorts of Underworld-related questions regarding lizards and dragons and spells cast upon people in the game, magic, and Patrick's "practice and belief."

Then Connell brought up how Patrick, as the four were charged with murder, went out and hired himself an attorney—one that had "negotiated with the commonwealth" for him.

"Yes," Patrick said.

"And you agreed to testify in exchange for not being charged—is that right?" Connell wanted to know.

"It was agreed that I wouldn't be charged for anything. . . ."

Connell paused. He looked up. He tapped a finger on the table. Then: "Is there a spell that would have protected you against being charged?"

"No, sir."

Connell indicated he was done.

Wexton had one question on redirect. It pertained to Connell bringing up the notion that Clara's computer could have been hacked, which might give jurors pause to think that someone might have set her up for a fall.

"In your experience within the Underworld," Wexton said, "who generally hacked into other people's accounts?"

"The only person that I was aware of that was actually hacking into other people's accounts was Clara."

Nothing but net!

CHAPTER 89

AS THE TRIAL carried on nearly two hundred miles north of where Kyle Hulbert was being housed in Waverly, Virginia, he felt detached from the entire process. He'd spoken and had pled the Fifth. Had done as his lawyer, according to him, had told him to do. Now he'd have to wait his turn. And Kyle's plan, he later claimed, was to mount an insanity defense once his case came up. It was the only option he saw, the only way for him to explain what had happened.

"I wasn't really thinking about Clara's trial at all while it was going on," Kyle explained to me. "Around this time period, I was pretty detached from everything. It was easier for me to focus on other things. . . . It all felt so out of my hands. I didn't feel as though there was anything I could do."

As far as an insanity defense went, Kyle believed he had a solid case.

"You know, seventy thousand pages of mental-health history," Kyle said, with a contemptuous laugh behind it, "I thought that was a pretty good . . . lock for insanity. That's what I *thought* was going to happen."

Kyle had gone through several psych evaluations since his arrest. He'd sat with doctors and psychologists and told his story ad nauseam, or until he just couldn't tell it anymore. It never changed. In all of his psych evaluation reports, it's clear that Kyle had stuck to the same narrative, by and large, where his life story was concerned. He told lies, no doubt about it. But they were lies to explain things away, not to try and get out of things. By all accounts, he was hearing voices and seeing dragons and having violent thoughts all his life— whether this was, in itself, all lies—well, that's another argument. If there was ever a case for insanity—which is very hard to win in a court of law in the United States, anyway— Kyle had a fairly good crack at it based solely on his case history.

His lawyer came to him one day, Kyle explained.

"And my lawyer told me, 'If you go to trial, if you fight this, you will be found guilty and you will be given a life sentence.'"

So Kyle had that to think about as he contemplated what to do next. According to him, the alternative was that if he pleaded his case out and avoided trial, he was told that he'd be given twenty years.

"I asked my lawyer, 'What do I do?' My lawyer told me Judge Horne has seen mental-health cases. 'If you fall on your sword'—and I told my lawyer not to use that phrase ever again—'and admitted to what you've done, Judge Horne, who has seen mental-health cases before, would understand. . . .' So I'm thinking, *'Okay, a guaranteed life sentence at trial or up to twenty years?'* I was told there was no plea bargain. I was pleading guilty to murder. This is what I was looking at. I looked at it as I didn't really have a choice."

It was a decision that would have to wait, however, until Clara's case was concluded.

CHAPTER 90

KATIE INGLIS'S TESTIMONY could go two ways for the prosecution: make jurors believe that she was an innocent party in all of this—as Patrick had already intoned—or she could come across as someone just saying what she was told in order to save her own hide.

Katie didn't look any longer like the old-school goth chick—Mike's trampy girlfriend—at least she didn't on this day. She presented herself well and played up that librarian look she had tried to work in the past.

Owen Basham asked Katie when she and Clara had become tight—you know, BFFs.

"We . . . didn't really become friends until our senior year in high school," Katie said.

As they talked through the relationship Katie had with Clara after high school, Katie told jurors several things that contradicted what Clara had been saying since the LCSO focused on her as the ring leader plotting and planning the murder of her father. Katie said, for example, that she had never seen bruises on Clara, but Clara talked about how her father had hit her. She also intimated that "on occasion" Clara would say she wished her father "was dead," giving context to the argument that Clara, long before she had met Kyle, wanted her father to die.

There were several conversations, Katie explained, that she had overheard between Patrick and Clara that told her they were planning on doing Dr. Schwartz harm. In one, Katie testified, "It was like, 'When are you going to help do something about my father?'"

Katie talked about that meal they had, when Clara thought her steak was poisoned. How Clara told Patrick he needed to see her father "one more time if [her dad] was going to die before Christmas. . . ."

Basham asked about the money—had Clara ever mentioned a monetary gain by her father's death?

"Yes," Katie answered. "She said she would inherit a third of a million dollars from her father."

Next came the times Katie said she spoke with Clara on instant message about her father dying.

As Katie testified, Kyle's name came up. Katie told jurors how they met him at the festival. She said Kyle would often sleep over Mike's house and sit in his room while she and Mike slept. Kyle spent most of his time talking on the computer to Clara. And as soon as Kyle became part of the fold, Katie added, he and Clara got closer and closer, nearly pushing her and Mike out.

"She started telling Kyle how her father had abused her and poisoned her and pulled out some of her journals and show[ed] them to him. . . ."

Katie's testimony was like a slow-moving dump truck full of allegations against Clara that picked up speed with each new question Basham asked. Through answer after answer, Katie told jurors that her onetime best friend had obsessed about the death of her father. What might have started out for Mike and Katie as a friend talking about a fantasy game—and the hatred a friend had for her father—became an all-out plan to kill the man. Yet, what was also clear in Katie's testimony was how she listened to this over a period of time; and as she began to believe it was real, she never once told anyone.

She simply let two people plan a murder and sat by and did nothing to stop it or report it to someone who could.

Her testimony moved on to that night they dropped Kyle off at Clara's and he camped in the woods. She talked about how that check was sent to Mike's house and they brought Kyle to the bank to open an account. Then she went on to how she and Mike went with Kyle to the Schwartz home on December 8, dropped Kyle off, waited, got stuck in the mud, and then went to a friend's house for pizza while decorating a Christmas tree.

Katie gave jurors details about December 8: the times, Kyle's demeanor when he returned from the house ("Shaken up . . . scary . . ."), how he sounded, and the comments he made. It was the first time during the trial that a first-person account of the night Schwartz was murdered had been given to jurors. Here was a girl who had spoken to the murderer minutes after he committed the act.

One conversation Katie told jurors she had with Clara was perhaps the most damaging testimony Katie could offer. While they were loading Mike's car shortly after she met Kyle, Katie said, Clara once stated, "Maybe Kyle can help me with my father." Yet, Katie admitted, "I don't know what kind of help she was referring to."

WHEN CONNELL'S CO-COUNSEL, Corinne Magee, got a crack at Katie not long after she made that comment, she began by asking what Katie was getting out of testifying for the prosecution. Magee pointed out: "Instead of the twenty-to-life offense, you're facing a one-dollar fine and twelve-months-in-jail offense?"

"And the eleven years for the conspiracy charge!" Katie snapped back.

Magee wanted to know if Katie had gotten involved with Clara's Underworld game.

She said she had. Most of the time she played, though,

was online, chatting with Clara. The testimony became tedious as Magee had Katie focus on screen names and where computers were located and who would use whose computer. Katie brought in several other names of friends that played the game with Clara, Mike, and her. Magee brought in transcripts from those e-conversations revolving around the game and showed, perhaps, by example, just how confusing it all was while they talked about fantasy and mixed the game with reality.

Katie was a bit scared of Kyle, she said. He came across as aggressive: a guy who would lie in order to pump up his reputation and ego. He didn't seem genuine. She said Mike drove Kyle everywhere and she didn't like it. She said Mike and Kyle became really tight. Katie said how she would get mad, even, when Kyle demanded to sit up front in the car with Mike. She'd have to tell him that her place was beside her boyfriend, in the front seat.

"Do you remember Saba, Ordog, [and] Nicodemus?" Magee asked Katie.

"I remember him mentioning Nicodemus. . . ."

"And were those [names] in relationship to his [imaginary friends] or something else?"

"I don't know what he was referring to. It could have been his pet dragons. He just had names for them."

"You didn't actually hear him speaking to his dragons as he was riding in the car?"

"No."

"Did he ever have a do-rag with him?" Magee asked.

"I don't remember. I didn't see one. It could have been hidden in one of his trench coat pockets."

"You never saw him with a do-rag?"

"No."

"Did you see him purchase gloves?"

"I . . . No. I remember him borrowing Michael's."

Magee was a smart lawyer. Through Katie's testimony, she was pointing out that a lot of what Kyle had said didn't actually happen the way he had said it did. What she was trying to do was show how complicated and messed-up Kyle was when he hung around them. It was as though whatever Kyle said was taken as gospel by the gang and no one challenged him.

"Did Kyle have a habit of making outrageous statements?" Magee asked.

"Not completely outrageous. I mean, they would be topics of conversation. I mean, he was usually very calm and didn't do outrageous things very often."

Magee finished with one more question concerning the "topics" Kyle often brought up, which Katie explained were no different than what they all talked about, "since we were all Wiccan. . . ."

CHAPTER 91

ON OCTOBER 9, 2002, it was time for the prosecution to bring in its arsenal of incriminating evidence against Clara. There was no better witness to begin that process than the well-spoken, seasoned LCSO investigator Greg Locke, who'd had the most interaction with Clara out of any law enforcement. Locke was a cop's cop, a man who carried himself not as some brassy, in-your-face detective badgering witnesses until they cracked, but rather as the fun uncle type, who made you feel comfortable when talking to him. Locke would immediately bond with jurors, and Jennifer Wexton knew it.

Locke talked of meeting Clara and Michelle that first time at JMU and explaining to them that their father had been found dead. Wexton asked how Clara responded to the news—had she exhibited any emotion?

"No, she did not."

From there, Locke explained the conversation he'd had with Clara, Michelle, and Jesse Schwartz that first time at the LCSO on December 12, 2001. What Wexton wanted to establish here was that Michelle, Jesse, and Clara all came in willingly and were not "restrained" in any way. They could have gotten up and left at any time they wanted. Locke didn't get into the content of the interviews too much, or talk about what was said. He, more or less, gave Wexton the opportunity to admit several pieces of evidence: phone records, online conversation transcripts, and other items that would bury any defense claim that Clara might lodge of not knowing about the murder.

Wexton asked Locke next to focus on a few specific things Clara had said to him about her father.

Locke explained that Clara admitted to not having a good relationship with Dr. Schwartz, how growing up was difficult for her, especially after her mother had passed away. Then he talked about how she said her father hated the way she dressed.

"And she stated that there was some physical abuse, that occasionally he would slap her. . . . One particular occasion, he punched her in the arm."

Then Locke added how Clara had said there was one instance of sexual abuse when she was in the ninth grade: how "he touched her butt. . . ." That was it, Locke said, as far as what she told him about any sexual abuse.

It was a butt slap as she walked by.

From that point forward, Locke talked about the entire content of the interviews he conducted with Clara after that first one and how she began to work Kyle into the conversations as a guy who perhaps took her stories a little too far and murdered her father by his own accord, simply to protect her.

Locke didn't believe it, of course, but he allowed her to talk and he listened. As the questions and answers carried on between him and Wexton, Locke basically went through just about everything Clara had told him during the interviews.

Ultimately, there was a lot of objection that did not hold water.

At one point, Locke talked about how Clara came up to him after the interview, in the lobby, and Wexton asked if there was anything that Clara had said to him as they ended the interview that day.

Locke talked about Clara pulling him aside, closing the door so Michelle couldn't hear her ask about the "estate" and if Michelle was going to be able to cut her out of her father's will. This set up the state's motive argument—Clara was driven by three things:

Money. Money. Money.

"'If Michelle's pissed at me,'" Locke recounted, speaking for Clara, "'can she cut me out of the will?'"

There was silence in the room after he said it. Jurors were undoubtedly astounded by the audacity of Clara for asking this merely days after her friend murdered her father (which was an indisputable, unimpeachable fact), asking this cop if she was not going to get her share of the estate.

After that, Locke explained how Jesse had called him on December 19 and wanted to know if the LCSO needed them to come in, because they were heading back to school. This allowed Wexton to place into the record the transcripts of the interview that Locke had stealthily recorded.

They talked about Locke participating in the search of Clara's dorm room.

The journals.

The trash.

The computer.

The conversations online with both Kyle and Patrick.

Then came the most damning line from the investigator: Clara had told him that she knew "in her heart of hearts" that Kyle would kill her father.

Confident the jury was getting a better, more well-rounded picture of who Clara Schwartz truly was, Wexton offered up the tape of the interview. Jurors could see and hear for themselves just how manipulative and uncaring this then-teenager had been.

When the tape finished playing for jurors and the gallery, Wexton said she was finished. What else was there left to say about a girl who, whenever she was backed into a corner, changed her story just ever so slightly in order to give the LCSO what they wanted to hear?

JAMES CONNELL BEGAN by asking Locke about the "death scene" and if he had gone to it.

Locke said he had.

Connell then brought up how the homicide was quite the media event, apparently suggesting that the pressure was on to solve the case of the high-profile scientist murdered in his own home.

That idea went nowhere.

Then Connell moved on to the visit on December 10 that Locke made with his colleagues to JMU. Locke had stated that Clara showed no emotion.

When she answered the door, Connell pointed out, "her eyes were red—correct, sir?"

"Yes, her eyes appeared to be red."

"As if she had been crying, sir?"

"Either an irritation or crying."

Connell became a bit abrasive with his sarcastic "sir" tag to just about every question he asked Locke. He was trying to put out that fire of Clara not being unhappy or sad at the news by making jurors believe that Locke and his colleagues might have been a bit pushy and judgmental right off the bat with Clara.

It didn't work. Locke held firm that he was only doing his job by notifying her and she did not respond the way in which they'd expect a daughter to react to such bad news—the way that Michelle had, in fact.

Connell pointed out that Clara actually hugged her sister and comforted her—"Right, sir?"

"Yes."

For the next half hour, Connell essentially picked and chose—what else could he do?—those moments during the interviews that might help him project a theory of reasonable doubt, which was his only hope here. He did this by saying how forthcoming Clara had been with information, which wasn't the sign of a guilty person.

Connell stressed how Clara gave up Kyle, gave up Katie and Mike, and gave up the fact that she had a storage unit with knives inside.

Locke agreed to all of it.

Yet, any mindful juror could tell that she gave up her knives because she knew she hadn't killed her father with those weapons. And she also knew that Mike, Katie, and Kyle were actually at the crime scene.

Sure, she helped.

Whenever it helped her.

The testimony became monotonous and mundane. Locke answered all of Connell's questions to the best of his knowledge. He said, over and over, that yes, Clara cooperated with the LCSO. Yes, she voluntarily came into the LCSO a few times to talk. Yes, she gave them pertinent information about Kyle and Mike and Katie.

Big deal.

Connell kept pushing back, trying to hammer the point home that Clara never "took Kyle seriously" when she heard him speak of killing or hurting her father.

Locke agreed—but only that, indeed, was what she had *said*. Still, the fact remained for Locke (and the evidence supported it) that she also said she sent Kyle $60 the day before the murder. Just a couple weeks before, Clara had Kyle stay near her house in the woods. And on the night of the murder, she knew who had done it, when, and how, but she did nothing to call the police and let them know. Time and again, Greg Locke spoke of facts as he'd uncovered them.

There wasn't much a defense attorney could do with a client who had spoken to the police on a number of occasions without a lawyer. Clara had broken the Golden Rule when being questioned by cops for anything: She had opened her mouth—several times—without legal counsel in the room to advise her. Here was that evidence in court now coming back to bite her in the ass.

The only real contentious issue the defense was able to pull from questioning Locke was to ask him why he hadn't recorded *all* of the interviews.

But Greg Locke had a great excuse for that. During those first few days, he said, they were simply on a "fact-finding" mission and not really sure who was involved in the murder, so there was no reason to record conversations or interviews. The more they spoke to Clara, however, the more they believed she might be involved. As a result, they then began to record the conversations whenever they spoke, to make sure they had a record of it.

CHAPTER 92

OVER THE NEXT several days, the prosecution got on a roll, calling expert witnesses to bolster its case against Clara along the lines of forensic (computer) and anecdotal evidence, explaining perfectly how Kyle might be a bit mentally incompetent, but what he said happened, happened. He wasn't making up things to try and pull Clara into a sinking-ship situation.

One of those witnesses was Brandy, Kyle's ex-girlfriend, who said there came a time when Clara called the house "every day asking for Kyle, no matter what time" of the day or night. Additionally, Clara never wanted to talk to her. "She always asked for Kyle." That is, Brandy told jurors, until the afternoon of December 8, 2001. Clara called and asked for Brandy and, out of the blue, wanted to chat for "two hours."

"She told me that she hated her father, her father was abusing her, and he was trying to kill her."

"Did you say anything about [how] he was abusing her?"

"Sexually."

Was there anything left to say after that?

CHAPTER 93

THE FIRST INDICATION that the trial might take a turn toward exonerating Clara came when her attorneys brought in what might have at first sounded like a dramatic bombshell. Attorney Connell called LCSO investigator Rob Spitler, who had done a comprehensive search of the computers inside Clara's dorm room and at her home. Spitler had testified for the prosecution already, but Clara's team had some questions for him pertaining, specifically, to what was found on a laptop computer that Robert Schwartz had used at home.

Spitler didn't mention who, but he said someone had made a "personal" request of him "asking" to check Schwartz's laptop for "additional information."

"And what in particular were you searching for?" Connell asked.

"Images depicting young children and any information related to these groups."

"Young children in general?" Connell asked, knowing quite well where this was headed.

"Depicting children, child pornography, or images of young children in various stages of undress or sexual activity."

If the defense could prove that Schwartz was downloading child porn, that information was certainly a game changer. Clara was walking.

So, was Robert Schwartz, as Clara's defense insinuated, a collector of child pornography? Was he a guy who surfed the Internet and downloaded the most vile images imaginable to most human beings—likely including the twelve sitting on the jury? If Clara's team could prove it, this one fact alone would destroy the man and his reputation. Jurors might want him dead, in other words, and truly think maybe Clara had been viciously and sexually abused. She'd pull the sympathy card immediately.

Investigator Spitler went on to say that while searching Schwartz's laptop, he found "three" different "newsgroups" that the computer had belonged to, each of which involved "kiddie porn" and "child pornography." These were sites dedicated to pornography of a specific type: teen girls and teen redhead girls. They also had an element of sadism and masochism to them. There were forty-one images in particular that the LCSO had found.

"Did you examine all forty-one valid images?" Connell asked.

"Yes, I did."

Connell asked what the images depicted.

"They depict minors, preteen minors, in various stages of undress and sexual activity."

"Are we talking about seventeen-year-olds?"

"I would say twelve and younger."

"Sir, did you come across one particular set of photographs involving a girl with a long braid?"

Spitler said he couldn't recall exactly what each image portrayed. He'd have to go back and look to be certain.

Connell handed him a list from the LCSO investigation.

"Braided hair?" Connell asked after Spitler looked at the list describing each photo. The idea here was that the defendant was sitting in the courtroom with a braid curling down the front of her blouse.

"Yes," Spitler agreed.

A few more questions and Basham took over for the state.

"Is this computer password protected?" Basham asked right away.

Spitler said he didn't deal with that side of forensic computer science. The answer, the prosecution proved, however, was no—anyone could have gotten into that laptop.

The other extremely important fact about this evidence smearing the victim of a homicide that was brought up by the defense became the dates in which the alleged files were created. That one photo, for example, the one depicting the girl with the braid, was created and last accessed (meaning looked at and downloaded) on the day Schwartz was murdered, December 8, about thirty minutes before Kyle knocked on the door. The earliest any of those photos was downloaded and viewed was December 5, 2001. That was three days before Schwartz was murdered, Spitler testified under cross-examination by the state. No pornographic images were saved to that laptop earlier than December 5 of that year. Schwartz had images on that computer's hard drive—family photos and other common photographs—dating back to 1997.

One might think that with pornography, it's not something an offender simply decides to do on one particular day, but it happens over a period of time. It's an obsession, really, that one cannot control.

MICHELLE SCHWARTZ THEN came in for the state sometime after Spitler and testified that Clara had access to that same laptop computer and that it was not password protected. She said Clara was home a lot. The computer was always on the table or on Schwartz's desk. It would have been easy for Clara to hop onto it and begin surfing the Internet.

What's more, the first time, Michelle said, that Clara ever mentioned anything to her about their dad hurting or poisoning her was right before that interview with police on December 20, 2001—the same one Michelle sat in on.

Perhaps the bigger question (of which no one brought up): Would Schwartz, if he was downloading child porn, leave a laptop, unprotected by a password, on the kitchen table— a computer that the family often used?

"Had she ever complained to you about physical or sexual abuse by anyone?" Basham asked Michelle.

"No, sir, she did not."

Had Clara Schwartz gone to such a length to cover herself as to download child porn onto her father's computer?

The prosecution never presented evidence of such a claim, but it would appear that someone besides Dr. Schwartz downloaded those images to the computer. It was either that or Dr. Schwartz had a secret he had kept hidden for those three days before he was murdered.

CHAPTER 94

ON OCTOBER 11, the state showed a videotape of the interview Greg Locke conducted with Clara. Locke then came back into the court and, through testimony, verified and validated everything he could about the interview. After that, and a few general conversations with the judge, the state rested. They had put on the best case possible by simply presenting the evidence that Clara herself had given them. They didn't need theatrics or fanfare, not even Kyle coming in and pointing a finger and telling jurors that she put him up to it. Jennifer Wexton and Owen Basham believed that Clara had dug her own hole in the sand and had put her own head into it by thinking she could outsmart the LCSO. It was that simple.

The defense could only do so much here with what they had in order to put on a solid argument that Clara had no idea her friend was going to murder her father. The best way for them to do it was to bring in Kyle's psychiatrists and see if they could get one or two to testify under oath that Kyle was quite capable on his own of committing a horrendous murder. He was a bomb with a short wick. He didn't need anyone telling him what to do, especially where violence was concerned.

In they came, one after the other, several of the psychiatrists and social workers and their supervisors that Kyle had seen.

And all of them read from, essentially, the same narrative: Kyle Hulbert had been in and out of foster homes. Kyle Hulbert was volatile and explosive. Kyle Hulbert was in and out of treatment facilities. Kyle Hulbert had behavioral issues all his life. Kyle Hulbert was prone to listening to Ordog and Nicodemus. Kyle Hulbert was quite capable of acting on his own. Kyle Hulbert had reported visual hallucinations.

Bottom line with all of this was that Kyle Hulbert could have easily taken what Clara Jane Schwartz had said and interpreted it as her telling him that she wanted her father killed. Still, it did not mean that Clara never asked Kyle to do it. And if he had gone out on his own to murder, based upon a threat to his friend, why hadn't Clara, after she realized what Kyle had done, gone running to the police? Why didn't she plead with them that her friend had taken it upon himself to kill her father after misinterpreting a game she had involved him in?

One school psychologist described Kyle as a "bright young man and very verbal and articulate." She said that was half of the person she evaluated. The other half was a person who "presented himself in a very mature way and then . . . would do things that were childlike—like one of the instruments that I administered involved use of manipulatives, blocks. And he would spin the blocks in a really childlike way that's typical of real little kids."

"Thinking and thought problems" were something most of the experts talked about when referring to Kyle.

As each talked through his or her testimony, it really wasn't clear whom this testimony was helping: Clara or the state?

One shining moment for Clara came when one psychologist described Kyle telling her: "I hear things that other people don't hear. I see things that other people don't see. I have strange thoughts. I have strange ideas. I collect things that I don't need."

Another expert testified that Kyle often misinterpreted what other people told him, and he based a lot of his decisions on those misinterpreted thoughts. There was probably some truth to the statement, but the perfect way it came out—and seemed to help Clara—made it sound contrived and conceived in a back room somewhere. And like a lot of the testimony that each expert witness provided about Kyle's mind-set, it didn't have an organic ring to it that made any difference in Clara's argument of Kyle acting alone. It just wasn't there.

However, what everyone waited on was: Would Clara herself, the ultimate narcissist, take the stand, look jurors in the face, and tell them that Kyle Hulbert took what she had said and misconstrued it all? She loved her father, despite what he had done to her. She cared for the man and did not want to see him dead, no matter what anybody said.

CHAPTER 95

IN THE END, Clara herself did not testify. How could she? If she denied anything, all the prosecution would have to do was open a page of her journals and diaries and point out how much she despised her father and had wanted him dead. No, Clara could not take the stand on her own behalf because her entire argument was a contradiction.

Maybe her *entire life,* for that matter.

By October 11, a Friday, Clara's attorneys wrapped up her defense, which hadn't amounted to much more than an attack on Kyle. What more, really, could her attorneys do? If the jury believed Kyle acted on his own, Clara walked. If not, she was going away for a long time.

After a long Columbus Day weekend break, everyone was back on Tuesday, October 15, 2002, the lawyers prepared for closing arguments.

The judge gave jurors twenty-five instructions and handed the first closing argument over to Jennifer Wexton, whose opening line seemed to summarize the case: "The truth just fits," Wexton intoned. Then she made a thunderous admission, telling jurors that she had plagiarized that sentence—that those words were not hers. She had not written them in some creative night of coming up with the right way to capsulize this case. Those words—"The truth just fits"—were spoken out of the mouth of the defendant, Wexton said, when she looked at Greg Locke during one of his interviews and explained how it all came down to Kyle and her.

From there, Wexton went back to her opening theme: "Clara Schwartz wanted her father dead."

The guy wound up dead.

Case freakin' closed.

Clara had put that energy out into the world, told people it was her wish, asked people to do it for her, and, by gosh, the job got done. She'd found the right stoolie.

Another important point that Wexton made, and quite smartly, was that "the commonwealth didn't pick these two gentlemen (Patrick and Kyle). Clara Schwartz did. . . ."

Closings are about reminding jurors of the facts that support your case. The perfect closing should be short, to the point, and entirely focused on the facts as they were rolled out during the course of the trial. The way Wexton and the commonwealth saw it, Clara Schwartz had sunk herself with her own words: in her journals, to Greg Locke, and to friends.

Wexton spoke of a concentrated plan on the part of Clara and Kyle, adding at one point, "The plan was that Kyle was going to take responsibility because he could be judged legally insane."

Then Jennifer Wexton appealed to the jury's intellect, placing them in a position of either being another victim of Clara's or a group of common, intelligent people able to figure her out. It was a bold move, in many ways—a call like this could backfire.

"By your verdict today, you can show her that she's *not* smarter than you are. . . ."

CORINNE MAGEE WAS up next. She focused her closing for Clara's side on Kyle and his ability to manipulate and bend the truth to support his lifelong claim of being mentally incapable of making the right choices in life. Magee started off by reciting a line from Kyle's confession in which he apologized to the Schwartz family for what he'd done, "especially my sister in spirit, Clara Schwartz." Then Magee asked if that sounded like the words of a plan between them to kill her father. If they had plotted this together, why would Kyle apologize?

Perhaps it was a fair question.

Magee asked that jurors put all of the statements made by the prosecution and by Kyle into context and see for themselves how they could be construed differently under different circumstances. It was all about functional background. How did Clara fit into the framework of an alleged plan by her? The evidence, Magee hammered on, supported Kyle hearing things from Clara and taking it upon himself to make her proud of him by taking out her father on his own volition.

"The commonwealth wants to lead you leaping to an illogical conclusion," Magee said. "They want you to believe that because Clara Schwartz had difficulties with her father, who expressed hatred to her father . . . and because Kyle . . . eventually murdered her father . . . that therefore Clara Schwartz must have gotten Kyle to agree to kill [him]. . . ."

Magee finally said Clara was "only guilty of *not* believing Kyle. . . . She did *not* see the logic behind Kyle's actions, and, *no,* she never will forgive him."

CHAPTER 96

THE JURY WAS excused after the commonwealth's co-counsel had a brief moment to offer a final closing statement. It was quick. Then the judge told jurors it was up to them to decide from here what course this trial would take next.

Within four hours of deliberations, the jury indicated it had reached a unanimous verdict. Because it had taken only a few short hours to come to this conclusion, it did not bode well for Clara. Innocent verdicts take time. People argue. Debates take place. Theories are hashed out. Conclusions are drawn.

But it appeared after a vote in the jury room, the jury had reached agreement.

Clara Schwartz was found guilty on all counts.

The jury recommended thirty years for murder, eight years for conspiracy, and five years for each solicitation count, for a total of forty-eight years. This was rather lenient, considering they could have sent Clara away for life.

There was a preliminary sentencing hearing right after the verdict, in which Schwartz's family members talked about what life had been like since he'd been gone and now one of their own was convicted for his murder. Most people there to support Robert Schwartz's memory cried—with the exception of Clara—as Jesse and Michelle talked about the good times with their father and how much they were going to miss him.

Judge Thomas Horne would ultimately decide Clara's sentence, but not until early 2003.

That December, several weeks after Clara's trial, Mike Pfohl pleaded guilty to second-degree murder (a mistake on his part) and was himself now awaiting sentencing.

Then, on September 8, 2003—after Judge Horne had sentenced Clara to the forty-eight years on February10, 2003, and Mike to eighteen years on July 8, 2003—Kyle Hulbert walked into the same courtroom, shackled and chained, ready to hear his sentence for admitting to murdering Schwartz in the first degree, the most severe murder charge on the books.

Judge Horne "did not hesitate," Kyle recalled, "as I stood there in front of him."

The sentence: life without parole for Dr. Schwartz's killer.

Kyle said he started laughing when he heard this.

The rest, he claimed, was a blur.

Two of those voices that were still hanging around at the time, Kyle explained, "must be getting a kick out of this."

Why did it sound like he just said I had a life sentence? Kyle thought. There was no way this could be. He had been told, according to his recollection, it would be twenty years, *tops*. If he fought it and went to trial, he'd get the entire judicial book tossed at him.

Which had just happened, anyway.

"I'm trying to process this," Kyle recalled. "As I stand there in utter shock, still laughing."

As Kyle stood, one of the deputies who had escorted him into the courtroom placed her hand on the switch to zap electricity through the belt that kept Kyle's hands latched. He was wearing a shock belt device and laughing at the judge who had just given him a life sentence. There was no telling what would happen next.

"I guess they didn't expect me to start laughing at being told I was going to be locked up for the rest of my life."

And just think, Kyle concluded, "Katie was sentenced to twelve months!"

Indeed, Katie Inglis got a year after pleading guilty to being an accessory.

CHAPTER 97

DURING CLARA'S SENTENCING, Michelle testified at the hearing. Something she said resonated with those involved. It was as if Michelle had come to terms with it all by the time Clara was about to hear her punishment. Michelle had figured it out, and yet the pain was worse now than it had ever been.

"It's been nothing but a nightmare since the first day I found out," Michelle testified. "It's hard enough it was my father, but on top of that to have my sister committing such a horrible crime."

Before Judge Horne officially sentenced Clara, who had been quiet throughout the entire judicial ordeal, he asked her, "Do you have anything to tell this court, Miss Schwartz?"

Clara paused. Then, looking down, she said: "Nothing that hasn't already been said."

The judge reaffirmed the jury's recommendation of forty-eight years.

Clara's appeal came back on April 19, 2005, and the Virginia Court of Appeals upheld the conviction.

She sits in prison now, at the Fluvanna Correctional Center for Women, outside Troy, Virginia, waiting for the day, November 2, 2051, when she can walk out—this after her conviction on all counts was affirmed by the Fourth District of the United States Court of Appeals on March 9, 2010.

It's over for Clara Schwartz. She has never spoken publicly about her case.

Why? you might ask.

Because, one can only guess, Clara has already said all that needs to be said.

AFTERWORD

THE GREAT PRAGMATIST and brilliant Russian novelist Alexander Solzhenitsyn, during a commencement address he delivered at Harvard University on June 8, 1978, said, "Truth is seldom pleasant. It is almost invariably bitter." When one begins a commencement address along those lines of thinking, his audience had better take a deep breath, sit back, and check their egos, because the rest of what this man is going to say is not going to be comfort food. Yet, it is probably what those before him should have said, but they likely did not have the guts.

When dealing with murderers and crime victims' families (I even hate to put the two in the same sentence), this same model Solzhenitsyn suggested during that commencement could be taken. Because when we talk about crime, the public's response to crime, the players involved, the facts as opposed to the supposition and rumor surrounding each and every case, we're dealing with the same set of criteria: everyone will have his or her truth. It might sound different or come out more astutely from one as opposed to the other; but when all is said and done, it is that truth that matters. That underlying *veritas* (truth) found in every case I have ever studied, written about, or profiled on my Investigation Discovery television series, *Dark Minds*. When you look at a case in hindsight and you've been given the opportunity to step back and study what everyone said and did, how the investigation transpired, what the guilty parties have said since their convictions, a new *veritas* emerges, rising to the surface like a scuba diver coming into focus from the black depths of the ocean. It's there—and yet only if you're willing to look beyond the fog and bullshit and accept it for what it is.

In this case—the vicious, brutal murder of esteemed biophysicist and DNA researcher Robert Schwartz, noted for his work on DNA sequencing—that truth was never more present and attentive. It was always directly in front of every player involved in this case. And those who could see it—well, look, they chose to do *nothing* about it besides let it manifest and transpire before their eyes.

"It won't happen to me."

How many times have we heard that?

As I began to call on people for this case, to ask if each was willing to enter into a dialogue about that truth, take a clear look at it now years later, I was met with mixed results. Some wanted to speak to me with an open mind and a willingness I admire, respect, and expect. Others wished to shun me, not return calls, not even give me the admonition of a "no, not interested"—one I think I have earned after writing twenty-five books. I contacted some people several times; others only once. It seemed to me—and the fact that a few didn't even want to acknowledge me—that there was something missing from the truth. Whenever a certain portion of people involved in a case doesn't want to talk, there is a truth within the story that these participants generally wish to ignore or leave undisturbed. Thus, this only made me want to dig in more, plant my stubborn heels deeper into the framework of this case, and begin to look at everything underneath a new, clearer light.

WHEN THE PRISON computer called my number, alerting me that a call from "an inmate in the Virginia prison system" is looking for me, there's a recording that Kyle made himself, letting the person on the other end (me) know who is calling. In other words, the prison computer calls your number for Kyle; you pick up; the phone says, "You have a call from [and the inmate's voice inserted here]. . . ." We might assume that, in this case, I'd hear, "You have a call from Kyle Hulbert."

But not when dealing with Kyle Hulbert. Nothing is that basic and simple. Picking up the phone, I was shocked and quite struck by this gem of a message from Mr. Hulbert: "You have a call from . . . 'I am the Kyle.'"

I thought this was a bit odd, as well as another thing I'll leave unsaid.

"I am the Kyle."

It sounds so, well, egocentric. So superficially hubristic.

I queried Kyle about it one day.

He laughed.

"Interesting you should ask. A friend of mine a long time ago once told me that Kyle is not just a name, but a state of mind. And so I took that and ran with it. I enjoy my individuality. And so, as far as I am concerned, I am the only Kyle. All Kyles that came before me and all the Kyles that might come after me are mere imitations of who I am. That's all. It's really that simple."

O . . . kay . . .

I look at Kyle Hulbert's life and what happened and I cannot stop myself from thinking that he could have easily been one of those people we see on the news all too often—the culprit walking gingerly into a school and spraying rounds of bullets at innocent men, women and children. I'm not an expert in this field, mind you, and my analysis here is based on my research into murder and murderers and my conversations with experts, but Kyle fits into this "ticking time bomb" type of person walking out of a mental institution with nothing in place to guide him and no place to go. Kyle had resources available, as many of these same people do—no doubt about it—but why didn't he use any of those resources?

It's a question we need to look at closely. True, Clara might have found a puppet to complete her task of executing her father because she didn't have the guts to do it herself; but how many Kyles are out in the world as we speak, thinking about violence as a means to an end? Where are they? What are they doing right now? Where do they live? We had one not too far away from where I sit and write this—Newtown, Sandy Hook. Three words that explain all that needs to be said about how that turned out.

Another part of this for me was the idea that Kyle could have been lying. Did he and Clara (from the very beginning, as some have suggested) plan and plot this, thinking they could get away with it based on Kyle's history of mental illness? This theory has to be considered.

"There's a certain amount of fallibility in my recollections, you have to understand that," Kyle told me.

When I told Kyle that those pornographic images found on Schwartz's laptop had been downloaded only weeks before the murder, Kyle became very quiet. I had not heard him like this—ever. And we had well over twenty hours of telephone conversations, along with letters to and fro.

"You there?" I asked. "Kyle?"

Crickets chirping.

"What do you think about that?" I asked.

"She set me up. She. Set. Me. Up. I didn't know that until you just told me."

During the course of our interviews, Kyle explained that he had been diagnosed with post-traumatic stress disorder (PTSD).

"And part of that is chronological displacement, or the misunderstanding of the order of things—a day here or there doesn't matter to me. Timelines don't matter. What doesn't change is the events that took place."

Kyle once said to me, "There's a monumental amount of trust being placed on you that you are on the level and are going to portray me as you say you are going to portray me."

What I told Kyle from the first moment we started talking was that I would tell his story as he told it to me, reflect back on the record to match it up where I could, and allow others to say what they needed to say. I also told Kyle that I sympathized with him. I know he is, was, and always will be mentally ill. He was in a terrible state of psychosis when he committed this crime. He has gotten help. He did sound somewhat stable at times when we spoke (but not all the time). I'm not saying Kyle is innocent or that I'd like to see Kyle move in next door or be out on the street—far from it. But I know that mental illness in this country needs a total postmortem. We need to look at it *closely* and, for crying out loud, do *something*. What I am grateful for is that Kyle Hulbert did not manifest his anger and violent thoughts and twist them into some sort of hatred toward society where he would walk into a school and shoot it up.

I then asked him about certain parts of this story that made me think Kyle knew a bit more about what he was going to do than he might have let on.

"As far as trying to get my sword sharpened the day before I murdered Dr. Schwartz," Kyle said, "it was a matter of convenience. We were going to the mall. I bought the sword there. I wanted it sharpened. I know how it looks, but it was nothing more than that."

It's likely Kyle doesn't recall the mind he was in back then, some twelve years before I interviewed him. He very well could have gotten his sword sharpened because he was set on murdering Schwartz and wanted to make sure he killed him with a sharp weapon. It fits.

"I honestly think," Kyle told me, "that Katie did know what Clara was doing with me. She grew up with Clara. It would not surprise me in the least to find out that Katie knew what was going to happen because Clara told her she was going to use me. Katie threw Mike under the bus to get out of it all, herself."

There were times when I spoke to Kyle and I heard a man

(now in his thirties) locked in prison, allowing the time to do him, not the other way around. As most inmates will say, "When you're down for life, you have to take things one day at a time." Kyle would say, "Mind-numbingly boring. That's the toughest part. There's nothing to do in here. A lot of stagnation."

As far back as he could remember, Kyle had wanted to be a writer. He cannot type in prison, however. So he would write out things he wanted typed and send it to people (prison groupies, friends, anyone willing) on the outside so they could type it for him. Lots of times it never materialized into anything.

"Comes a point when I have to say, 'Universe, I am listening, you don't want me to do this.' Einstein described insanity as doing the same thing over and over and expecting a different result."

I told Kyle that Bill Wilson, who founded Alcoholics Anonymous (AA), used that same saying as a core principle for his program of recovery.

"Well, they got it from Einstein."

Writing is the only "constant" in his life, Kyle said.

"Sucks that I can't get anything done with it."

CLOSING REMARKS

AN INNOCENT MAN lost his life in a very violent manner. A man, it needs to be noted, who could have gone on to make greater discoveries in science than he had made already. The world lost a brilliant scientist. I have no doubt about that. It's appalling to me that a group of teens decided that their dreary, drab, and shitty lives were more important than his. These kids believed they were entitled to bigger and better things because they were "different." The world owed them something. No one understood who they were on the inside.

Boo-hoo-hoo.

It's all hogwash. I've heard the goth sob story before, one too many times. *"Society doesn't understand me. I'm different."* Yeah, yeah, yeah. We get it. Now get over it and lead a productive life. I did everything I could not to inject my own feelings about Kyle Hulbert into this book, only because I believe that mentally ill people should not be branded "psychopaths" and/or "sociopaths." They suffer from real disorders and, in this case, true paranoid delusions and do not need the likes of crime experts and television talking heads (like myself!) bantering about them. On top of that, we don't take care of the mentally ill as we should in this country. We continue to do nothing but close mental hospitals and cut "patients" loose before they're ready for society on their own. How many more images will it take of kids being led out of schools with their hands in the air, parents running toward fire trucks and police cruisers, doubling over in gut-wrenching emotional pain, and headlines of more death by the hand of a mentally ill person on a rampage with a gun? If we haven't done anything now—suffice it to say after those horrifying images from Newtown—we are *not* going to do anything.

All that being said (as I step down off my soapbox), I wanted some final thoughts from Kyle within that theme. Mostly, though, I wanted to know if Kyle was sorry, regretful, and, most of all, remorseful for what he did to Dr. Schwartz. I've interviewed a lot of killers—none like Kyle Hulbert. I was curious what he thought about himself, Dr. Schwartz, Clara, and the rest of this case.

"Dr. Schwartz should not have died," Kyle explained during a final call between us. "He did not deserve that. It's tragic in a way that can never be described." He stopped talking. Thought about what to say next. Then he offered his own version of justification, adding, "Because, had Schwartz been molesting her, had he been doing the things Clara claimed . . . yet, all indications, all evidence I have, say he was not doing those things. . . ." He stopped there. Concluding the thought with: "And that's a burden I am never going to escape."

To me, Kyle stopped just short of saying that had Schwartz been proven to be molesting his daughter, he should have been killed. The act of him committing a crime against his daughter would have justified those thirty stab wounds.

Kyle had done some writing and it was posted by a friend on the Internet. He got lots of hate mail, he said. I asked about his response to the hate mail.

"I wish I could tell them all, if I was let out today, I'd still be paying for what I did."

He said the pain and guilt of the murder he puts himself through is far worse a punishment than any court could ever dole out. He has lived with the guilt of the murder every day.

To the Schwartz family, Kyle said, "'I'm sorry' doesn't even begin to cut it. I don't think there is anything I have a *right* to say to them. I took their father, their brother, their uncle, away from them. *I* did that. Regardless of the manipulation and how Clara set this up, *I* did it. . . . The only thing I would hope for is that they understand how sorry I am. . . ."

Kyle said he "wishes" he never met Clara.

I asked Kyle to ponder a hypothetical: Had he never met Clara, let's say, did he think he would have committed a violent act, such as murder? My thought was that Kyle, newly released from being a ward of the state, was on a fast track toward a violent ending. He was destined to commit some sort of violent crime based on his behaviors when out of state custody.

"It's possible," he said. "It's quite possible and, according to some people, it was likely."

Then I asked if he considered himself in the same category as those who walk into schools and shoot innocent kids. Was this something Kyle believed he was capable of? I added how, if we are to believe what Kyle claimed (that he shouldn't have been emancipated and should have been monitored), then we have scores of similar people walking out of court-rooms and into society, thus creating the opportunity for these mass shootings at schools to continue.

"While I understand mental illness, even with my under-standing I find it hard to grasp how a person can justify in their minds these mass shootings."

What if Nicodemus and the other voices had repeatedly told him, I asked, to walk into a classroom and shoot it up—what would he have done then? Over and over, I said, there they were, in his head, telling him to walk into a school with an arsenal of weapons and fire.

"What would you have done, Kyle?"

"Once your perception of reality alters to the point where you cannot distinguish what's really happening," Kyle said stoically, "it's a very dangerous place."

I took that as a "yes."

Had Kyle considered himself at that breaking point (we'll call it) when he was released into society from the state?

"Depends on who you ask," he said. "When I'm off my medication, my world gets very, very, very, very dark—and very dangerous for me."

Kyle then broke into a long monologue about the dark side of foster care and how the world treats the unwanted, concluding, "Do you have *any* idea how different my life would have been that, instead of putting me on medication, someone sat me down and just spent some time with me?"

It sounded trite. So much like the perfect thing to say now, after the fact.

"Isolated," he said of the mentally ill. "We feel so alone. Nobody takes the time to understand." He then said the "Columbine kids" were a good example of what he meant. He was referring to the shooters, not the victims. "These kids went to the adults and said, *'Look what is happening to me.'* Nobody listened. While I don't agree with what they did and would never condone it, I do *understand* their mind-set. . . . *They felt they had no choice.*"

Many would argue with that statement—including myself.

I moved on to Clara. I wanted to know what he would say to her now.

The line went silent. For quite some time. Then: "I don't know that I would say anything." But in true Kyle Hulbert fashion, he could not leave it there. He added: "I don't think I can trust myself to speak to her. Knowing what I know now, I don't think I could trust myself *ever* being around her. She is the cause of a lot of people's misery. She ruined the lives of a great many people. I'd have nothing to say. If I could make her feel the things that she's put everyone else through, I'd like to do that."

Kyle wanted to tell Mike, "I'm sorry. You didn't deserve any of this. Aside from Dr. Schwartz and the family, Mike was blameless. And he is a victim, just as much as anybody in this. He didn't know. He had no *fucking* idea what was going on. . . . He gave me a ride because I *asked* him to.

He is only in prison because that harpy Katie . . . [needed] to save her own skin."

Within every convicted murderer I have ever spoken to is the strong, inherent belief that he or she will one day be awarded a new trial, or some sort of miracle lawyer will fall out of the sky and get the inmate released for some reason other than why he or she has been incarcerated. I asked Kyle about this, thinking that his aim would be to fight for a life in a mental hospital. As we spoke, Kyle's lawyers had just finished writing his habeas corpus argument. A habeas is a petition, essentially, to the court, asking that the detained person—inmate—be brought back into a courtroom for a hearing on whether his or her incarceration or detainment is lawful. One legal definition describes a habeas this way: *The writ of habeas corpus serves as an important check on the manner in which state courts pay respect to federal constitutional rights.*

"If the judge accepts our argument, it starts over," Kyle explained.

"What is that argument?" I wondered.

"Ineffective assistance with counsel. My court-appointed attorney never pursued an NGRI (not guilty by reason of insanity)."

Seems to me Kyle has a good point here. He should have brought his case to trial and pled not guilty. Those types of defenses are long shots, sure; but Kyle had a chance at being found not guilty by reason of insanity simply based on his past history. No one can deny that. I, personally, would have liked to see what a jury thought of that case.

Without being asked, Kyle then began a long narrative detailing his mental-health history (of which I had heard and read many times already), adding how documented that history is. He talked, on and on, about how his mental illness had stopped him from doing anything he had ever tried to do in life. He talked about how his records proved that through-out his life doctors and psychologists have evaluated him and made the claim that he was a "very suicidal boy with . . . thoughts of homicide and suicide," quoting from his psych evaluations. He was spot-on with his analysis—there were plenty of quotes in the thousands of pages of psych reports I had read to back up what he was saying.

My final question: "What is it that you hope will come from your habeas?"

"'Hope'?" Kyle said right off. "A chance for freedom. A chance for a life."

"When you say 'free,'" I countered, "what do you mean by 'free'—or 'freedom'?" I was confused. Did he mean free from the chains of guilt? From being found guilty of first-degree murder? Free from the corrections system? What was he saying?

"Free!" he said, clarifying. "Look, I am sure there'll be some time for me spent in a psychiatric facility." (You think?) "But I have geared the last twelve years of my life toward rehabilitation—toward being able to be a member of society. But if the best-case scenario is that I get out and have to remain in outpatient therapy . . . with some sort of psychiatry, well, okay . . . but then maybe, well, if not, the next best thing is removal from DOC (Department of Corrections) and placed in ment (a mental facility). And there, eventually, they would see where I am ready for society and I am able to have a life."

He saw himself on the outside with friends. He saw himself leading a "normal" life. He saw himself working and socializing and being a productive member of society. He saw himself putting the first thirty years of his life behind him and starting over.

But he murdered a man. He had admitted it. He had pled guilty to it.

"You have to understand," Kyle then added, "it's something I have never had—an actual chance at a life. Like someone saying, *'Here, you're on an even playing field. Let's see what you can do with it.'* I've never had that. The deck has been stacked [against] me since day one, and I have had to make shit hand after shit hand work. And I have been doing that for thirty . . . fucking . . . years."

SHOULD WE LISTEN to Kyle's concerns, his dreams, his ideas, and take him seriously? Or should we allow Kyle to fade into the obscurity and dust of the prison system? I have asked myself this question many times while getting to know him. Speaking for myself, I think Kyle is mentally incapable of understanding the totality of what he has done. He butchered a man. *For no reason.* Then comes back and claims he's never had a chance at a real life. Well, he did, actually, when he was released from being a ward of the state. That was Kyle's chance. He blew it. When you stab a man to death, you don't get a do-over.

On the other hand, I don't think Kyle understood the sum of his actions before he committed this crime. I also feel he was manipulated by Clara far more than we will ever know. Then there's a part of me that thinks maybe Kyle and Clara entered into this together and believed they could get away with it because of Kyle's mental history. So, as is often the case in these types of crimes, I am conflicted.

One thing I know for sure: Kyle Hulbert should be locked up somewhere and never be released—ever. It is my belief that he would hurt someone again. I feel that the cycle for him would begin the moment he was released back into society.

THANKS

I WOULD LIKE to extend immense gratitude and my biggest appreciation to my readers. You continue to support my work and I am humbled by your presence every time a new book is published. I am, as always, at a loss for words when trying to say "thank you," because nothing I can say is, in my opinion, enough. You are the most important part of my work. I am grateful to each and every reader.

Also, to my fans of *Dark Minds* on Investigation Discovery: I am honored by your dedication and willingness to watch the series and support it. Thank you.

My publisher, Laurie Parkin, and the entire team at Kensington Publishing Corp.: I thank you for the passion and confidence each of you put into each book.

I would like also to give my sincere appreciation to everyone at Investigation Discovery and Beyond Productions involved in making *Dark Minds* the best (nonfiction) crime show on television. It takes a lot of good people to produce a television series: Andrew "Fazz" Farrell, Alex Barry, Colette "Coco" Sandstedt, John Mavety, Peter Heap, Mark Middis, Toby Prior, Peter Coleman, Derek Ichilcik, Jared "Jars" Transfield, Jo Telfer, Claire Westerman, Milena Gozzo, Cameron Power, Katie Ryerson, Inneke Smit, Pele Hehea, Jeremy Peek, Jeremy Adair, Geri Berman, Nadine Terens, Samantha Hertz, Lale Teoman, Hayden Anderson, Savino (from Onyx Sound Lab in Manchester,

Connecticut), David O'Brien, Ra-ey Saleh, Nathan Brand, Rebecca Clare, Anthony Toy, Mark Wheeler, Mandy Chapman, Jenny O'Shea, Jen Longhurst, Anita Bezjak, Geoff Fitzpatrick, John Luscombe, Debbie Gottschalk, Eugenie "Jeannie" Vink, Sucheta Sachdev, Sara Kozak, Kevin Bennett, Jane Latman, and Henry Schleiff.

My entertainment lawyer/business manager, Matthew Valentinas, a warm thank-you for embarking on this journey with me.

I am immensely grateful for Shirlina Mann's assistance. Shirlina is an excellent researcher; all of the running around she did for me at the Leesburg Courthouse was extremely helpful. Thanks, Shirlina!

Lastly, my family: Mathew, Jordon, Regina, and, especially, April, whose dedication to her schoolwork and sports is a true inspiration to me.

Don't miss the next exciting real-life thriller by
M. William Phelps

TO LOVE AND TO KILL

Coming from Kensington Publishing Corp. in 2015!

Keep reading for a preview excerpt . . .

CHAPTER 1

FOOTSTEPS. THE SOFT, spongy slap of rubber work shoes against the scratched, unwaxed, filthy surface of a tile floor.

One after the other.

Pitter-patter.

Squeak, squeak, squeak.

Waitresses take perhaps thousands of steps during a shift. Always coming and going, while patrons bark orders, make crass comments and groundless, tasteless judgments, before getting up and leaving squat for a tip.

The South is full of roadside diners serving up high cholesterol and diabetes—all you have to do is walk in, sit down in a booth sporting ripped, waxy seats and grimy checkered tablecloths, and the journey into the greasy-spoon experience has begun.

Heather Strong had been a waitress at one of these places for nearly ten years, though she mainly worked the register as a cashier these days. She took to the job because it suited her character—outgoing, loud, always on the move—and put food on the table for her children. In February 2009, Heather, a beautiful, blue-eyed, brown-haired, twenty-six-year-old mother and soon-to-be divorcée, was working at the Petro Truck Stop, out on Highway 318 in Reddick, Florida. The Iron Skillet Restaurant inside the Petro was a busy joint.

It was one of those just-off-the-freeway pit stops filled with tired, hungry, dirty, foul-mouthed, penny-pinching, smelly men coming in off the road, piling out of their musty Mack trucks, looking for cheap fast-food saturated in grease. Heather drew the eyes of most of these men because she was so stunningly gorgeous in a simple American-girl kind of way. Sure, she had the figure of a swimsuit model, but that exterior beauty was juxtaposed against an inner abundance of innocence and purity, a warm heart. Still, for anyone who knew Heather, there was no mistaking the fact that this young woman could take care of herself, if necessary.

There was also a hidden vulnerability there within Heather's forced smile: You could tell she had struggled in life somewhat, but with the right man by her side (whom she had found just the previous year, but had let go after getting back with her husband), Heather could find that picket-fence happiness all young women in her shoes longed for.

"What's a hot little thang like you doing in a place like this?" was a common remark Heather endured more times than she could count. She hated it every time. Paid no mind to men that spoke to her disrespectfully like that. She had a job to do. Kids to feed. She was making ends meet. It didn't mean she had to take insults and sexually aggressive comments.

"Give me your check and let's get y'all cashed out?" Heather would snap back. "I ain't got all day."

Heather seemed tired on this particular day. She'd been having a rough go of things lately, to say the least. Most of those problems stemmed from the relationship with her children's father, twenty-seven-year-old Joshua Fulgham, a rather complicated and volatile man with a past. They'd separated and Heather was now living with a new boyfriend, but the leash that Josh had around his wife had not been severed completely. Josh wanted his kids, was afraid Heather would one day take off with them, and promised a nasty custody battle coming down the road. He was also enraged at the fact that Heather was living with a man whom Josh saw as a danger to his children.

"You seen Heather around?" Heather's boss asked a coworker a day after Valentine's Day, February 15, 2009. It had been a normal day at the Petro: regulars, new customers, broken coffee machine, dirty dishes coming from the kitchen, stains on the silverware. About the only thing different was that Heather had not come to work. It was so unlike her not to show up. If there was one thing about Heather Strong, work was first and foremost. She needed the money to support her kids—and that darn husband of hers? He rarely gave her anything to help out, but he always seemed to have the cash to buy weed or go out and have a good time.

"She always called," Heather's boss later explained.

"I haven't seen her," Heather's coworker said.

"Hmm," Heather's boss responded. "If you do, tell her to call me."

Heather generally worked the morning shift, although she did sometimes take on a double. On most days, she'd come in and set up the salad bar and then go about her ordinary duties.

She should have been in by now, thought Heather's boss, looking at the clock in her small office, trying to shake a bad feeling that something was terribly wrong.

CHAPTER 2

HEATHER'S FIRST COUSIN, Misty Strong, was at home in Columbus, Mississippi, where Heather grew up and had lived most of her life. Misty, equally as beautiful as Heather, could pass for Heather's identical twin. The two girls really did look so much alike.

"Heather was like a sister to me," Misty later said.

A few weeks had gone by and Misty had not heard from her cousin. This was odd. Heather and Misty kept in touch. However streetwise Heather had become over the years, especially while living in Florida, she was green in many ways of the world, Misty knew. It seemed that Heather had only one man most of her life and he had taken her to Florida: Joshua Fulgham.

Josh and Heather had met in Starkville, Mississippi. Heather was fifteen, waitressing after school at a local restaurant; Joshua, one year older, was a customer. Josh was that tough, rugged, overprotective, and overly jealous type. He was known in the Mississippi town where he grew up as a bruiser—a tough, troubled kid. Josh was five feet eight inches tall and weighed about 175 pounds—one of those physiques people might say he was born with—a guy who could eat anything and would never gain an ounce. Josh generally wore his hair shortly cropped, but he had turned to an entirely shaved head later in life. For Heather, Josh fit the image of a badass she liked so much. Heather felt comfortable around Josh. She felt protected. The two of them hit it off right away on that day inside the restaurant.

From the start, Misty Strong later observed, Josh and Heather had issues. He was rough with her. He liked to man-handle Heather a lot when he wanted his way. The cops were often involved. After meeting, dating, and then living together as teens, Heather having a child, with another on the way, Mississippi didn't seem to suit them as it once had. So Josh and Heather made the decision to move to Florida. It was 2004. Josh had potential job prospects in Florida—or so he said. He had family down there. The move felt like a step forward. Heather wasn't thrilled at going, moving away from her family in Mississippi, but she thought, *What the hell! Why not give it a try?* They could always move back if things didn't work out, she figured.

Misty knew with Heather moving away, there was little she could do. Once Heather was gone, in fact, Misty had lost touch with her for a time, and Misty believed it was Josh holding her down, keeping Heather from contacting her family. One more way for Josh to govern over Heather and keep her tied down.

"He was just too controlling," Misty explained. "He didn't want her around any family or anybody that cared about her."

Heather didn't even have her own cell phone or computer back then, during their early days in Florida. She had been totally cut off from everyone back home.

Just the way Josh liked it.

Then, in early 2008, after nearly four years of living with Josh, raising two kids and going through hell and back, Heather showed up in Columbus one day.

"I've finally left him," she told Misty.

"Thank God."

Misty and Heather's grandmother was sick at the time. She was actually dying. So they bonded over that family crisis.

The two women picked up their "sister" relationship from back in the day and stayed in touch daily. Misty kept telling her cousin it was all going to be okay. There was no need to worry about anything. She'd help with the kids. She'd help Heather start over. The key to it was for Heather to stay the hell away from Josh, who was still in Florida. If Heather could do that, she had a chance. Everyone in her family believed this.

There was one day when Misty went to see their grandmother, who was in her last days. When Misty returned, Heather was gone.

And so were her bags.

Damn.

"Josh had . . . brought her back to Florida," Misty later recalled. No one knew it, but he snuck into town, convinced Heather she needed him, and drove her back.

Heather had gone willingly, apparently. She wanted to work things out for the kids' sake. That was Heather: She always was yearning to find that pristine image of the American family unit on the other side of a dark rainbow. What mother, after all, doesn't want her children's father to be a part of their lives? Maybe Josh was changing. He was angry and sometimes violent; but when he was good, he was a nice guy. They got along and loved each other.

Or was Heather locked in that same fantasy that many abused women see in their dreams and pursue in their minds?

I'll give him just one more chance. He'll change. You'll see.

Things didn't work out for Heather. Josh *didn't* change. So Heather moved out and found someone else to live with in Florida. She thought it would be better for the kids if she stayed in the state this time. The place she found had a computer. Heather now had a cell phone. She and Misty were in contact just about every day, sometimes several times a day.

"Myspace, cell phone, e-mail," Misty said.

But then, suddenly, it stopped. *Boom!* One day, Heather wasn't communicating anymore. Misty and Heather had been talking for months. Heather was saying that Josh had a girlfriend now. He was letting go. Heather had someone new, too. There had been some issues between Heather and Josh's new girlfriend. Josh sometimes seemed to want to reconcile with Heather, but Heather was saying things were beginning to settle down. They had finally figured out that maybe they just weren't meant to be together. Josh seemed to accept this.

Now Misty was concerned, however. It was late in the day on February 25, 2009, and she had not heard from Heather in well over a week. Misty knew damn well that something was up. It was so unlike Heather not to call or e-mail for this long a period.

So Misty called Heather's brother, Jacob, and asked if he had heard from her.

"No," Jacob said.

"Any idea where she is?"

Jacob responded, "I got a call from [Heather's friend]. She was concerned."

"Concerned? How so?"

"Well, Heather had all her belongings over there at her friend's. Now all of her stuff is gone and she is missing."

"'Missing'?" Misty answered. She felt her stomach turn. Her body was now numb. Then that life-will-never-be-the-same-after-today feeling came on all at once. Misty felt it.

Missing? Misty pondered.

That word no one wants to hear. It sounded so final.

So dangerous.

So deadly.